Two-Buck Chuck &
The Marlboro Man

Two-Buck Chuck &
The Marlboro Man

THE NEW OLD WEST

FRANK BERGON

UNIVERSITY OF NEVADA PRESS *Reno & Las Vegas*

University of Nevada Press | Reno, Nevada 89557 USA
www.unpress.nevada.edu
Cover art by Journie Kirdain
Cover design by Frank Bergon
Author photo by Holly St. John Bergon

LIBRARY OF CONGRESS CATALOGING-IN-PUBLICATION DATA
    Names: Bergon, Frank, author.
Title: Two-buck Chuck & the Marlboro Man : the new Old West / Frank
    Bergon.
Other titles: Two-buck Chuck and the Marlboro Man
Description: Reno ; Las Vegas : University of Nevada Press, [2019] |
    Identifiers: LCCN 2018039126 (print) | LCCN 2018041047 (ebook) | ISBN
    9781948908054 (ebook) | ISBN 9781948908061 (cloth : alk. paper)
Subjects: LCSH: Central Valley (Calif. : Valley)--Social life and
    customs--21st century. | Central Valley (Calif. : Valley)--Social
    conditions--21st century. | Cultural pluralism--California--Central Valley.
Classification: LCC F868.C45 (ebook) | LCC F868.C45 B47 2019 (print) |
    DDC
  979.4/5--dc23
LC record available at https://lccn.loc.gov/2018039126

FIRST PRINTING

Manufactured in the United States of America

For Aleksandra, André, Kaitlin,
Gretchen, Caleb, and Madeline
my nieces and nephews

Contents

Mule-drawn wooden float used on San Joaquin Valley ranches into the 1950s

Introduction

To think about the American West in the twenty-first century astonishes me when I look at an old black-and-white photograph taken on my family's California ranch when I was five. I'm wearing a straw hat and sitting in a wooden "float" used to compact and smooth vineyard rows for raisin drying. Next to me, a ranch worker from Oklahoma in a small-brimmed Stetson fedora holds the reins to a mule dragging the scraper and us through a vineyard.

Now in the twenty-first century, mechanical harvesters roar through the night from dusk to dawn picking wine grapes in similar vineyards. Against the racket of this mechanized harvest, the remnant of the Old West in the photo glows as if from a distant galaxy. Less distant is how the Dust Bowl migrant behind the harnessed mule and today's Mexican immigrant on a night harvester might think and feel, sharing Old West beliefs in the power of individual resilience and the future rewards of hard work. In the rural West, core beliefs change more slowly than the surface of people's lives.

This book is a personal portrayal of how California's Great Central Valley breaks down distinctions between the Old and New West to create America's True West, a country where the culture of a vanishing West lives on in many contemporary Westerners, despite the radical technological transformations around them. I write about rural and small-town Westerners, some with ties to Nevada, Oregon, Idaho, New Mexico, Arizona, Wyoming, Oklahoma, and Texas, whose lives have intertwined with mine, all shaped, as I was, by California's Great Valley, a place itself shaped in large part by migrants and immigrants. Many I write about see themselves as part of a region and way of life most Americans aren't aware of or don't understand. In their myriad voices I hear a vibrant oral history of today's rural West.

I was born in Nevada, lived in the Colorado Rockies, taught in the Pacific Northwest, and came of age in the San Joaquin Valley, where I grew up on a Madera County ranch as a Californian and an American Westerner. I didn't always understand these connections. One morning as a kid I was riding with my dad in his pickup down a country road when he waved to a lone driver approaching in a black truck.

"Who's that?" I asked.

"I don't know."

"Why'd you wave to him?"

That's when my father explained the significance of his greeting, not so much a conventional wave, really, as a flick of the fingers upward—the heel of his hand still rested on the steering wheel—in half-acknowledgment, half-blessing. "That's the hospitality of the West."

We were in the center of the San Joaquin Valley. It and the Sacramento Valley form California's Great Valley, 450 miles long constituting nearly three-fifths the length of the state, an area larger than Rhode Island, Connecticut, and Massachusetts combined, a massive country of farms and ranches, and—as I was told—the richest, most productive agricultural region in world history.

Nevertheless, a few months earlier, after moving from Nevada, I'd asked my dad when we were going back to California.

"We are in California," my father said.

I'd thought California was Los Angeles, where we'd lived briefly before moving to the center of the state.

Once I got my geography straight, I had no doubt that California was the West and I was a Westerner. I lived on a ranch. It had horses, mules, sheep, and cattle. It also had cotton, grapes, and alfalfa, but nobody said farm in those days. Everything was a ranch, as in "cotton ranch" or "dairy ranch." My grandfather and dad were ranchers, even after the cattle business went bust and they farmed the dirt.

To put a twist on what my old teacher Wallace Stegner told us at Stanford, rural California is like the rest of the West, only more so. As a region, the San Joaquin Valley in its extreme otherness from the state's tourist and metropolitan haunts has caused native-son writers like Gerald Haslam and David Mas Masumoto to distinguish this rural country as "The Other California." It's this other California that best illuminates what playwright Sam Shepard dramatizes in *True West,* a play set in a rural California ranch house next to an orange grove, forty minutes east of Hollywood at the intersection of a sprawling suburb and a desert of yapping coyotes. Shepard as a boy lived on a ranch in nearby Duarte, raising sheep and avocados, and he later worked as a ranch hand and a lay-up stable boy near Chino. "The California I knew, old rancho California, is gone," he once explained. "It doesn't exist, except maybe in little pockets. I lived on the edge of the Mojave Desert, an area that used to be farm country."

This interpenetration of a vanishing Old West and an emerging New West creates the True West, as it always has, dramatized in the aspirations and disappointments of two brothers in Shepard's play. "There was a life here then," says one brother with regret about the disappearing ranch country. The other responds with dismissive toughness, "There's no point in cryin' about that now." What's true about their

West emerges as paradoxical. A mythical Wild West still exists in their minds, somewhere out in the desert, only to become a violent, immediate reality when the brothers end up viciously fighting each other. An equally mythical West manifests itself at the dawn of a new day as one brother exclaims with a Western whoop of can-do optimism, "It makes me feel like anything is possible. Ya' know?" The other brother seeks fulfillment of his True West desires, but elsewhere, farther West, as it were, in the San Joaquin Valley, where embodied in his memory lives a beautiful green-eyed woman he desperately tries to phone but hangs up in True West disappointment because he can't remember whether she lives in Fresno or Bakersfield. He only knows she's somewhere in the truer West of the San Joaquin Valley.

Shepard describes the ranch country where he grew up as "a weird accumulation of things, a strange kind of melting pot—Spanish, Okie, black, Midwestern elements all jumbled together." The San Joaquin Valley is also such a weird accumulation, only more so. Traditions of nineteenth-century Mexicans, Californios, Chinese, and Japanese, plus twentieth-century African Americans and Okies, as well as more recent Mien and Hmong have all shaped the Great Valley, along with dozens of other ethnic groups, like Assyrians, Azorean Portuguese, Volga Germans, Russian Molokans, and my own family of Basques and Béarnais.

What's remarkable about this valley's earlier frontier is its nearness to recent history. When I was a boy riding in a wooden float pulled by a mule on my grandfather's ranch, I didn't know I went to school in a town that only seventy-five years earlier didn't exist. The forty-acre place where Madera at the time was being laid out in auction lots was described as "then a barren, dry waste...devoid of verdure...with the exception of a strangling growth of wild oats...a person could drive a herd a hundred miles and not find any kind of habitation." Fourteen years later, after the U.S. Superintendent of the Census officially announced that the frontier had "closed," it hadn't quite closed in Madera, where civilization blessed the growing town with a lumber mill, a hotel, a post office, a school, two churches, and twenty-two frontier saloons with open gambling and prostitution.

A frontier mentality noticeably marked the valley through my high school and college years. When reporting on the Filipino and Mexican grape-pickers' strike of the 1960s, John Gregory Dunne portrayed the San Joaquin Valley as "largely insulated from what industrial America thinks and does and worries about.... The prevailing ethic is that of the nineteenth century frontier." Dunne didn't know that for target practice new Western historians who'd never visited the valley were preparing to hang in quotation marks the concept of "frontier" and leave it shredded with bullet holes as an antiquated artifact. Neither did Mexicans who crossed *la frontera* to pick the grapes. Nor did Armenian, Italian, Croatian, and other immigrant children who owned the vineyards their parents had planted in an arid frontier inhabited by jackrabbits and rattlesnakes.

The West of California and Nevada where I grew up continues to be a land of immigrants. While California gold and Nevada silver initially attracted people worldwide, farming was the subsequent lure for immigrants and migrants, who often found themselves in a triangular squeeze of resentment, rejection, and accommodation. While many who came to exploit the land found themselves exploited, many moved to a better life their parents only dreamed of. Not melted into a homogenous American society, they stamped California, Nevada, and by extension the West as pluralistic. Nearly two out of three people currently in the San Joaquin Valley are minorities, and more than two out of five minorities are foreign born, almost like the frontier West once again, when the states with the largest percentage of foreign born were all in the West.

Ethnic stereotyping informed certain proverbs about ranch work and hiring practices during my boyhood: "Nobody can herd sheep like a Basque, nobody can prune vines or pick olives like a Filipino, nobody can irrigate like a Sikh…" A Sikh? Yes, turbaned Indians from India were once more common to ranch life, at least during my dad's youth, than were Native Americans. Yokut mortar bowls for grinding acorns and grass seeds popped up in freshly plowed fields on my family's ranch along Cottonwood Creek, accusatory reminders of the not-so-distant Indian past in the valley when some fifty Native American dialects thrived there, before pestilence and guns obliterated native life. Anthropologist William Wallace noted in the Smithsonian *Handbook of North American Indians*, "No large section of California is so little known ethnographically as the lower or northern San Joaquin Valley. The lack of information concerning the aboriginal inhabitants of this region is due to their rapid disappearance as a result of disease, missionization, and the sudden overrunning of their country by American miners and settlers during the gold rush years."

In the hills, remnants of Chukchansi, Miwok, and Mono survived. Some moved back into the valley to work. Indians played in our town's softball league, including a Chukchansi with an 85-mph underhand pitch that struck out ninety percent of batters. In contrast, the entire Nevada Battle Mountain Band of Te-Moak Western Shoshone lived a few blocks from my grandparents' house. Today in Wyoming, modern Wind River Arapaho share sweat lodges with Anglo ranchers.

—ɯ—

We're now in a tumultuous period in which a controversial and sullied presidential election has revealed a widening gulf between the country and the city. The rift isn't just between elites and the working class but between city and country people of all social classes and ethnicities. The people in this book are immigrants, migrants, their children, or grandchildren—rich, poor, and in-between, of several races and ethnicities. Some have been featured in *The New Yorker, The New York Times, Harper's, Sports Illustrated*, and *People*—in short, figures of national interest. Others should be of equal interest: Chicanos, Okies, Mexicans, African Americans, Italians, Asians, Native Americans, and Basques of my heritage, all commonly evolving into a shared identity as Californians and Westerners. A California-born sixth-grader drove home this point about ethnic transformation when he told writer Gerry Haslam, "Oh, my dad used to be an Okie."

In the new millennium, the Great Valley as a place of individual freedom and economic opportunity achievable through hard work, a belief American at its core, remains Western in its intensity, though now harder for many to maintain beyond a wistful dream. A fair shake is all Westerners wanted and still want, in the phrase's original meaning—a fair-and-square shake and roll in a craps game. The always-suspect dice though appear increasingly loaded against economic fairness. Some workers, like my former school friend Joe Alvarez, found their way out of the fields, as many still do, through military service, though not out of a constrained life of labor. Now when everyone in the military is supposedly considered "Our Heroes," many still aren't treated that way.

Problems from the past still haunt the twenty-first century. The Great Valley made California an agricultural state and the engine of its economy for nearly a hundred years. Today the richest harvest of crops in history accompanies the extreme impoverishment, depopulation, and bankruptcy of valley towns. California's massive construction of dams, aqueducts, canals, and reservoirs that created an agricultural paradise also altered the land to a greater degree than anywhere else in the West. The problem of vanishing water—a defining characteristic of both the urban and rural West—mars farms and ranches to an extreme. Droughts, acute pollution, silting and toxic salts on a sinking earth have accelerated to the point of threatening a new Dust Bowl and the destruction of agriculture, worse than anywhere in the West. The disappearance of the valley's underground water and the impossibility of restoring it promise to shock the entire economy of the West, the nation, and world geopolitics.

Today the ranch I grew up on is long gone, its disintegration a kind of explosion that flung my two sisters to the northern and southern extremes of the state, my brother as far away as Colorado, where he landed as a farrier, and me to the East Coast where I taught. As a kid I climbed up into a saddle and waded a horse across Cottonwood Creek to gather cattle from a pasture. Now rows of grapevines and almond orchards cover the dirt. The valley's farmland disappears at an astonishing rate under suburban sprawl. The northern San Joaquin Valley merges into an extension of the San Francisco Bay Area. In much of the new millennial West, the old extractive industries of logging, mining, and ranching have given way to second homes, vacation resorts, retirement communities, and tourist haunts of the new Recreational and Environmental West. This is the West—and America—today, a region in conflict with itself.

The West, as John Updike once noted, has seemed to this country the essence of itself. The West I write about represents America in the extreme. It's a land of both bounty and poverty, a country of large history and even larger myth. Certainly the legendary image of the Marlboro cowboy in the famous advertising campaign reflected widespread beliefs nationally and abroad about

America and its origins. Behind Marlboro Country's mythic veneer and carcinogenic reality, the main Marlboro Man riding across four decades was an actual cowboy, who worked on ranches in the San Joaquin Valley, where I came to know him in my teens.

The image of the Marlboro Man was recently and wrongly invoked when the Wild West rose up again in the New West. In 2014, Nevada gun-toting ranchers faced down federal officers in a confrontation over grazing rights. In 2016, Oregon blue-collar rage against economic unfairness sparked a "Rebellion in Marlboro Country" when armed cowboy "patriots" seized a federal wildlife refuge for six weeks, ending in a standoff with the FBI and state police until a protester in a cowboy hat was shot and killed. In Idaho, a rebellious hero—or antihero—for this Old West–New West conflict emerged thirty-five years earlier when a self-styled, freedom-loving mountain man gunned down a game warden and a wildlife biologist.

As heirs to this Sagebrush Rebellion, my cousins' Nevada ranching family ended up on the front page of *The New York Times*, when they illegally released their drought-starved cattle onto public land. Their populist anti-government anger burns across many regions of today's West. Like a lot of people struggling to make a living in the rural West they feel left out and looked down upon. With their voices unheard, their stories untold, they continue to saddle their horses and graze their cattle, while their livelihood and way of life vanish.

What abides in the San Joaquin Valley is an Old West code of toughness and hard work that I saw my grandparents and parents continue to believe in: a communal allegiance to Western dreams of freedom and opportunity, an optimistic fortitude coupled with physical endurance, a respect for work with your hands, a disinclination to complain or give up, all the time knowing that the demands of the code in confrontation with the harsh cyclical reality of agricultural disappointment might leave you crushed. Or possibly renewed. It's what I still hear when talking to a Basque American rancher and former neighbor, whose buoyant pride in the achievement of hard work echoes my father's conviction that everything turns out for the best, despite the certainty that in ranching disappointment and failure are always part of the deal. An African American ranch girl reinforces that belief when talking about how in a racist society her hardworking father from Alabama found respect in the West. A pervasive Western code of resilience and work as the source of her character is what a Korean immigrant believes she shares with the post-Steinbeck children of Dust Bowl migrants portrayed in *The Grapes of Wrath*—ethnic Scots-Irish, working-class Americans, whose ties to the American soil go back to colonial times, and sometimes earlier. Many are also of mixed Choctaw or Cherokee or Muscogee or other Native American heritage, like the celebrated Indian novelist Louis Owens. Their roots and adherence to Old West values define much of California's rural culture and that of the Intermountain West and beyond to provide an understanding of a widespread but neglected base of the nation we live in.

In the Old West, a California settler said about the Great Valley in the 1870s, "People generally look on it as the garden of the world or the most desolate place in Creation." They still do, only more so. Too often the West gets jammed into popular stereotypical extremes of the Mythic West or the Debunked West, one legendary and romantic, the other brutalizing and empty, both cartoonish. More complicated entanglements of myth and fact shape the lives of Westerners beyond the technology altering the world around them. The Old West lives on in the valley long after it was declared dead, enlivening the way people think and feel, not so much clashing with the New West as blending into it.

In the San Joaquin Valley, values of the Oklahoma Dust Bowl migrant who became the Marlboro Man overlap with those of the grandson of Italian immigrants, Fred Franzia, my high school classmate and legendary creator of the best-selling wine in history, popularly known as "Two-Buck Chuck." His agricultural sidekick, Sal Arriola, a Mexican immigrant who illegally crossed the border with his family when he was three, now farms the biggest vineyards in the country. What's amazing is how much a current Mexican immigrant can sound like an Italian immigrant of a hundred years ago in what both believe to be opportunities in California's Great Valley.

I'm now looking at two photos. One is of Darrell Winfield on horseback as a working cowboy in the San Joaquin Valley when I first knew him. In the other I'm standing next to him on his Wyoming ranch some forty years later, when he was still being photographed as the Marlboro Man. In both photos, he looks to be wearing the same silverbelly Stetson, the same cowboy white shirt, and the same boots. In both photos, he's basically the same guy, spanning five decades of drastic change in the American West.

While the label of Marlboro Man has been applied to a murderous wannabe cowboy and a gun-toting rancher, the real Marlboro Man was nothing like the individualistic, gunslinging, macho rogue so popular in Western fiction and film. Darrell Winfield, featured in the famous advertising campaign, emerged from California's San Joaquin Valley as an actual American cowboy who behind the ads exemplified the communal values of today's True West.

CALIFORNIA

The Cornucopia of the World

ROOM for MILLIONS of IMMIGRANTS

43,795,000. ACRES of GOVERNMENT LANDS UNTAKEN

Railroad & Private Land for a Million Farmers

A CLIMATE FOR HEALTH & WEALTH WITHOUT CYCLONES OR BLIZZARDS.

I

Working the Dirt

The Vision of Two-Buck Chuck

A friend from my high school days told me, "Given that Fred is our most famous classmate, you should write a book about him." Famous for what? "He's brought wine into the homes of more people than Gallo or Mondavi or any other winemaker. In Napa his name is anathema. They don't like good wine at two dollars."

He was talking about Fred Franzia and the wine called Charles Shaw, better known as "Two-Buck Chuck," introduced at California Trader Joe's in 2002 for $1.99 a bottle, thus earning its two-buck moniker as America's most popular wine. Without advertising, the wine set a record for a new label within a year when sales shot up to a million cases. Thirteen years later, in 2016, sales hit more than a billion bottles. No wine in history has ever sold so much so fast.

"People create too much mystery around wine," Franzia has said, pointing his barbs at pretentious Napa Valley vintners. "No wine is worth fifty bucks a bottle."

Franzia transformed the wine industry in the twenty-first century. For bringing inexpensive wine to so many people through the acclaimed miracle of Two-Buck Chuck, Franzia was compared to Jesus Christ changing water to wine, while several magazine articles contrastingly painted him as a jowly, bullying, gruff-talking Devil Incarnate for scourging California's elite wine country. I had a hard time connecting these two disparate mythological figures to my memory of the small fourteen-year-old kid from the San Joaquin Valley I first met at a Jesuit boarding school many years ago.

It didn't take me long to see the kid again one October morning in 2011 when a mischievous-grinning, barrel-bellied, silver-haired, sixty-eight-year-old Fred Franzia duck-walked into the coffee shop of the Madera Valley Inn. Outside, the town's big water tank towered against a clear autumn sky with an arrow-pierced heart painted on it to show we were dead center in California. Fred doesn't like the broad term "Central Valley" applied to what he advocates as the special distinctiveness of the San Joaquin Valley, where he rules as the most controversial winemaker and the biggest vineyard owner in the United States.

I was hesitant to follow my schoolmates' advice to write about Fred, especially a book; such journalism wasn't my kind of writing. At the same time, I had an insider's perspective: we'd both grown up in the valley and I'd known him since he was a schoolboy. No article I'd seen had explained how he'd managed to create his successful bargain wine. He'd refused to cooperate with the writers and publishers who'd approached him about a book. "Not interested," he told Penguin and other New York publishers. His fundamental method, it seemed to me, had revealed itself back when we were high school housemates. As we'd learned from studying the poet Wordsworth in our senior English class, "The Child is father of the Man."

I recall a 1991 high school class reunion barbecue in San Jose, when Fred energetically waved his arms and described to Bill Sterling, a Boston architect, a dream of building an imposing future home in the center of a vineyard. He gestured toward areas of the patio and excitedly shaped designs in the air with his hands to create models of how and where he wished the house to be built, his expletive-rich speech reinforcing the intensity of his desire. In his somewhat cryptic, arch, offhand way, he asked Bill to drive a hundred miles with him the next day down to the San Joaquin Valley to look over the site and give him some ideas, an offer Bill deflected. He wished to remain near the coast with his former classmates and to continue drinking the wine Fred had donated for the reunion.

Twenty years later, his dream home started but unfinished, and his family business bringing in nearly $1.5 million a day, Fred serenely hunkered behind a café table in Madera at mid-morning, wearing rumpled khakis, an unbuttoned green polo shirt, and white New Balance running shoes, covered with field dust. He asked the waitress, "Do you have a Bloody Mary?"

It was 10:30 a.m., the bar wasn't yet open. I was a little surprised at his order because he was known usually to drink Diet Pepsi during the day.

"Do you have a Virgin Mary?"

"Can't do that either," she said.

The coffee shop behind her was empty; the chatter at the long window table where retired farmers gathered every morning had quieted hours earlier. Breakfast dishes had vanished from the other tables, crowded that morning with fifty Egyptians on a bus tour through the valley to study pomegranates. I'd watched farmers stare outside at a Muslim kneeling on the grass and bowing his forehead to the ground in prayer while his veiled wife stood looking on.

"Do you have tomato juice?" Fred asked. She did. "And Tabasco sauce?" She nodded. "Ah!" Fred leaned back, reminiscent of a mischievous, satisfied broad-faced Buddha in silver-rimmed spectacles slipping down his nose. "That's what I really want. I like the heat."

Plenty of heat has come Fred's way in his anti-elitist battles against his disdained wine hypocrites of Napa Valley, who scorn the grapes and juice from the San Joaquin Valley. Napa wines are supposed to be at least seventy-five percent made from Napa grapes. Accusations of Fred's purloining the word Napa from California's famous wine region are a source of angst to the wine elite but enjoyment to Fred, although at some expense and litigation. A 92,000-square-foot bottling plant he built in the southern Napa Valley allows him to sell Charles Shaw as "cellared and bottled in Napa," although the grapes come mostly from the San Joaquin Valley.

But Charles Shaw a.k.a. Two-Buck Chuck is only a part of Franzia's wine empire. The Bronco Wine Company—the family business he owns with his brother and a cousin—is the largest vineyard owner in the United States and, with six separate locations in California, the fourth-biggest winery. It produces more than two hundred brands sold in over ninety countries. When the Napa Valley Vintners Association launched a six-year court battle to close a loophole in California law to prevent Fred from using non-Napa grapes with the appellation Napa Ridge, a winery he bought for forty million dollars that had been legally following that practice for years, he immediately produced a wine with Napa grapes called Napa Creek. It sold for $3.99 with the nickname "Four-Buck Fred."

"That's when everyone went nuts," Fred said. "These fucking guys have no mind-games capability."

Most wine critics initially responded to Charles Shaw with niggardly reviews and ratings.

"Fuck the critics," Fred told me in the coffee shop. "We don't need 'em."

He's certainly right in terms of success since two-thirds of the triumvirate determining value in the world of wine are in his camp: the consumers and the judges. At Trader Joe's in Berkeley, I watched one shopping basket after another come to the cash register with several bottles, or often cases, of Charles Shaw, advertised in the store as "The World's Best Selling Wine" and sold in eight varieties: Cabernet Sauvignon, White Zinfandel, Merlot, Chardonnay, Sauvignon Blanc, Shiraz, Nouveau, and Pinot Grigio.

Critics taste wines out of labeled bottles, knowing what they're drinking before it hits their palates. Crotchety independent judges at blind-tasting competitions don't know the brand beforehand. Such judges, often winemakers themselves, have given seven varieties of Charles Shaw wines major awards, like best of class in both the 2011 Pacific Rim International Wine Competition and the New World Wine Competition. At the Twenty-Eighth Annual International Eastern Wine Competition, judges tasted over two thousand wines and gave a top prize—a double gold medal—to Charles Shaw Shiraz.

In July 2007, I received an email invitation to our high school class's summer BBQ in San Jose and was told, "We'll enjoy some of Freddie's finest....Top Chardonnay in California to be served." Indeed, Two-Buck Chuck had beat out 350 other Chardonnays to win a double gold medal and the best of show at that year's California Exposition and State Fair, an event the local paper announced as a "Two Buck Bombshell" and another paper headlined "The Judgment of California," a comparative reference to the 1976 competition in Paris when French experts unhesitatingly judged California wines superior to the best of French wines, both red and white, to stun the world's wine industry with what came to be called "The Judgment of Paris."

In subsequent years the awards have rolled in. Two-Buck Chuck won three gold medals at the 2013 Orange County Fair Wine Competition, one of the state's wine events where most of the judges are winemakers. "What makes this especially significant," the director said, "is that we hold the largest competition with only California wines, over 2,500."

The June 2013 *Consumer Reports* ranked Charles Shaw Chardonnay third out of ten wines costing up to ten times as much. It was also ranked "Best Buy."

Well, how did he do it? How did Fred achieve his success? Ever since he was a kid he'd always found a way to succeed. His talent, in short, resides in his niche-finding genius.

In the coffee shop, I looked across the table at Fred, who, though still rotund, had kept his weight down after dropping sixty pounds—at one point he'd ballooned up to over 260. As the years fell away, I once again saw the boy I knew in high school, not much over five and a half feet tall and 145 pounds. His older brother, Joe, a much bigger though quieter, unassuming, popular student, was a year ahead of us, our football team's star running back with powerful legs that didn't stop churning when he plunged into hapless tacklers. "Many fans," the Bellarmine school newspaper declared about Joe, "have been amazed at his ability to keep driving when smothered by a host of tacklers. He just puts down his head and starts plowing." In his senior year, Joe led the league in rushing yards and our team to an undefeated season.

In contrast, Fred didn't play football during his first two years of high school; he worked sequentially as student manager of the junior varsity and varsity teams. He then figured out a way to become a football player.

"I knew I wasn't big enough to make the team," he told me when I brought up the subject. "Look at you. You were twice as big as you are now." His observation proves an interesting reflection on the vagaries of memory because when I later checked a football program from our senior year, "Vallejo Apaches vs. Bellarmine—September 16, 1960," I'm listed at 5-11 and 191 pounds, probably only an inch and five pounds more than now, certainly a false listing since the weigh-in occurred at the beginning of the season when we returned heavier from the summer. Like some of my teammates, I'd also chugged down a quart of milk before stepping on the scales, wearing clothes and shoes, a strategy, we believed, to produce intimidating statistics when our opponents saw them.

In that same program, Fred is listed at 5-8 and 155 pounds, no doubt an exaggeration, though his size was irrelevant for our team's placekicker. During the summer between his sophomore and junior years he taught himself to kick. "Maybe Joe helped me," he now recalls about his brother, and he practiced until he was good enough to make the junior varsity and then the varsity. During our afternoon team practices, Bill Sterling, then the team's all-star center, remembers Fred in a square-toed shoe repeatedly kicking the ball through the goal posts. "Not many kids would practice alone that diligently" Bill said. "He had a tremendous work ethic."

Fred was listed on our team as a halfback, because in our day placekicking wasn't a specialty position. When Bill went to practice for the North-South All-Star Game in Los Angeles Coliseum, no kicker had been selected for the team and the coach asked if anyone could fill in. Fred had found a niche before there was one. "He became a very good extra-point and field-goal kicker," Tony Morici, our all-league quarterback, said. When I asked Fred, "What was your most memorable kick?" he replied, "In Kezar Stadium." The thrill, as Tony said, was that we got to run through the tunnel and play on the turf of the San Francisco 49ers. Tony was the holder for Fred's field-goal attempt. "It was forty-three yards," Fred recalled. "I think I missed." Actually an opposing lineman blocked the kick. "The guy hammered me," Fred said.

"Fred was good enough to play college ball," Tony told me. "He made the freshman and varsity teams at Santa Clara." Although a kicker, Fred was still listed as a halfback and once got to carry the ball on a running play. He scampered forty-five yards to score an apparent touchdown. It was called back, a source of future teasing from his friends. Tony told him, "Fred, you made the longest run of your life, but you were out of bounds."

Two other football players on our team were John Filice, whose family then owned San Martin Wines, and Mike Mondavi, whose father was Robert Mondavi, the winemaker most responsible for persuading Americans to see Napa Valley as a wine region comparable to the best of France. Fred and his brother, Joe, were heirs apparent to their family's Franzia Brothers Wine Company.

After high school, Fred remained friends with John, Mike, and Tony when they went down the street to attend Santa Clara University. John Filice recalls, "When we were at Santa Clara, one late afternoon I went to Fred's room to tell him that we were all going out to Dinjo's, a bar in San Jose. I found him in a sports coat and tie. We agreed to meet later that night as he had to go to a Wine Institute meeting in San Francisco. At nineteen, he'd signed up for some institute committees, since after serving on various committees and working his way up through the chairs he knew he'd be in line to become the Wine Institute president. While the rest of us were thinking about girls and drinking, Fred made a considerable commitment to the Wine Institute and eventually became its youngest president. At nineteen, he was already planning his ascension. It made quite an impression on me." He also later made a splash as president with some choice remarks about French wines during the institute's annual tour of Europe's wine-growing regions, causing one venerable member of the institute to ask John, "Has Fred always been so outspoken?"

At our team reunion in the fall of 2010, Mike Mondavi offered to supply wine for both the Friday tailgate party and the next day's lunch, but the reunion organizer wondered what would happen if Fred made the same offer since he knew the two old teammates were friendly rivals in the wine business. Mike replied to all of us in an email, "If Fred offers some wine I'd be happy to work with him—no problem—just that mine will taste better!"

Fred couldn't attend, however, because, as he said in an email, "This is our harvest season. I hope everyone has a great time."

Tom Abts, who was arranging events, wrote our teammates, "Somehow I have a hard time seeing Fred out picking grapes at his age."

"Leave Fred alone," a valley grape buyer told me; "he works hard. He works all the time." Which is true. I once exchanged a round of emails about a project with him and his PR man on Christmas morning and New Year's Day. I told the grape buyer that a lot of Fred's former teammates would like to see him at the reunion, and the buyer passed back Fred's reply, "Fuck those guys."

Perhaps you need a Jesuit boarding-school education to understand how we greeted this taunting language with good-natured chuckles. Competition was intense in our high school in both sports and the classroom—the entire top half of the fresh-man class was hierarchically ranked after each of eight exam periods, and the results were sent to our parents. In upper grades, only the honor roll was published. Guys with size felt pressure to play football. Fred was sassy and fearless, a cocky guy with a charming smile flashing as quickly as his impulse to say "fuck you" in a way we didn't take personally. No fistfights took place in the schoolyard because our splenetic moods found vent in language or athletics. The old notion of the spleen as the source of both anger and mirth fits Fred well: he said "fuck you" with a smile.

I heard from an insider about his meeting with a ten-billion-dollar glass container manufacturing company. The CEO projected a three-percent decrease in wine production over the next ten years, while Fred was projecting a ten-percent increase. Fred picked up a bottle of drinking water from the table. "Look how stupid you are," he said. "What business are you in? Glass? And you serve me water in a plastic bottle? I'm insulted." He stood up, walked out of the meeting, away from the lunch prepared for him, and went out to eat tacos.

"He's a complex guy," our classmate Joe Claassen said about Fred. "He has always been witty and quick, comfortable in his own skin—with a half-under-control vain streak that I always found Chaplinesque and touching."

Like an irascible Jackie Gleason in the TV sitcom *The Honeymooners,* who fumed, doubled his fist, and asked, "Do you want to go to the moon, Alice?" a mocking threat his wife met with a blank response, Fred blusters and postures in a way that can't hide an underlying streak of sweetness. If you're not in tune with reading between his lines, his social skills are reminiscent of a charging rhinoceros.

"A terrible story on Fred was in *The New Yorker*," Fred's PR consultant, Harvey Posert, told me. "The woman reporting the story appears to have been turned off by Fred's mouth and behavior because she started out by saying how she was 'on his side.' She learned nothing about his innovations." She also didn't get his sense of humor. Fred was profiled as a brash provocateur with a peppery tongue. Bragging about the risk he took grafting new vines every year, he said, "The average farmer would shit in his pants." Posert, a former newspaperman from Tennessee, came to the Napa Valley from Memphis via Yale and the University of Chicago Law School, and earned respect for his brilliant strategies and gracious charm. "Well, fuck *The New Yorker* piece," he told me. "It showed a shallow, blaspheming side of Fred without the deep work ethic and agricultural commitment."

One of our teammates thought Fred was lucky to have outgrown certain characteristics he'd seen while working with "predelinquent" boys. "These kids acted out against all authority figures without reason. They couldn't read their own emotions. Almost all they could express was anger. If they felt embarrassed they got angry; confused by a school problem, they got angry; jealous of someone else getting attention, they got angry. They all had either an absent or a weak father in the home before the age of eight. That may be an angle to investigate in Fred's early childhood experience."

A public clash with his father came after Fred graduated from college with a finance degree and returned to the valley to begin his advance in the family business, working in sales and then the company's wholesale division. He passed through one door after another, until the next expected door didn't open; it wasn't there to open. Against Fred's vehement protest, his father and four uncles sold the family winery to the Coca-Cola Bottling Company of New York. Their wines became part of The Wine Group, the world's second biggest winery at the time. The sale included the family name. Today, no Franzia brand has anything to do with Fred Franzia, including the popular innovation of wine in a box.

Fred refused to work for Coke. Enraged at his dad—seeing him as weak and not a fighter like himself—Fred set out with his brother and a cousin from square one. "We started with nothing," he told me in the coffee shop.

"You had some money from the sale, right?"

"We didn't have much money, but we had knowledge."

Fred gained much of his knowledge from his grandmother Teresa, who emigrated from Italy as a twenty-one-year-old mail-order bride, arriving on the Fourth of July in 1900. The San Joaquin Valley was then a remnant of the Old West—a region increasingly depopulated of native people and sparsely filled with newcomers of many ethnicities, races, and religions, who came to make a living off the land. Many Italian immigrants worked for the Miller & Lux cattle empire in the arid valley, others in the mountain timber sawmills, while Teresa—with her husband, Giuseppe, who'd immigrated to California in 1893—planted a vineyard. When her husband was back in Italy, where he annually spent six months, Teresa mortgaged the family vineyard in the San Joaquin Valley during the Great Depression for her five sons to start the Franzia Brothers Winery, in Ripon, north of Modesto, where Fred grew up. His grandmother had a talent for discovering profitable niches as he would later on. In 1933, Teresa helped another winery get started in Modesto by loaning $5,000 to a twenty-year-old boy married to one of her daughters and later Fred's uncle and mentor, Ernest Gallo, who with his brother Julio started the E. & J. Gallo Winery, now the biggest in the world.

Fred started from scratch. He'd learned from his immigrant grandmother Teresa the importance of hard work. Even as an old woman she put in long shifts on the winery's bottling line. From his uncle Ernest he learned how to stay grounded in the details of the business.

In 1973, in Ceres, a small town near Modesto named after the Roman goddess of agricultural fertility, Fred bought a cow pasture with his brother, Joe, and his cousin John Franzia to set up construction-site trailers as headquarters of the Bronco Wine Company, a name shared with the mascot of their Santa Clara University football team on which Fred and Joe played. Fred as Bronco's CEO, and Joe and John as co-presidents, launched their business as wine distributors by signing as their first client their old school friend's father, Robert Mondavi.

Due to Robert Mondavi's success in bringing prestige to Napa Valley wines, and by extension to those of California, several wineries had trouble keeping up with the public's shifting demand for whatever might be currently popular, as when White Zinfandel became the rage. Fred's Bronco company filled the niche by quietly entering the bulk wine business and anonymously selling to established wineries. Fred became a trader, both buying and selling grapes, juice, and wine. "Trucks brought in empty bottles," George Taber writes in his book, *A Toast to Bargain Wines,* "Bronco filled them, and then other trucks hauled them to the client winery." Without the name Bronco anywhere on the labels, Fred's wine ended up in Napa Valley bottles of Sutter Home, Beringer, and Robert Mondavi wines.

To move from bulk wine into retail sales with his own brands and labels, Fred, who'd lost control of his own name, began buying up defunct, bankrupt, or failing brands, acquiring labels cheaply without any clear idea if or when they might be glued onto bottles. One name in his collection of labels was Charles Shaw.

Eight years later the label appeared in Trader Joe's chain, and the following year, at the 2003 United Wine and Grape Symposium in the Sacramento Convention Center, it was described as creating a new category of "extreme value" wines and Bronco was named "Winery of the Year." The crowd erupted with hoots and jeers. Four years later, after setting a record for the fastest-selling label of all time, Charles Shaw, a.k.a. Two-Buck Chuck, began winning medals and prizes.

Journalists have been unable to connect the dots in the story of how Fred produced a popular wine at such a low price because he works behind a haze of obfuscation as thick as any tule fog in the valley. I've looked through books and articles to see how obscured glimpses of his process produce mostly distortions and speculations. One widespread myth about Charles Shaw in 2002 was that Fred bought up all the good wine the airlines had dumped because they could no longer use corkscrews after the terrorist attacks of September 11, 2001.

Even his friend Robert Mondavi couldn't figure Fred's success. According to Julia Flynn Siler in *The House of Mondavi: The*

Rise and Fall of an American Wine Dynasty, the ninety-year-old wine king of Napa Valley confronted the younger winemaker, "Fred, I just don't know how you do it. How can you make money selling wines so cheaply?" Siler reports, "Franzia deflected the question and revealed no secrets." He didn't reveal that he was buying good wine in bulk from several Napa wineries, including from Mondavi's own son Mike, at fire-sale prices because of a market slump and a storage glut. Wineries had to rid their tanks and barrels of unsellable wine before the coming harvest. Mondavi didn't know, and Fred wasn't telling.

Trader Joe's is as secretive as Fred about the origin and terms of their union, producing more speculation about how Fred arbitrarily picked the label Charles Shaw and told the chain store how to market it. In truth, Fred says, the retailer sets the price, something he learned when he tried to get restaurants to lower their prices of his wines by lowering his own. What actually happened, he told me, is that "we were already distributing a $2.99 imported Argentine wine to Trader Joe's when the salesman told me he wanted me to find one for a $1.99." Rather than look for an inexpensive Chilean or Argentine wine to import, Fred went to his brother and said, "I think we can do this ourselves."

He also didn't pick the label Charles Shaw on a whim. "I went through my labels," he told me, his fingers flicking the air as though looking for a greeting card on a store rack. "I wanted an Anglo name that was easy to remember." It helped, of course, that a decade earlier Charles Shaw had been known as an elite Napa wine before he and his wife divorced and the company went bankrupt. Fred always refers to the wine as Charles Shaw, never Two-Buck Chuck.

The glut of decent wine available for Charles Shaw certainly helped its popularity among consumers, but it wasn't enough to guarantee a profit. An executive in one of the big three wineries told me that they couldn't do what Fred did even if they'd wanted to, despite the worldwide glut of grapes. The cork and bottle alone would've cost a dollar, and the cost of distribution at thirty percent would've wiped out any profits since the retailer also takes thirty to forty percent. According to the executive, Fred told Trader Joe's he wouldn't give them forty percent; he would give them five percent, but in turn they would have the exclusive they desired. Another executive claimed Fred offered three dollars a case.

"Is that close to right?" I asked Fred.

"Nothing is ever right a hundred percent," he replied. "We work hard at having competitively priced wine of quality and good prices in everything we negotiate so that by the time we get to the packaging no one can compete with us. The proof is in the pudding. Now we're trying to farm forty thousand acres of grapes organically, and no one else in the state wants to tackle it. Most growers don't do it because it takes extra effort and work, but once you get through the knothole and get control of the weeds and don't use chemicals, the vines are healthier."

"We've gotten off the subject," I said. "The thing is that Trader Joe's does have the exclusive for Charles Shaw, and you gave them that."

"Yeah, hell yes."

"But they didn't get as big a cut, the regular forty percent."

"What they got is what everybody wants—an item that consumers want to buy and you can only buy at one place. Trader Joe's is known for good food, good prices, organically grown food, and when we match that up with our operation and go as direct as we can and keep those prices down, they just blow that stuff out of there."

"What about the person who said you gave them five percent and the other who said three dollars a case?"

"They don't know. Nobody knows."

"So what is it?"

"There is no answer."

"Didn't you give them something?"

"Well, I gave them a price that's fixed. Let's say I sold them at eighteen dollars a case and they sold at a $1.99 twenty-four bottles a case so they made six bucks a case or fifty cents a bottle. We give a price and they sell at whatever they want."

"So it would be wrong to say you gave them five percent."

"It wouldn't be accurate."

"Ten percent is closer," I said as a statement.

"Yeah, closer."

The principle remains that the retailer took a lower cut in exchange for an exclusive. An example of how Fred is also able to "go as direct as we can" was his ability to avoid the distribution costs of other wineries because his brother, Joe, was his distributor in California. In distant states and those where the law required a third-party distributor, Charles Shaw sold for $2.99 and $3.99. By continuously looking for ways to cut costs, such as changing wine-case boxes from white to brown cardboard, Fred kept the price of Two-Buck Chuck constant in California for twelve years. He created his own trucking company and spent a million dollars to run railroad tracks directly into the Ceres winery. In 2013, the price went up to $2.49, still only two bucks plus change. In 2018, it was $2.99.

What most people don't know, a company insider told me, is that bulk wine, not Charles Shaw, continues to be "Fred's cash cow." Bronco crushes some 500,000 tons of grapes a year, which would produce fifty million cases a year if all the wine was poured into Bronco bottles, but Fred sells half as bulk wine that ends up in bottles of other companies. "That's easy money," I was told. "Fred's turning the inventory so fast, a month later the juice is Pinot Gris, and the checks roll in from Gallo."

One of Fred's early deals, I was told, was when he agreed to supply someone with bulk wine before he had a winery to make it. "He got someone to commit capital for the bulk wine up front," a company insider told me. "So he cut the deal without having the infrastructure to make the wine. He then used the money to build the facility to make the wine. Nobody knows about that deal. Well, I think a few people know. Fred says, 'That was my greatest deal of all time.'"

Driven by the loss of his family winery—he didn't speak to his father for seven years after the sale of the Franzia name—"Fred became like the General Patton of winemaking," according to his friend John Filice. "In building Bronco from scratch, he did what was necessary to first survive and then prosper. If a rule or industry protocol was in his way, he ignored it. He worked harder, longer, and more aggressively than anyone, save his uncle Ernest. I think Fred will be like his uncle and his friend Robert Mondavi in that he'll continue to work 24/7 until he's ninety. They will wheel him out of that trailer office. Fred has it much better than General Patton. He will never run out of wars."

Many battles took place in protracted lawsuits and court clashes, one over a distribution contract with Robert Mondavi, but the most serious occurred in 1993 when the Bronco Wine Company and Fred Franzia were indicted for mislabeling grapes over a five-year period, bringing a federal charge of conspiracy to defraud by selling loads of cheap grapes as more expensive Zinfandels. According to the feds, Franzia instructed workers to disguise the falsely labeled loads by scattering Zinfandel leaves on top of the cheaper grapes, an act Franzia reportedly called "the blessing of the loads," supposedly a mocking imitation of the inaugural religious ritual at harvest time.

I'd heard of farmers mixing berries or falsifying field tags, but using leaves to disguise loads struck me as far-fetched. Who notices differences between grape leaves? "You've been around wineries long enough," Fred told me. "If you're shipping 400 to 500 trucks into the winery a day, how do you do this? You'd need a wind machine trying to put leaves and shit in there. It wouldn't work. When they get you and squeeze you, they want you to say you're guilty of something you might not have done, but it stops them."

The larger charge of misrepresenting five thousand tons of grapes and a million gallons of wine was another matter. "We had the government for eight years chasing us down," Fred said. "They wanted to indict six other guys here, who had to get their own attorneys. I mean they break you. They won't stop. In business you have to get smart, take the hit, and shorten it. They wanted one guy to plead guilty. I did, and that was it."

Fred paid a $500,000 fine and served five hundred hours of community service at a child-abuse-prevention center under the pseudonym Ralph Kramden, the name of Jackie Gleason's working-class bus driver in *The Honeymooners*. The Bronco Wine Company pleaded nolo contendere and paid a $2.5 million fine. The combined fine was the court's biggest in what had been a widespread scandal in the grape industry when the popularity of White Zinfandel elevated the price of Zinfandel grapes to ten times that of somewhat comparable varieties, creating the temptation to substitute. "Everyone was doing it," a winery VP told me. Unlike half a dozen other valley grape and wine dealers breaking the law—or rather the half dozen who were caught—Fred didn't have to go to jail or sell his company stock. The U.S. prosecutor accepted his plea-bargain contention that if he were jailed the company might fail and the community would suffer economically from layoffs, though he did have to step down as

CEO and was technically banned for five years from company involvement in winemaking.

After the trial Fred and his legal team were eating at Morton's in Sacramento, and all his lawyers were ecstatic because he hadn't gotten any jail time. Fred later told a mutual friend of ours, "I felt like throwing up. I'd just pled guilty to a crime and they were all celebrating on my dime."

The sting of the felony conviction led him in later years to try to get a presidential pardon from George W. Bush, but he was rejected. As with the loss of the family winery, the incident remains galling. "We work very hard to give consumers a hundred percent of what we say they're getting," he told me. "We run the cleanest operation in the country. Yeah, we got tattooed, but that was twenty-five years ago."

Near noon, in Madera, I rode shotgun with Fred in his dusty Jeep Cherokee to a Mexican carnicería and taquería at the edge of town, called Don Chuy, where there's no table service and just about everyone speaks Spanish. Jim Unti, a former grape buyer for Constellation Wines and my friend since the first grade, drove to the taquería with Sal Arriola, Fred's field boss for the vineyard division of Bronco, named West Coast Grape Farming. In 1986, when the wine industry was in a severe slump and growers were pulling out grapevines in response to projections of bad times ahead, Fred found a new marketing niche by doing the opposite. He began buying land and developing vineyards throughout the San Joaquin Valley. Bronco's enormous capacity for crushing, bottling, storage, and distribution required a lot of grapes. When land prices were cheap Fred saw a way to achieve more self-sufficiency and control over his source of grapes by owning his vineyards instead of leasing them, as he'd been doing, or buying from farmers who wanted high prices. He and Sal were now on the road to meet with workers at the vast vineyards between Modesto and Bakersfield, more than forty thousand acres, debt free and expanding, more acreage than all of Napa Valley's vineyards put together.

"I think he's always appreciated farmworkers," Sal later told me about Fred. "I think he's always made an effort to say 'I understand what they do for me,'" but when he was building his business, "he was too removed from what they actually do and now he's made a point to look at his farming operation and to be personally involved."

In speaking out for immigration reform, Fred gave the March 2013 keynote address at California State University in Fresno for ninety growers, contractors, and congressional and senate representatives. "The farmworker is a viable and important part of our being in the San Joaquin Valley," he said. He called for reform to protect their rights and prevent them from "being on the dodge and acting like they're some criminal element." On other occasions he has spoken out in ways that blunt accusations of his disguising a self-serving need for workers in his fields. "We benefit from their labor," he told a group of reporters; "they benefit from our jobs. Our laws should acknowledge and reflect this reality, not deny it." He talked about earlier "ignorant discrimination and racism," saying, "I am sure many of you can relate to how other ethnic groups such as Italians, Irish, and Japanese were labeled as criminals and mafioso." He went on, "Historically, the best results have come from providing more legal ways to enter the country."

—⁂—

In the Madera taquería, the tangy smells took me back to the many months, and even years, I've lived in Mexico. Fred handed

Sal a hundred-dollar bill and told him, "You know what I like." With great detail in Spanish, Sal explained to the women behind the service counter exactly how he wanted Fred's *carnitas* prepared. I ordered the *lengua* and spicy *barbacoa*. Like Fred and Jim, I pulled a chilled Diet Pepsi out of the stand-up cooler.

Before going to work for Fred, Sal had worked ten years for Jim as his right-hand man at what is now Constellation Wines, the world's biggest winery behind Gallo. I'd often heard from Jim how Fred would drop by his office to drink Diet Pepsi and get local news. "The first time I met him," Jim said, "a guy came running into the office about a helicopter landing." Fred had roared into the valley and landed in the Bisceglia Winery, where Jim then worked as the field rep.

"When he was younger," Sal said about Fred, "I can imagine what kind of bulldog he was. I've seen him change over the past five years."

While we ate at Don Chuy, Fred talked about his plans to fund a wine institute to research vineyard development in the San Joaquin Valley. "We almost have enough money to do it," he said. "I've got a million from Gallo and commitments from others."

I asked about the ongoing study of winemaking and vineyard technology at the University of California in Davis, and at California State University in Fresno, and Fred replied, "Ah, they don't get into the fields. They don't get out and talk to the workers." He didn't mention that six years earlier he gave CSU Fresno a million dollars to endow the Bronco Wine Company Viticulture Research Chair in the Department of Viticulture and Enology. He also anonymously picked up payments for another chair.

He and Sal were now traveling through the valley all the way to Tehachapi.

"I want to find out about the wild grapes in the Tehachapi

Mountains," he said. "That's why the area was called Grapevine." Like most people who grew up in California, I'd assumed (as does the *Wikipedia* entry on "Grapevine, California") that the term *Grapevine* referred to the treacherous curving ascent of old Route 99 (and now Interstate 5) twisting like a grapevine from the valley's southern endpoint up through Tejon Pass into the Tehachapi Mountains. When I was a boy, drivers from the valley to Los Angeles strapped canvas water bags to the fronts of cars for their soon-to-be overheated radiators on the winding mountain climb through three-digit heat, whipping winds, or impenetrable tule fog. Everybody knew someone who'd broken down on the Grapevine.

The name actually came from wild grapes growing in the mountain pass, causing Catalan explorer Pedro Fages in 1772 to call a canyon near the summit Cañada de las Uvas, or Canyon of Grapes.

Fred pointed across the table to Jim Unti. "I want Jim in the institute. He's an encyclopedia." He said Jim had been out in the fields. He wasn't someone who'd spent all his time trying to develop a little garden vineyard. The numbers may sound far-fetched, but Fred buys a hundred tractors at a time, spends three million dollars a year on owl houses for rodent control and another twenty million on pesticides. "You need fresh knowledge from the fields to make money," he said. He grew enlivened in summing up his business philosophy. His wide-open eyes flashed behind his rectangular glasses. "I'm in the money-making business. What's a guy going to do who's not making money? Jerk off about how good his vineyard is?"

Now he was sounding like the old, salty-tongued Fred, energized by his Diet Pepsi and caricatured in many published reports as driven by America's primary measurement of success: money, and the belief that only money matters, money to buy more and more things.

After lunch, as we stood by his Jeep Cherokee, he surprisingly countered the spouting of a money-driven tycoon and even echoed the eremitical tradition of the third-century Desert Fathers of Egypt, as he extolled the value of work over money. He talked about classmates we both knew, who, he said, have never really had to work because of inheritance. That was part of the reason for his setting up his new institute and for figuring out other ways to put his money to use. "It's no good just to leave it all to your kids," he said. "Inheritance isn't good, if you don't have to work."

I gave him a thumbnail sketch of my family's monetary fate in California ranching over three generations, starting with my great-grandfather's coming from the Pyrenees to farm in Los Angeles and ending with the loss of our family ranch in the San Joaquin Valley. Fred gave me a sidelong look, a crooked grin, and then threw a quick punch into my arm. "Hey," he said, "that's the best thing that could've happened to you."

He told me that he liked the world of work I presented in my novel *Jesse's Ghost*, which dramatizes valley ranch life in the 1960s. He said a mutual friend of ours, Mitch Lasgoity, a Basque American rancher in Madera, who sells his grapes to Fred, recommended the novel to him. In turn, Fred passed along copies of the novel to others.

"A farmer friend of Fred's," Jim Unti had told me, "is reading your book. Fred gave it to him." The farmer wrote poems on coffeehouse napkins and read them at a local writers' group where Jim also read his own autobiographical essays. "Madera is getting strange," Jim said.

Several scenes in *Jesse's Ghost* take place along Cottonwood Creek, which runs through our former family ranch and near where Fred now owns Cottonwood Creek Winery. After asking me several questions about the process of writing and publishing, he mentioned how affected he was by the pain of divorce in the novel. "Have you ever been divorced?" he asked.

I told him no, and he said he could hardly believe it, given how it's dramatized in the novel. "That's about the worst thing that can happen to you," he said. "Divorce—and maybe losing your whole business."

I sensed no anger in his voice, only grief. Fred was twice divorced and had five children; two sons and a daughter then worked with him in the family wine business. In that moment, I thought of the injunction from our former classmate—more than one, actually—to write a book about Fred. Something in me still resisted. As we talked, though, I began to feel differently because of our shared connection to the valley and our beliefs about work and inheritance.

The complexity of Fred's feelings during our conversation suggested to me a way to write about both him and San Joaquin Valley agriculture. I knew he'd be reluctant. He had little interest in publicity. When the PR consultant Harvey Posert first came to work, Fred told him he wanted no press. Harvey had worked for Robert Mondavi who'd wanted all press. "It was the other side of the moon," Harvey said. Only recently did Fred allow Harvey to set up a website for the company, an antiquated one with no social media. He'd become more reticent and reclusive over the years. He didn't socialize or take vacations: both infringed on time better given to work. His dream house, he said, was for his kids and grandchildren. He lived in a Modesto condominium, the same one since his second divorce twenty years ago.

"He works out there in that dump," Harvey told me about Fred's headquarters in Ceres, still the original construction-site trailers of some thirty-five years ago. When I last visited him the original industrial carpets still lay on the floor, some with saucer-sized holes exposing bare particleboard, others patched with duct tape. In his dilapidated trailer, Fred sits in homage to a vanished older West of his grandmother's era. "Hell, he could fix it up," Harvey said, "but he just wants everything the way it is. He wants it to be like in *Jesse's Ghost*—like the old days—and he's the *patrón*."

I asked Fred about his role as boss of the company. I'd heard that he was mainly responsible for sales while his cousin and brother handled production and distribution.

"Nah," he said, "we do pretty much everything together." He gave me that mischievous grin. "But I go where the heat is."

As he was about to climb into the Jeep Cherokee to resume his journey south toward Bakersfield, I mentioned that some of our classmates wanted me to write a book about him. He looked at me skeptically. I amended my suggestion. "Maybe I'll just do a sketch," I said.

He waved his hand dismissively and pointed to his field boss, Sal Arriola, walking our way toward the Jeep. "Write a story about Sal," he said.

Illegal Immigrant to Valley Farmer

Sal Arriola illegally crossed the border from Mexico with his parents when he was three and later worked in vineyards not far from where I met him one October afternoon at the Franzia Cottonwood Creek Winery outside Madera. Sal was in charge of the Franzias' forty thousand acres of vineyards in the San Joaquin Valley and more than three thousand fieldworkers at the peak of the season. "I didn't see it coming," Sal told me. "I was destined to connect back to where I started."

Sal, who'd just turned forty, exuded the energy of a six-foot-three former athlete as he bounded along grape rows. Although his family name is of Basque derivation, he proudly proclaims his *mestizo* heritage from Mexico. Dressed in a white shirt and blue jeans, he has black brush-cut hair, a bold nose, and dark eyes that can be both intense and dreamy. He'd left his parked Cherokee running by the side of the vines, the sound of the rumbling engine in sync with his fast-talking, gravelly voice. "I've got six hundred acres here of organic grapes," he said, pointing to Cabernet, Zinfandel, Pinot Noir, and Tanat. "I'm the one who found the spurs for Tanat. We're now the largest growers of Tanat in California—in the world maybe."

A designated twenty-acre research plot contained a half-dozen red varietals from all over the planet. Out of the plot Sal grew several acres of a new red-blended Cabernet. "This is Cab

Dorsa. It's supposed to be as dark as a Ruby Red. It's a vinifera varietal. I don't know where John Franzia found it, but this guy's going to be a twelve-to-fourteen-ton red producer. We'll pick it in August with twenty-five sugar."

John Franzia is the winemaker and does the research, but his cousin Fred determines what grapes he needs. "One thing about Fred," Sal said, "is he doesn't minimize the importance of his partners"—his brother, Joe, and his cousin John. "Fred doesn't say 'I, I, I.' He says, 'My partners and I.' But he's the driving force. What the market is calling for—whatever Fred's short—that's what we're going to put in. We grafted two thousand acres over the last couple of years with Zinfandel."

Sal grafts from a thousand to fifteen hundred acres of vines every year to meet shifting demand—"one of the secrets of our success," Fred has said. Sal explained how a new vineyard can be created, not by replanting but by grafting canes of a different variety onto an older rootstock. In one year an entire vineyard can be transformed. Sal showed where Muscat canes were originally grafted onto the trunks of Zinfandel grapevines because Fred needed Muscat grapes, but when Fred became short of Zin the Muscat canes were cut off and replaced once again with spurs of Zinfandel.

"What's unique here," Sal said about the organic vines, "is that when we want to switch varieties, we do the research for two or three years, then we cut off the canes and graft new varieties. This is Pinot Noir organic, and here we have 120 acres of grafted Cab. We cane-pruned it and decided we were going to get creative."

They grew two varieties on the same grapevine trunks. The grafted Cabernet canes went on the top wire and the original vines on the second wire. "It's Triple Blanc underneath," Sal explained. "We put Cab on top and—*voom!*—twelve tons the first year after the graft."

Cottonwood Creek Winery is a CCOF-certified organic winery, which means it produces wine made with organic grapes. It's not organic wine. "That's impossible," Sal said. "Without sulfites it would go bad in two weeks. Then you're screwed. It's wine made from organically grown grapes." Besides Cottonwood Creek wines, which are available on the general market, Fred introduced a less expensive label in 2010 called Green Fin made with organic grapes and sold exclusively at Trader Joe's for $3.99. In 2016, the U.S. Zero Waste Business Council honored the Bronco Wine Company for its outstanding recycling program.

Franzia's goal is to make all his vineyards organic. In the spring of 2018 he introduced an organic Charles Shaw Pinot Noir and four other varietals, all with a cork that twists open with a *pop!* On April 19, 2018, the Master Sommelier Emmanuel Kemiji wrote that he'd "tasted the Shaw organic wines today which I must say, specially the whites and the rose, were spectacular for the price."

"The biggest obstacle to all organic growers is weeds, Bermuda grass," Sal said, "but my cleanest block of vines through the season is organic, and I don't use any chemicals. It's all mechanical. I've got five or six plows. I'll tell you what: that French plow works. I plowed five hundred acres last year. We can only do about ten acres a day. It's real slow, so we also put a double tiller on the same frame as the French plow."

The irony here is that Sal never learned to drive a tractor. "Yeah," Sal said, "that's the irony. I'm the farmer. I never drove a tractor. But I bought four hundred since I started here. Spent millions and millions of dollars. I never saw it coming. I didn't want to be here. When I got out of school I thought I was going to interview with some corporate law firm, thinking I wanted to work in an environment that allowed me to put a suit on—or a bank because I like numbers. Never did I think I'd loop back into agriculture. I completely revamped the way they run a farming operation, and my father will ask me every time he talks to me, 'You still don't drive a tractor, do you?'"

Sal's father, Miguel Arriola, inauspiciously began work as a farm laborer the first time he illegally crossed the border into the U.S. in 1969 with his wife's father and brothers and migrated up to Washington to pick apples. He arrived at the apple orchard on a Friday and was busted on Sunday by the border patrol before he could get in a day's work. Deported with his relatives to Tijuana, he was again walking across the border a week later, this time more successfully establishing a migratory life until he found more permanent work with Frenchy Montero on the Leonard Creek Ranch in Nevada. After a couple of years, he returned to Pihuamo in the state of Jalisco and wended his way back to the U.S. through the Tijuana hills with his wife and four children when Sal was three.

Ramón Montero Orquin and Michel Bidart started their Leonard Creek Ranch when Nevada was the leading immigrant state with the largest percentage of foreign born in the country. The former Basque sheepherders bought seven thousand acres from Miller & Lux, first running sheep and then a thousand cattle on 150,000 acres of private and public land that remains in the family. "They were into rodeos," Sal said about the Bidarts and Monteros, "and old-style ranching. When I was six, we'd go horseback riding for days. I thought it was play." Frank Bidart is in the Buckaroo Hall of Fame. More recent Monteros have won cowboy honors. In 2001 and 2003 Suzanne Montero was a two-time national college all-around champion cowgirl. Her brother Dan told me how the old-time ranching Sal was exposed to continues today. In the fall of 2017, Dan was helping with branding. His seventy-four-year-old mother was castrating a calf when its hoof slipped out of the rope and kicked her face. "She was bleeding and most anyone else in the corral would have been down for the count," Dan said, "but she pretty much refused any help not forced on her and was back castrating about ten minutes later."

Sal's family began to migrate from the Nevada ranch to pick grapes during the fall harvest in the San Joaquin Valley, where he recalls helping his parents lay out raisin trays in vineyards when he was five and a half and going to kindergarten in three different schools, two in Madera and the third in Nevada, a one-room shack on the Leonard Creek Ranch. Sal's family chased work, as he says, jumping from town to town. When he was eight, his parents quit migrating and settled in Madera, where they still live.

Of the vineyards Sal now farms for the Franzias, five thousand acres are in Madera County. The Cottonwood Creek Ranch is fifteen hundred acres, including the six hundred of organic grapes. Sal led his former boss Jim Unti and me to a farmhouse that serves as the ranch headquarters near Cottonwood Creek, which winds through my family's vanished ranch, where I grew up. Sitting at a table in what's called the Creekside Office, Sal talked about his experience of growing up in the valley.

"Every summer and in the winter when school wasn't on, we'd be working in the fields." Everything earned went into the family pot. When his three older sisters were ten, fourteen, and sixteen, "they were pretty good at flipping raisin trays." After school at three o'clock his parents would pick them up, and his sisters could flip a thousand trays in an evening to make twenty or thirty bucks, pretty good money, that went into the pot.

"I remember thinking, man, I can't wait until school starts," Sal said. He learned to love school because it took him out of the 105-degree heat when he was either trying to lay down trays or hide in the shade when his parents were looking for him. During Christmas break when his parents pruned vines and it was too cold to be outside he remembers crawling into the car and turning on the heater. He began to seek other outlets.

"When junior high came around," Sal said, "I realized school's the only way out. I didn't want to be on the ranch. I didn't want to be on the farm." He looked at his parents' struggles and didn't want them. "That's what got me hooked on school."

He began moving away from his farm-labor crowd, guys who wanted to go down to Bonanza 88 and shoplift or do dope. He was smart enough, he said, to surround himself with smarter friends, like Jim Unti's son Eric.

"They just weren't Caucasians. Black, brown, blue, it didn't matter. We had a mixed bag. I had Latino—Mexican—friends, like Omar Davina who went on to Yale and Jesús Rodríguez who went to Stanford and is now a doctor in Fresno. The race card was never there. What we had in common is we wanted to do well. We peeled ourselves away from those who were going to hold us back."

In the eighth grade, when he visited his friend Eric's house on Barnett Avenue, he talked with Eric's mother. "Tina Unti was the first nonfamily member who took a genuine interest in me. There were positive things she would share with me." She talked to him about the importance of doing well in school and excelling in sports. When he was a freshman in high school she told him, "You're not the average fourteen-year-old kid." She didn't say he wasn't merely Latino or Mexican. "She didn't play that card. She was always telling me I wasn't the average fourteen-year-old. She told me it's not just what you know but it's your confidence that's going to persevere."

That year when he was fourteen stands out because in high school other people "started making you conscious," he said, "of how different you are, but why you're different is because you're of Latin descent. Everybody seemed fascinated that I excelled.

It wasn't supposed to work that way. How the hell can you be so smart? Early on I never felt as intelligent as the other kids. You didn't have the support system when it came to education back home, so you had to work that much harder. But that was a motivation. I always need a target to shoot for. I had to work harder to keep up with the other kids."

In high school, he made the junior varsity basketball team and the varsity volleyball team in his freshman year. "My approach to sports was the same way. There's going to be kids better than me, but nobody's going to outwork me."

Teachers, principals, and coaches took an interest in him. "They gravitated toward me, not because they liked me, but because I made them look good. They wanted a success story, but I didn't buy into it. To me it wasn't about making them look good, it was my escape. I was laughing at them. You guys are my ticket out. I'm not going back to the farm."

When he was fourteen, Sal realized for the first time that he was still working during the summer when many of his friends were playing hoops, going on family vacations, or holding only part-time jobs. *Hey, this ain't fair,* he thought. While a couple of his good friends decided to go to a Notre Dame basketball camp with Digger Phelps in Indiana, Sal had another target to shoot for. He wanted his own bed. With three sisters, he was the kid on the couch. Now that his family was moving into government-subsidized housing with several bedrooms he wanted a bed. And he got it. For a month, he worked at a peach-packing shed, until it was discovered that he was a minor. He left the house at 4:00 a.m. and returned home at 8:00 p.m. with more money than his father was making. "I think my mother still has that bed," he said.

"When we come back to school I'm telling these guys about the hours I've been working and they're telling me about how they got yelled at by Digger Phelps. I think that's cool. I didn't hold it against these guys but, okay, we're not quite the same."

After his sophomore year he picked table grapes during the summer and by noon could have fifty or sixty bucks in his pocket. "In my junior year," Sal said, "we tried to transition out of the fields." His uncles opened a restaurant called Rancho Madera. "It was a traditionally owned family operation, an outlet for all the family." Sal's mother was the cook, and during the summer of his senior year Sal bussed tables and washed dishes, working alongside his sisters, aunts, and cousins. They never returned to the fields. Only his father remained a farmworker, though no longer a pruner or grape picker. "He'd elevated himself to a tractor-driver classification," Sal said, "which is higher than farm laborer." Sal continued to do well in sports, playing varsity basketball for three years and making all-league his senior year. By his sophomore year he was a star in volleyball and runner-up as the league's most valuable player. He went to a volleyball tournament at UCLA his junior year, and recruiters started appearing from colleges like Stanford, BYU, Rutgers, "schools I'd never heard of." He took breaks from work to go to weeklong basketball camps at Fresno State and volleyball camps at UC Santa Barbara, Albuquerque, and even Toledo, Ohio. "I didn't pay for anything. I'm just a poor Mexican kid out of Madera. Tina got involved." She raised sponsorship money for his trips.

He graduated from Madera High with a 3.87 average as one of the top fifty volleyball players in the country and was accepted at UCLA, Berkeley, Long Beach State, and elsewhere but chose the University of California at Santa Barbara for its Division I volleyball program and a scholarship covering room and board, tuition, and three-thousand dollars each quarter for pocket money. "The whole nine yards," Sal said.

He was seventeen when he started college and went to

preseason varsity volleyball practice. "The only mistake I made was thinking I was as good as people made me believe." He'd taken the summer off from practicing. He was six-three and could jump pretty high, touching eleven feet, but at UC Santa Barbara everyone was impressive. "Everybody was good, tall or short. That's why it's the cream of the crop. In Madera I'd played on raw talent." Here were kids from L.A. and Manhattan Beach, who'd been coached and had perfect form. A sophomore on the team would later go on to win an Olympic gold medal.

The team coach told Sal that like other first-year players he'd be red-shirted as a freshman, meaning he'd practice with the team but not play games and still have four years of eligibility. Sal said, "That was the first time someone told me I couldn't do something. The first time a door closed. It didn't sit well. I felt I wasn't being given a chance. I transitioned myself to say sports got me to this point. The next level is to get a university education."

He graduated with a degree in business economics. Commencement was on Saturday, and on Monday he started work as an inventory analyst at the pistachio-processing plant of Paramount Farms outside Bakersfield. "I'd never seen a damn pistachio except in snacks." But the company had lost a million pounds of them—they'd just magically disappeared—because of computer system problems. The professional engineer he replaced didn't have an accounting background like Sal and couldn't speak Spanish with ninety-nine percent of the company's employees, who were Mexican.

"Now I'm a Latin middle manager," Sal said. "Every employee was coming to me complaining about not getting a raise in three years." Management told Sal to fire them. "It wasn't just management I had a problem with." Older supervisors with the company for years were loath to take orders from a twenty-two-year-old kid. Management told Sal to fire them, too. "I was the brown guy who was supposed to fix everything up, but I wasn't the right guy for the job. I knew I wasn't going to succeed because of the culture and my age. Now if I'd been thirty-two, maybe it would've been different."

After three months he left the company and went to talk to Tina. Jim Unti was then a VP in charge of grape management and grower relations at the Canandaigua Wine Company, later named Constellation Wines and the second biggest in the world after buying the Robert Mondavi Corporation for a billion dollars. Jim told Sal, "I can't pay you very much, but why don't you show up?" When Sal pressed for a description of what he was supposed to do at the winery, Jim replied, "Don't ask so many questions. You sign up for the commitment, not the job. Pave your own way."

This was 1995. Sal said, "I saw that my ticket was the computer. I arrived at a perfect time when the technology was just coming in—Gore had just invented the internet! Programmers didn't understand the grape business, and computers were foreign to grape buyers. Nobody had closed the gap. I wanted to do things nobody else could do: start using computer technology to advance the business front. I set about learning the business, learning computers." He went on, "I didn't have a knowledge of grape growing. I didn't have a knowledge of shit. I'd picked grapes but knew nothing about the business component. But I saw they had to automate the system to expedite the business. That's what I think I accomplished." He automated grape management at the winery.

One of the winery's biggest problems with grape management was with Fred Franzia. Constellation had a contract to deliver twenty thousand tons of grapes to Fred for crushing, but Sal said that every time grapes were ready for delivery, "Fred told them to go pound salt." He wasn't ready. Then when Fred wanted grapes—so many reds, so many whites—Constellation didn't have them, or he didn't want the ones they had. "I won't take another pound of Carignan," Fred would say. It was a Catch-22. A senior VP at Constellation worried that Fred was going to sue for breach of contract since the company hadn't brought him any grapes. Sal took over scheduling and when Bronco was ready for delivery he scrambled to allocate grapes from different wineries and growers, "taking from this pocket to that pocket," he said, "moving enough fruit around not to piss off too many people." He got twenty thousand tons to Fred.

Fred, known for keeping his ear to the ground, followed his habit of showing up in Jim's office to drink Diet Pepsi and get news about local grapes and wine until he sometimes dozed off in the chair. "Jim was the only one at Constellation Fred would talk to," Sal said. "Unbeknownst to me, he's eyeballing me." He saw this young kid, a Mexican kid, seemingly with a good head on his shoulders.

The next year Constellation had a contract with Bronco to deliver forty thousand tons. With only a few weeks left in the season Sal saw they weren't going to make it. Again Constellation worried about Fred bringing a lawsuit. Sal asked the Bronco scheduler to have Fred call him. Sal had learned that Fred actually didn't need the grapes—his crushing plant was full—but Fred didn't let on when he phoned and asked, "Hey, Sal, why do you feel so inclined to have to bring me so much fruit?" *What?* Sal thought. *Why do I feel so inclined?* He told Fred he had a mandate to deliver forty thousand tons.

"Where are you at?" Fred asked.

"Nineteen thousand."

"Well, that's enough."

Fred took to calling Sal at home on Sundays. "I can't find you guys in the office," he told Sal. "Don't you work on Sundays?"

He even offered Sal a job in front of Jim when they were all in the Jeep together after eating at Don Chuy. "I can use a man like you," Fred said, "if you need a change of pace."

In 2007, Sal had worked at Constellation for twelve years, and Jim thought Sal might take over from him, but Constellation was expanding under new management, Jim felt pressure to retire, and Sal sensed he wasn't making progress because of the expansion.

Fred invited Sal to visit him. "We didn't have a formal interview," Sal said. Fred just told him, "We think you can run this farming operation," which was a hundred-million-dollar business. He also told Sal not to worry about his salary, the money was going to come. He pulled out a book and said this was their fifty-year plan. Did Sal want to be on board or stay at Constellation and try to figure out who his next boss was going to be?

Knowing that Fred squeezes everybody, Sal told him he had to negotiate a contract. Fred asked, "What will it take?" Sal, not thinking he would leave his job with Jim or get what he requested, wrote down more than twice his current salary.

Fred tossed the paper back and said, "I don't pay people that kind of money." Sal didn't tell me the number, but Jim said he'd asked for a hundred thousand dollars.

"But I can do a nickel less," Fred told Sal.

"You mean ninety-five thousand?" Sal asked.

"That's right," Fred said.

When Sal told Jim about the offer, which also included a transfer allowance and other perks like profit sharing, he advised Sal that he'd be crazy not to take it, but he emailed me, "I'm happy for Sal, but Fred better not show up in my office for a while and want his free Diet Pepsi."

When Sal asked for a description of his new job, Fred waved

his hand around the room and said, "You figure it out. I'm running a company. Do you think I've got time to run grape management?"

What is this? Sal wondered. *Jim Unti all over again?* There's a desk. You figure it out. Pave your own way.

Six months later Sal had completely revamped Bronco's computer system. At the first big company meeting Sal attended, Fred stood up after three minutes and said, "Sal, I think you've got this meeting" and walked out.

"He's a different kind of guy," Sal said. "Either you can work for him or you can't. He's just a moneymaking machine. He's so vertically integrated. Somewhere in his life he connected all the dots." When he was faced with a problem he learned to fix it and make money along the way. "Those are the buzzwords," Sal said. "Fix it, save money, or make more money, and you're in gold with Fred."

At first Sal didn't have a title. Fred told him, "I'm the CEO, CFO, COO. I'll find some bullshit title for you." That title eventually became CAO, or chief agricultural officer, one of the company's highest-ranking nonfamily officers and one level below the owners. If there's trouble on the ranches, Sal said, "I'm the guy who hires the field contractors. Now that I'm an officer in the company I can really get screwed, the guy they can put in the slammer."

Here's what he was talking about. A year after he began working at Bronco, in late spring of 2008, a young farmworker named María Isabel Vásquez Jiménez suffered a heatstroke while tying vines in a Bronco vineyard and died two days later. The seventeen-year-old illegal immigrant, who came from Oaxaca to join her boyfriend in Madera, was two months pregnant and became a cause célèbre. Governor Arnold Schwarzenegger attended her funeral. The contracting company that employed the girl, Merced Farm Labor, was shut down, and the business owner, Maria De Los Angeles Colunga, and her safety coordinator and brother, Elias Armenta, were charged with involuntary manslaughter for not providing adequate water and breaks for workers but pleaded no contest two years later to a misdemeanor of failing to provide shade. The deputy district attorney told the press the case was problematic because there was drinking water available and workers did receive breaks. Fred and his company were not brought to court, although United Farm Workers called for a protest against Trader Joe's.

When news of the teenager's death initially reached Jim, he worried about Sal. *Oh shit,* he thought, *they're going to throw the Mexican into the fire,* but he later learned that Fred called Sal into his office and said, "There's going to be some heavy heat coming this way, but you don't have to be involved, unless you want to."

Sal replied that he'd signed on for everything and would be involved. He saw it as an opportunity to learn. "Fred understood that," Sal said. "He told me the times he learned the most about his business and how to run it differently was when he was in a jam. 'And you will do the same,' he told me." Sal didn't realize, though, how the learning process would begin almost immediately when Attorney General Jerry Brown had his office speed-dial Sal about possible criminal charges.

Fred vehemently broadcast his empathy for fieldworkers. He maintained that a water truck, driven by the girl's uncle, was available that day, as they always are in his fields. After Isabel collapsed, no one called 911, and the foreman, according to Fred, delayed too long in getting her to the hospital for fear of her discovery as an illegal.

In 2005, Governor Schwarzenegger had passed a heat regulation law to protect California's 450,000 seasonal farmworkers, and after the death he announced, "I fought to adopt the strongest and first heat regulations in the nation because worker safety from heat illness must and will be protected in California."

Later that same summer after Isabel's death five more field-workers at other California farms died from heat sickness.

For his part, Fred funded an association for farm-labor contractors to improve working conditions in agriculture through the enforcement of regulations for shade, water, and safety. All contractors working in Fred's vineyards must belong.

"We took a negative and turned it into a positive in the way we operate the ranches," Sal said. "We made a lot of changes for the better."

I asked about the United Farm Workers' claim of Franzia's abuse of farmworkers. "There's no truth to that," Sal said. "We go beyond what a normal grower does, and we were probably already one of the better ranches, but that gave us the leverage to really make a change and have the highest reputation with everybody who works for us in terms of contractors.

"The UFW," he went on, "is a dying union with a very small membership, but it has a very big voice in Sacramento because it goes back to the César Chávez days. I'm not minimizing what César Chávez did—he improved working conditions for farm-workers." Chávez's activism spurred passage of the Agricultural Labor Relations Act when Jerry Brown was first governor, a law to protect farmworkers from abuse and help them organize.

"But they've done what they're going to do," Sal said about the UFW. "After all the smoke and mirrors you see they don't really represent farmworkers. They have their own political interests. They find some perfect story—the gal who dies on our ranch—and claim there's farmworker abuse. They get lawyered up and try to make somebody out to be the bad guy."

Sal was deposed for three days by six lawyers. One of them was a Latino like himself. He asked Sal his title and said, "It sounds like you've done very well for yourself. I applaud you." He told Sal how they'd both been farmworkers, they both had a lot in common. *No, we don't*, Sal thought. *Fuck you, because you want to put me in jail. Let's skip the chitchat and get down to the investigation.*

"I've never been so uptight in my life to really dislike anybody. Not as a person. I disliked his motive and approach. He tried to make me out to be the bad guy. That's what UFW culture is all about. I never felt so threatened in my life as when they said, 'You were negligent in control. You're guilty.'"

Five years later, in the Creekside Office, Sal became vehement as he narrated his reaction. "I'm guilty? I go, 'Hey, it could've been anybody else. It could've been on another ranch. Have they ever thought about how the girl was sick? I'm not taking personal responsibility simply for her going to work when she shouldn't have gone to work.'"

Sal went on, "We already do more in ag than in construction or anywhere else. The UFW doesn't represent anybody. They don't do anything. If they were doing good, there would be guys like me lining up to support them."

Sal was thirty-four when he started working for Fred. "Just imagine," he said, "I see all these people—twenty-five hundred—three thousand people—who work on the ranches. I see my aunts and my uncles and all these people I grew up with. They're not my family but they remind me of twenty-five years ago. How can I not want to make it better? So I started."

He streamlined the ranches to become more efficient. He cut back on expenditures and hired fewer people. "I always tell the story I can't worry about the twenty percent of the people you may shave to downsize to get more efficient. I got to worry about the other eighty percent, and my guys got it. They bought into it. I run a ranch of five thousand acres here in Madera with twenty people, full-time guys." On Cottonwood Creek ranch he has five or six tractor drivers, three or four irrigators, and one supervisor. "We streamlined and keep these guys employed year-round, and, I mean, they'll do anything for you."

Sal said when he was a kid his parents would tell him, "We have to go find a farmer." They had to like working for a farmer, someone who wasn't mouthy or overbearing. "They wanted someone to respect the work they were doing, appreciate the work, and be fair with the pay. That's how you'd rate growers. Not someone who would micromanage us. They'd let us do our job. That's all people wanted. To this day that's what everyone wants."

Sal talked about the intangibles he can offer his full-time workers. When he's hit with demands for raises, he usually doesn't go up. A tractor driver will forgo a quarter raise, he says, if you can give him new equipment. "Guys want new tractors." He says his workers also understand when he tells them, "This year if we save those quarters for all you guys out there, then we can potentially go and buy another ranch. Guess what? We buy ranches; we buy tractors. In about twelve months these guys are pulling me aside as the tractors roll in and tell me, 'Sal, we understand what you're trying to do.'" Sal tells them we need the Fred Franzias. "The way to get more work for your family members is to get more ranches. We keep adding dirt."

Sal said Fred's way was better than enforced legislation. Sal found himself in the governor's headquarters in Sacramento with lobbyists, talking about a proposed farm bill that he didn't think would help workers. "I was one of two brown guys surrounded by Caucasians," he said, "I was a farm laborer, I told them, and ninety-five percent of farm laborers wouldn't vote for this bill." He went on to say, "I never thought of myself as a spokesman, but this was a bad bill, hurting the persons we're trying to protect."

Later a grape grower told me, "I'm not sure many farmworkers would agree about not raising their wages. I got to thinking, *Sal, now you're the Man.*"

That's one way to think, shared with urban dwellers, and not without justification. Here's another. Forty miles south of where Sal and I talked, David Mas Masumoto and his family grow eighty acres of peaches and grapes. Jim used to buy their grapes for Constellation Winery. Mas also writes books. *Epitaph for a Peach* captures the world through a farmer's eyes. While his Japanese grandparents and parents began valley life as field laborers, Mas now hires Mexican work crews for his organic crops. "Am I now the boss and exploiter?" he asks in *Letters to the Valley*. His father, also accused of exploiting farmworkers after he returned from a Japanese incarceration camp and bought a forty-acre farm, answered for him: "At least these hardpan farms created jobs for a people hungry for work."

As Mas discovered, "Paying more for farm labor cannot be simply an expense that farmers pass on to the consumer." Prices for his crops are dictated to him. In 2002, when he tried to adjust to demands to boost production, cut expenses, and become efficient—"Be lean; be mean," as he said—low prices and a grape glut banished profits and wasted an entire year's worth of labor. He concluded he would've been better off not growing a single grape.

"My farming creates work," he wrote. "I remember my first summer after college at Berkeley. I wanted to solve the problems of poverty and inequality immediately. I adopted the popular idea of thinking globally and acting locally by doubling the prevailing wages for our workers. After calculating expenses and income for that month, I realized we had lost thousands of dollars. My idealism was then moderated. I concluded that providing jobs was the best contribution I could make to the world. Now I try to pay a little more than the prevailing wage and I work out in the field alongside the workers."

Even so, as a small farmer paying the same or even higher wages, Mas can't always get field hands when he needs them because "work crews satisfy the larger places first, farms that give them more work throughout the year."

In 2017, Governor Brown's chairman of the board overseeing the Agricultural Labor Relations Act resigned, saying the law was "irrelevant to farmworkers." In the previous three years, only one petition had been filed by a union. Part of the reason was that more than half of California's agricultural workers were undocumented and didn't want to get involved with the government. Farmers negotiated agreements with contractors. Wages had gone up and the average hourly farm wage was higher than the state's minimum. Yet when adjusted for inflation, real earnings were lower than forty years earlier.

Everyone seems to agree that the Agricultural Labor Relations Act has been a failure. The California Institute for Rural Studies published a report calling for a new paradigm in agriculture. The institute founder and farmworker-and-civil-rights activist, Don Villarejo, maintains that since most of consumers' food dollars go "not to farmers" but to food processors, supermarkets, fast-food outlets, and other sellers, "it is increasingly apparent they must share responsibility for the wages of those who produce food products." For example, pressure on Wal-Mart in Florida to supplement tomato harvester earnings by an additional penny per pound helped increase workers' wages up to seventeen percent, "depending on picker productivity," but "all Florida tomato workers benefited."

Altogether Sal has three thousand employees when seasonal workers peak during pruning season; ironically, none are grape pickers. Even so, complaints regularly appear online about Franzia's abuse of fieldworkers who handpick his grapes. "We don't pick anything by hand," Sal said. "Everything is automated."

Jim added that ninety-five percent of wine grapes are machine picked. A smaller acreage of table grapes, including his own, is picked by hand, but just about the entire wine-grape harvest in the San Joaquin Valley is mechanized. "Fifty percent of Napa Valley wine grapes, too," Sal said, "though they don't like to admit it." Giant harvesters roar through the night, when grapes are firmer in the cool air, and shut down in the morning as the day heats up. Not so with mechanized harvesters of other crops. While riding with Jim in his pickup, I saw a huge machine churning up rows of green vegetation and spewing out of an elevated tube into a truck what looked like roots and sticks.

"What's that?" I asked Jim.

"Carrots."

At Jim's house, Tina said, "I didn't know they grew carrots in Madera."

—〰—

The popular notion of valley farming as historically dominated by "factories in the field" from the Gold Rush to the present continues to influence professional historians of California agriculture. It irks Jim and Tina how a view of monolithic corporate agribusiness of mostly absentee owners misrepresents the history of their own families and the diversity of today's farmers. During the harvest season of 2016, I helped arrange a tour of San Joaquin Valley ranches and farms for board members and donors from the University of Colorado's Center of the American West. We visited Sal and Fred at the Cottonwood Creek vineyard and winery. We talked to David and Marcy Masumoto about their eighty-acre farm. We visited an almond-packing plant run by my cousin's brother-in-law, Denis Prosperi, who started out as a third-generation valley farmer when he was eighteen after planting fifty acres of wine grapes. We'd planned to talk with Mexican workers picking Jim's table grapes, but the crop had ripened early and the harvest was finished. Olives, though, were still being harvested.

When our tour bus arrived at the olive grove that Jim's grandfather had planted a hundred years earlier, a few workers were on ladders in the trees picking olives. A crude cardboard sign hung on a gate by the road. Jim had earlier photographed the sign and emailed it to me, saying: "My guy Max is advertising for olive pickers. Is this 'old school' enough?"

Scrawled on the sign with a magic marker were the words:

PICAR
TuE olivo
Olivo PiSCAR
MARTES

Nearly fifty of us were no sooner off the bus and out of a car at the grove when I overheard Jim telling the center's director, Patricia Limerick, what he thought of a book she'd assigned for the tour, *Industrial Cowboys: Miller & Lux and the Transformation of the Old West, 1850–1920.* "I haven't read it," Jim told her, "but I'm pretty sure I'm going to hate it."

I had read the book and found fascinating much of the historian David Igler's original research about how Henry Miller stitched together his valley cattle empire. What was reductive and forced was the book's main point about how the Miller & Lux Company represented agriculture among the railroad, timber, and mining corporations that industrialized the West. "The West had a 'machine in the garden' that moved across the region with shocking speed,"

Igler writes. "Large-scale industrial enterprises fanned out across the West and plundered its public domain and natural resources.... Among the top corporations directing the region's industrial activity was Miller & Lux."

Yet the book destroys its own argument by showing that Miller & Lux wasn't typical or representative of ranching in the West. The company was an anomaly. No other ranching or farming operation in the country came close to it. In 1917, "Miller & Lux was the only agricultural corporation ranked among the nation's top two hundred 'industrial enterprises,'" Igler writes. The industrial aspect of the company was primarily its large San Francisco Butchertown operation. The two German immigrants had created a vast urban slaughterhouse and meatpacking conglomerate. In 1871, when criticizing "the landed aristocracy of California," the political economist and reformer Henry George included the two men he labeled as "Miller & Lux, San Francisco wholesale butchers."

Calling Miller and Lux "Industrial Cowboys" bothered Jim. "I guess 'Industrial Butchers' wasn't sexy enough," he said.

Jim's grandfather had emigrated from Lucca, Italy, in 1911 and worked for Miller & Lux near Dos Palos, driving wagons and breaking horses. At that time four-fifths of the workers on the Dos Palos ranch were northern Italians, part of the biggest group of European immigrants working for the cattle company. Jim's grandfather eventually planted his own vineyard and orchards on forty acres, where the CAW tour group tasted olives and sipped wine a hundred years later.

After hearing David Igler talk to the group the following night about Miller & Lux and about California as a Pacific Rim state, Tina was disappointed. "If someone wants to write a book with a lot of information from documents and other books, that's fine," she said, "but it's too narrow. It doesn't tell the whole story."

Valley ranchers and farmers have long felt misrepresented in books and the media to the point of being dismissed and unseen. When the Center of the American West published *The Atlas of the New West* with a feature essay by Limerick, it excluded California's Great Valley. In the tour's brochure Limerick wrote that as a child she'd driven many times with her family on Highway 99 through the San Joaquin Valley but never purposely visited it or stopped to chat with farmers or farmworkers. The tour was to be a rectification of such an oversight.

We talked with Michele Lasgoity about her family's ranch. Michele was the Madera County Cattleman of the Year in 2012. Her paternal great-grandparents were Basque immigrants. Her maternal great-grandfather had emigrated from Tuscany to work for Miller & Lux in Firebaugh. There he met his wife, also an Italian immigrant, working in the company boardinghouses.

We also visited the cattle-and-horse ranch of Dusty and Clay Daulton. Clay's great-great-uncles were two valley ranching brothers, Thomas and Emphrey Hildreth. In 1863, Henry Miller bought a Hildreth herd, ranch, and the famous "HH" brand that became synonymous with Miller & Lux cattle throughout the West. We talked with the Ken Schmidt, whose Volga River German grandparents immigrated in 1892 to farm in the valley, where Ken still lives and works as a hydrologist.

After visiting with third-, fourth-, and fifth-generation California family ranchers and farmers, I was surprised—*shocked* is a better word—when a Coloradan on the tour found agreement from others after announcing on the last day how it helped to understand California not as a Western state but as part of the Pacific Rim. In a later email to the group, his wife reinforced how "the idea that California is not a western state but more a Pacific Rim state explained a lot." To counter this dismissive view, Jim sent me a photo from the local newspaper showing

Michele Lasgoity on horseback with three of her cowboys riding into a sunrise after a roundup. "The West lives," Jim wrote.

California, of course, is *both* a Pacific Rim and Western state. It has big family farms and ranches like those of Franzia and Lasgoity and smaller ones like those of Unti and Masumoto. The average farm and ranch size is more than a hundred acres smaller than the national average. David Vaught in his book *Cultivating California: Growers, Specialty Crops, and Labor, 1875–1920* documents the diversity of valley ranchers and farmers who historically weren't big landowners. Despite the uncharacteristic size of Miller & Lux, Henry Miller was an obsessive micromanager who maintained personal contact with many vaqueros and field hands, while his partner Charles Lux reportedly checked the San Francisco slaughterhouse each morning and greeted many workers by name.

That can't happen in the same way on most big ranches today. Besides machines, laws impose an industrial system on aspects of farming. Sal hires the contractors who hire the workers. "Legally I can't talk to any of my employees," he said, "but I can talk to their management staff." In Madera he meets with the ranch supervisor, who's hired by the contractor. "By law, he's management, so I can give him instructions. I give him work orders but the rest of the people understand how this game works."

I asked Sal about Fred's more personal relationship with growers, which hearkens back to rougher days in the West. I'd heard different stories: that if you have a good relationship with Fred, it's great, and if you don't he's worse than the bigger wineries.

"Fred has a different style of buying grapes," Sal said. He doesn't need a contract. Just as in the legendary Old West, he'll buy on a handshake. He then talks prices in September after the harvest. He wants growers to make money, Sal said, but it can't be too high because he has to compete globally. He works on a thin margin and sells by volume. Nobody looks at the industry the way he does. He talks to the farmer about the global market and the grower gets too much information and feels beat up. *I'm getting fucked,* the grower thinks. *Fred just worked me over for a hundred bucks.* "Not the case," Sal claims; it has to do with the global market, adding that he's seen Fred tell some of his best, most loyal farmers, to take better offers when they get them. "If some stupid winery wants to pay those prices," Fred says, "I'll increase my bulk wine."

"Fred didn't plan to become the biggest grape grower in the world," Sal said. "He couldn't get growers to plant enough grapes for him. They wanted these outrageous dollar amounts, so he started buying land. He saw the problem and fixed it. We overwhelm people with our scale, but we really do try to run it like a small operation." Farmers who buy two tractors a year can't understand how Sal can buy 120 tractors in one shot. "It's just a number," Sal said. "Just add a digit."

Sal said he struggles to find good management people, good Latino bilingual students to put into internships or middle-management positions. "They shy away from ag." He goes to Fresno State and Cal Poly to discover that out of fifty people in a viticulture department only four are Latino. "Given the statistics of Latinos in California," he asked, "why aren't more Sals in agriculture, guys who have gone off to college and got educated? Talk about an opportunity people are missing."

With a booster's enthusiasm, Sal maintains that children of farmworkers, whether of the first or second generation, have to look past the struggles of their parents, the hard work, the difficulties with poverty, the stigmatization of farm labor, and see the opportunities. "It's about the American Dream," Sal said. "My parents don't have an ounce of resentment toward the farmers they might've worked for. They didn't care if it was in garlic or picking grapes. It's honest work, honest hours. They don't feel abused, and this is going back thirty years." His parents saw the opportunity in agriculture to hand off to their kids the chance to use education as an outlet to move ahead.

Sal talked about the possible effect of his own story on some young kid struggling with school, contending with his parents working through poverty, who might realize "Sal found his way back to agriculture. It's his saving grace. He was destined to connect back to where he started. Damn it, there's an outlet here. You just have to come full circle in some way."

It's a disservice, Sal maintains, the way we push these kids into the social sciences, into criminology. They become probation officers, corrections officers. "We have to expose them to the opportunities of staying in ag."

Sal stopped to reflect. "Sometimes I don't get it. Maybe I'm not the guy to be talking." His own wife, a schoolteacher for the last sixteen years, "was a psychology major, like all other Latin women," he said, and his four boys "are never going to set foot on a vineyard." Sal himself, as he repeatedly says, didn't anticipate he'd ever return to agriculture. He'd picked grapes, he'd worked in the fields, but he'd never been exposed to the business.

"That's why the kid who slept under the grapevines never saw it coming until he was exposed to it. By who?—Fred Franzia—a visionary."

Sal sees Fred as a visionary who wants to make a difference in the entire industry. "He can talk about money being his motivation," Sal said, "but money isn't his motivation. He wants to change the industry."

Sometimes Fred will ask Sal, "When was the last viticulture book written? How can the biggest grape-growing region in the world not have books? Why aren't we writing the book in Spanish?"

"You want to be around him when he gets going?" Sal asked. "He wants to write the viticulture book. I say, we can't write the book. No one could understand the way we farm. But he wants to write the book."

Fred doesn't want to be a Robert Mondavi, Sal said. He doesn't want to spend all his life like Mondavi trying to convince people how rich or intelligent he is. "That was all a front, a façade." Fred talks about impacting the industry and making a change. "That's why he's involved with the universities," Sal said. "He pounds on Fresno State and then gives them millions of dollars; he pounds on Davis. He's probably the biggest donor to the nonprofit American Vineyard Foundation." With a major donation from Fred, Sal helped the Fresno State viticulture program to replant a teaching vineyard of French Columbard wine grapes.

"He puts his money where his mouth is," Sal said, "but he can't get things changed enough, so he says he's giving up on the universities and going to get twenty million dollars and start his own research institute. Anybody else, that would be far-fetched, but if he puts his nose to it, he'll make it happen." Fred was then seventy. "He's just going to run out of time," Sal said.

I asked how Sal saw himself in ten or twenty years.

"I don't know," he replied.

Fred had given him a lot of authority, more than to some of Fred's family members.

"I didn't ask for that," he said, adding that Fred just wants motivated people who make his business better. "He doesn't favor his own children. He holds them to the same standard, but the succession plan is what it is." Nine family members including the owners now work for Bronco, down from sixteen. "I would be the first one they smoke," Sal said. "Either I'm going to land very nicely on my feet with the next generation, or if it doesn't work with them I'll position myself to go somewhere else." In 2018, Sal was promoted with two family members and five others to become a managing director of the company.

"It's the same story," Sal said. "Not too many guys are going to outwork me."

Basque Dirt

Like Sal, Mitch Lasgoity grew up speaking English as a second language. "As a kid I spoke Basque with my parents," Mitch told me. He was then living on the San Joaquin Valley ranch his grandfather bought eleven years after leaving the Basque Country.

In many ways Mitch was like European Basques who traditionally identify themselves as Euskaldunak, meaning "those who speak Basque," an ethnonym Mitch embodied as an American boy in California schools, even when he spoke to himself. "I never realized that until maybe I was in college," he said. "I thought in Basque."

Mitch was still vigorous at eighty-two, with quick blue eyes and the identifiable stocky build of many younger Basque men. He spoke about the acquisition of his family's original forty acres in Madera County with a pride I've heard when European Basques talk about their *basseri-etxea*, or ancestral home, a concept bearing the connotations of both land (*herri*) and house (*etxea*).

"People in this day and age don't realize how little money there was around at that time," Mitch said. His grandfather came to herd sheep with his brother for a rancher who later went broke and had no money to pay the brothers for back salaries. Instead, the brothers accepted three hundred hogs they shipped to Stockton for sale in order to buy a dryland vineyard. That was in 1892. Mitch's grandfather sold his share to his brother, who returned to the Basque Country to get married. In 1903, his grandfather bought the forty-acre home ranch where Mitch's mother was born three years later and the family raised grapes and peaches in addition to running sheep.

"I now own the Bonita ranch," Mitch added, meaning the ranch where his grandfather had herded sheep and obtained hogs more than a hundred years earlier. He has kept both that ranch and the forty-acre home ranch in his family.

The house and vineyard where Mitch grew up are less than two miles from my family's former ranch. Mitch told me, "My dad used to rent your grandfather's alfalfa for his sheep in the winter."

Mitch remembered times as a kid going with his dad to see my Béarnais grandfather. "The first thing your grandfather did was pour us a highball."

"For an afternoon snort?" I asked

"Oh, no," Mitch said, "morning, afternoon, whenever."

I recalled the Lasgoity sheep grazing in the fields of alfalfa stubble outside our ranch house. The sheep wagon and Basque herder with his dogs in winter fog inspired one of my first short stories in high school. I remembered seeing the sheep not only in those fields but farther west in what my grandfather had named the Bank Ranch in honor of the bank manager who'd bought it for him with no money down.

"That was a good piece of dirt," Mitch said. "There's a beautiful almond orchard on it now."

When Mitch went off to college, he didn't know if he'd return to ranching. He'd been accepted at Stanford, but a family friend named Sodie Arbois, a Béarnais who ran 150,000 sheep for Miller & Lux, was a 1908 Santa Clara grad and promoted the Jesuit college to Mitch's dad, who himself as a boy in the

Basque Country had attended a Catholic boarding school in St. Jean Pied de Port.

Mitch graduated from Santa Clara University with a major in business and a minor in philosophy. He'd gone to school with Mickey and John Laxalt, the brothers of the Basque American writer Robert Laxalt and the future Nevada governor and senator Paul Laxalt. "I also knew your uncle," Mitch said about my mother's Basque brother Lou Mendive. "He was my age, maybe a year older. He was a great basketball player, a guard at the University of Nevada.

"I had a classic Jesuit education," he added. "Those original Jesuits could sure teach."

He was accepted to Santa Clara Law School, but in the fall he decided he was sick of school. His father said he could do what he wanted, but he couldn't go out drinking every night and carouse around. Mitch suggested to his dad, "How about if I help you with the sheep?"

For three years Mitch and his father were partners raising sheep until the summer of 1956 when his father offered to sell Mitch his half of the business. Mitch's mother had died when he was a college sophomore. His father had remarried another Basque woman, and they intended to go to the Basque Country for the summer. His father told Mitch, "I'm not going to finance you. Go to the Bank of America and see Cesar Perini."

"I thought the son of a bitch is going to want to have my dad co-sign," Mitch told me about the banker. "I thought if he does, I'm not taking the sheep. Fuck it. I'm going to law school."

Cesar instead asked Mitch if he had a budget. No, he didn't. He didn't know how much he'd need to run the sheep business. Cesar put him in touch with a man in Fresno who helped estimate his expenses, then Cesar loaned Mitch the money with no co-signer.

"The first year I borrowed $56,000," Mitch said. "No wonder at Cesar's retirement party, two-thirds of Madera were in Hatfield Hall. He lent money to people. Go down to a bank today and see if they do that."

That summer on a blind date for a 20–30 Club dance he met his future wife, Rosemary, who was also from a ranching family and had a summer job at the Fruit Basket while attending San Jose State. A year later they were married.

Ever since he was a kid, Mitch was aware of living in a Basque community. Through the valley stretched his mother's extended Basque family of Ospitals and Biscays. His dad had been president of the San Joaquin Woolgrowers Association, as was my grandfather, and later Mitch himself. The group had a big picnic every spring. "There was that picture in the Basque Hotel," Mitch said, of his dad and my grandfather barbecuing lamb over an open pit. The hotel was where Mitch continued his dad's tradition of hiring sheepherders from the Basque Country.

Over the next twenty years Mitch's sheep business grew until 1976 when it peaked at fourteen thousand sheep in both California and Nevada. "We had a ranch in Ely," he said. "Your dad and mom had lived there." I added that I was also born in Ely. The sheep company surrounded the Nevada town. On that ranch Mitch ran nine thousand sheep and five hundred brood cows.

"Rosemary inherited a half-section, and I started cotton farming. Little by little I kept buying pieces of dirt."

I mentioned how I'd heard that he had just bought another ranch.

"Fourteen hundred and seventy acres," he said. "A beautiful piece of ground over at Four Corners near the Urrutias, where your grandfather was partners with Miguel Urrutia. It has a classic old ranch house on it. All told, we have about thirty-three thousand acres. We farm every inch of it ourselves."

Mitch's daughter Michele, after twelve years with Hewlett Packard, manages the family farms and cattle. His son John owns the sheep business which has more than two thousand sheep. John also owns the original forty acres, where he continues to grow grapes and lives in the first family home with his wife Alyson and three children. On the ranch he and Alyson had a boutique winery with a tasting room called Chateau Lasgoity. Winemaking isn't new to the family. Mitch's grandfather and father made wine from local grapes for the family and their sheepherders, who boarded at the ranch.

"You can't run sheep the way we used to," Mitch said. "We haven't got the alfalfa. It's all been developed into trees and vines." Mitch was on the board of the Western Range Association and used to import a lot of herders from the Basque Country. "Before you knew it, Basques were becoming engineers, doctors, lawyers, the whole bailiwick." Sheepherders are now Chileans, Peruvians, and Mexicans.

—⁂—

On an overcast October morning, I joined Mitch in his Mercedes 550 SUV to drive into the foothills where Michele was meeting three truckloads of cattle from Oregon. Mitch wore a blue button-down shirt, brown pants, and his usual straw cowboy hat.

"We buy the cattle mostly on videos," Mitch said. "Here we have about seven hundred brood cows and nine thousand yearlings."

After calving season, Mitch sells the unproductive cows and half the calves. He breeds the remaining heifers and buys other yearlings in the fall for a total of roughly ten thousand head.

He showed me the list of more than six thousand steers and heifers already bought that year at sales in Nevada, Oregon, Idaho, and California, almost all certified natural and with what's called ASV ("Age Source Verified"). Mitch likes to buy as many steers as he can, letting them roam the hills and put on a 100 to 110 pounds before the grass dries in late May or early June.

"We buy all blacks, if we can," Mitch said.

"Because people think Angus beef is best?" I asked.

"Well, that's a lot of bullshit," Mitch said.

"Like brown and white eggs."

"If that's what people want, that's what they're going to get. It's the same with grapes. People think they want Zinfandel."

We headed into the foothills on the road leading to Yosemite. Nothing so much as the tawny hills of fall, with their granite outcroppings and live oaks, evoke for me an essential California landscape out of the past, for I know I'm seeing something reminiscent of what the Chukchansi saw when they gathered acorns, what the first Spaniards confronted on horseback, and what a mountain man like Jedediah Smith and a naturalist like John Muir might have wondered at when they came out of the mountains and saw the last ghostly hue of native summer grass before winter rains turn everything brilliant green in California's distinctive reversal of seasonal beauty.

Sandhill cranes flapped in the gray sky and hawks soared as we turned off-road and climbed uphill on Mitch's ranchland. Vistas opened and waves of pale yellow grass on bald hills rolled westward into the distance. A barbed-wire fence surrounded a hilltop cemetery. We walked around dilapidated tombstones and looked at burial markers, fragile remnants of people who'd come and gone.

On the way downhill, Mitch called his daughter on the car speakerphone. Reception wasn't good in the hills. "Where are you, Michele? We're just leaving the Pate Cemetery."

She wasn't far and would meet us at a crossroads where she'd unloaded the cattle. "They closed Donner last night," she said.

An October snowstorm had shut down the pass over the Sierra. "Two loads got here; number three got stuck. I unloaded the two and then we goosenecked the steers back over to the Chase."

"Okay, fine," Mitch replied. "Where's the other truck?"

"They called me about an hour ago and will be here about noon. They'll call from Modesto and I'll go unload them."

"All steers?"

"That load happens to be all steers." The other two loads were light.

"What'd they weigh off-truck?" Mitch asked. The car phone crackled and the connection broke. "I lost her," he told me.

Downhill, on the flat two-lane road, two cattle trucks roared toward us, one without a headlight. No sooner had they passed than Mitch was back on the phone. "Michele, one of the trucks has a front headlight out."

"Oh, really? Okay, I'll look at that."

We pulled up to where Michele stood next to her four-door Ford pickup by a ranch gate. She wore a straight-brimmed vaquero hat with a braided red-and-white band, a lithe, athletic-looking ranch woman, relaxed with a quick smile but in charge. On round-ups, Michele rides horseback through the hills with her cowboys. As a little girl she rode with her dad to tend cattle or sheep and heard his advice: "Sail your own ship and never sell the land." That morning without comment Mitch had handed me the newspaper article announcing Michele as the upcoming Madera County Cattleman of the Year. The "cattle women" in the cattlemen's association don't want the words *cattleman* or *cattlemen* changed.

Mitch asked Michele about the stock she'd unloaded.

"I turned them out in the Collins Field," Michele told her dad, who inquired again about the off-truck weight, the individual average of the two light loads. "About four hundred and eighty," she said.

Back in the car, we drove toward a ranch yard with barns and cottonwoods visible from the hilltop cemetery. "This is the Chase Ranch," Mitch said. "It's a good ranch"—5,371 acres. "Where there are oak trees, the soil changes and becomes granitized. It's still good but not near as good as these bald hills." He pointed out the renovated ranch house. "This was the Chase house. I redid these barns. I put in that rose garden. I like to replace everything just the way it was in the old days."

With his memory for physical and historical details about his own and seemingly everyone else's ranches in the county, Mitch talked about another ranch of his we drove onto, called the Sherman Thomas Ranch, and the story of Sherman who came to California from Arkansas with nothing and built up a ranching empire, with the main headquarters in the valley near where Mitch and I had grown up.

"Have you been to Buchanan before?" Mitch asked as we climbed out of the SUV to look at some bare ground. "This was the first settlement here. We had a brass thing to mark it, but some son of a bitch stole it." A remaining plaque did say that Buchanan was founded in 1863 as a copper-mining town and peaked ten years later with one of the first post offices in the state. The ore ran out. Nothing of it was left. Mitch pointed to a bare piece of ground. "The smelter was right over there."

We drove down into what was the Buchenau Ranch, a place I knew from the time as a kid when my family visited Herb and Elsie Buchenau. Elsie was Rosemary Lasgoity's aunt, her mother's sister. To me at that time a visit to this ranch in the hills represented a trip to the Old West, despite its outdoor swimming pool and tall skinny palm tree. "I just redid this main barn," Mitch said, "and that old barn—it goes back to the 1870s—and the old bunkhouse just like it originally was but only with a bathroom and shower. We rebuilt the corrals. We still have the big house to work on. Rosemary and her sister inherited it, and then her sister sold her portion to Michele."

Michele is now renovating the big house, built in 1865 by sheepman Henry Clay Daulton and originally called "Shepherd's Home." Daulton's two brothers-in-law built similar southern-style houses on their nearby sheep ranches. All three of these oldest working ranches in the county are now owned by the Lasgoitys.

Besides cattle ranches, Mitch grows cotton, alfalfa, almonds, and grapes on the valley floor. "We borrowed all we could lay our hands on to buy the dirt," Mitch said. "In the last ten years or so we've been paying off these ranches. I told Michele, every year we'll get that debt down. It takes a long time. We'll pay off the Thomas Ranch and the almonds this year." The Chase Ranch is already clear, bought with cash from a trade in grain commodities. "Our goal is to try and get more and more ranches free and clear. There are still two cattle ranches in Madera County that would cost a lot of money but that I would buy, even as old as I am."

"What's your motivation?" I asked.

"Oh, I don't know. I just like the dirt." He laughed. "Somebody's got to own it."

"So the dirt is more important than the money?"

"Exactly. Oh, absolutely. Once you acquire the dirt there's a good feeling to it. You want quality ranches. We don't buy any shit."

Good prices for crops like almonds and grapes helped Mitch pay down his loans. He has 845 acres of almonds and 2,880 acres of vineyards.

"What we got for our grapes this year," he said, "is almost indecent. The highest price in my lifetime."

What would account for that?

"I think everyone got a little panicky. We've had two years of relatively short crops. It's worldwide—the Australians, the Argentines. A lot of the prices for two or three years were under the cost of production. Europe is short this year. Spain, Italy, and France have the shortest crops they've had in a long time."

Mitch sold twenty-eight thousand tons of grapes to several different buyers, including my old high school classmate, Marko Zaninovich. "He's tough but straight," Mitch said about Marko. "He's a good trader." Zaninovich is one of the valley's big table-grape growers. "I think they have between twelve and fifteen thousand acres of table grapes. They make a fortune, but they take risks, and it all could collapse on them. I don't like table grapes. I don't like putting more than the land is worth into the crop, because every go-around you're betting the whole ranch. With what we do the returns aren't as great, but the risk isn't either."

Mitch punched buttons on his car phone and when Marko's voice came through the speaker Mitch told him I was in the car. "I wondered why you were calling, Mitch. I heard you picked the grapes, we bought them, and now you're going to put me in the poorhouse because we have to pay for them."

Marko was a year ahead of me in high school and at the time owned a Bonneville. On the phone, he and I reminisced about our drives into the valley. "I don't think you ever drove it into the valley under a hundred and ten," I said.

Marko corrected me. "I always say fifty, fifty-five. We never went to jail and we all lived through it."

He mentioned a few classmates he was still in touch with. "I talk to Fred Franzia and Joe Franzia."

I said I'd also recently talked with Fred.

"I hope he had a sense of humor. He may be a little cranky at times but in the big picture he's got the wine business going."

"I think he's mellowing."

"You think he's mellowing?" Incredulity gave rise to Marko's questioning voice. "Oh, hell, we've reached the millennium."

This year Mitch sold a little more than one-fifth of his crop— six thousand tons of grapes—to Fred Franzia and his Bronco Winery but nothing to the three biggest wineries. "With Gallo, Constellation, and the Wine Group, you don't even have the possibility of making a fair deal. Gallo is the biggest, but I think the worst is Wine Group to deal with as a grower." About these wineries, Mitch added, "They think we're their pissing posts."

I mentioned hearing that Fred, whose winery is the fourth biggest, was supposed to drive tough deals with growers.

"If you didn't have some kind of relationship with him, he'd be worse. But once he knows you're going to try to sell to him he has a totally different approach. I've always been able to arrive at something reasonably good with him. We sold him all our Cabernet, and he bought all the Merlot this year. He's a worker, a very, very intelligent man. For all the public business he's in, he's a private person. A lot of people can't get along with him, but once you have a deal with him he's very fair." The next year Mitch would sell all his grapes to Franzia.

Not far from Mitch's foothill ranches heading into the valley is one of Franzia's vineyards. "This is Fred's shop. There are twenty-seven or twenty-eight hundred acres here. They're all well managed. Excellent farming. His man Sal is very capable." Mitch launched into an aside about Sal Arriola who runs the ranches and how Sal's father worked for Frenchy Montero in Nevada, not far from my cattle-ranching relatives. Mitch went on with his usual, quick memory for details, saying that Montero, who had both sheep and cattle, partnered with his brother-in-law Frank Bidart, a Basque not related to the Bakersfield Bidarts and the poet Frank Bidart. The Nevada Bidarts ranched between

Denio and Winnemucca, past the Quinn River, at Leonard Creek, and so on. Back on the subject of the Franzias, he said, "They know what they're doing. You don't see Fred Franzia buying any off-quality ranches."

I mentioned that someone told me Fred had just bought another big ranch—the Houldings' Cantua Ranch on the dry Westside of the San Joaquin River Basin—three thousand acres to add to Fred's vineyards, now pushing fifty thousand acres. The new purchase exceeded all of Mitch's vineyards.

"You didn't hear how much he paid for it?" Mitch asked.

"I heard thirty-six million," I said.

"Thirty-six million?"

"That's what I heard."

"So that's over ten thousand an acre."

"He plans to put grapes in over the next three years—one-third, one-third, one-third."

"He's got the money," Mitch said.

"It's nice ground I heard."

"Oh, excellent. And one thing about that piece at Cantua is the underground water is pretty decent. Way better than just a little bit west of them."

At Cantua, the famous Mexican bandido Joaquín Murieta was killed and beheaded after a shootout at his Arroyo de Cantua hideout. At least a California Historical Marker claims he was.

Soon Mitch had Fred Franzia on his speakerphone. He told Fred he was riding around in foothill cattle country with me, Frank Bergon.

"Frank Bergon! Jesus Christ," Fred told Mitch, "you're scraping bottom."

After I told Fred that our classmate John Filice wanted to treat us and a couple of others to lunch at Cole's Chop House in Napa, a place Fred likes, he replied, "We'll do that."

"Hey, Fred," Mitch said, "I heard you bought the Houldings' in Cantua."

Fred admitted that he had.

"That's some of the best water on the Westside."

"We wouldn't buy it if it wasn't."

"How deep is that water, Fred?"

"I don't know yet," Fred said. "We have people checking."

"That's a good piece of dirt, too," Mitch said.

After we'd hung up, Mitch didn't say anything for quite a while. We drove in silence out of the hills back into the valley until he said, "You know I'm surprised at those Houldings. Shit, they're all much younger. They're about your age. What the hell's the matter with them?"

I said I'd heard that one of the three brothers didn't want to sell but two did. Majority ruled.

"They ought to be ashamed of themselves," Mitch said. "They'll never have another ranch like that."

"It's the farming you like?"

"Yeah, and the dirt. I like dirt. Once you own a piece of dirt, if you're in agriculture and you have good water on it—I've been up against the wall more than once—but let me tell you, even then, when you drive your car or pickup or whatever on your own piece of dirt, you're boss. There's something about the ownership of land that's true here or in Europe—it doesn't matter where. It gives you a feeling of—oh, how the hell would I describe it? It's the pride of ownership, of course, but there's something there. It's different than when you go on someone else's dirt or the county's dirt. I guess that's because I'm a Basque. I have an affinity for the dirt."

Drought in the Garden of the Sun

Two years later, in the fall of 2014, I visited Mitch and his wife, Rosemary, at their Madera home. It was ninety-six degrees in October under a cloudless blue sky, one of five record-setting days of heat that week. The drought approached its fourth year and people wondered if it would ever rain again. Jim Unti emailed me: "We need a Rachel Carson to wake up this country about what's happening to water. All anybody wants to plant are almond trees which take fifty percent more water than grapes and there isn't any water." Amid reports of wells drying up and many farmers going out of business, I discovered that Mitch and some other ranchers were finding ways to survive, though in the long run valley agriculture itself looked doomed.

Mitch, who was then eighty-four, had taken a downturn since we'd driven through cattle country. He'd then weighed 210 pounds. Now he was 135 after suffering what appeared to be a seizure in the middle of the night. On his return from the hospital, Rosemary said, "He took about ten spills around the house. He was getting weaker and weaker and went to the neurologist, had bone scans, an MRI, everything. By then he was getting completely wacko and really weak."

Mitch spent ten days up north in the Stanford Hospital but doctors couldn't find anything wrong with him. Now he was getting a little better.

We talked about cattle gaining weight in the drought-ridden hills. "Last year we didn't have much gain," Rosemary said, "but the price was really good so we actually came out okay but, of course, there's nothing up there now, no feed in the hills." This season they'd ordered fewer incoming steers and heifers, scheduled to arrive in a month.

"We haven't bought all we need," Mitch said.

Mitch's upbeat desire to buy more cattle despite the drought didn't surprise me nor my friend Gene Dellavalle, who grew up on a ranch close to Mitch's and mine. "In hard times, most guys pull back," Gene said, "but Mitch doubles down. That's called 'The Basque Hedge.'"

Mitch's daughter Michele later told me that her dad's normal position is that *more is better*. A newspaper article titled "Valley Ranchers Trying to Stay Afloat Amid Drought," reported that Madera County cattle rancher Michele Lasgoity couldn't bear to look at the dry grasses that blanket the San Joaquin Valley's parched rangeland:

> "It does not look good at all," said Michele Lasgoity, whose family has been farming in the region since the 1920s. "It just makes me sick."

Drought isn't unusual in the San Joaquin Valley. It comes in cycles, and in fact every year for up to nine months, when farmers normally can count on uninterrupted sunshine, hence the valley's epithet: Garden of the Sun. As a boy when heat regularly hit the valley, I caught desert horned toads between grapevines. California is the only state with a clearly defined rainy and dry season, just like Chiapas, Mexico. Storms and heat usually arrive on schedule, except in extreme drought years when we went to church to pray for rain. Then the floods arrived to help us forget the droughts.

Floods are what I remember most about extreme weather in the valley when I was growing up. "Get up and help your dad," my mother called into my bedroom one morning. I was seven. My father was already cranking up the sump pump to drain our flooded basement. Outside our ranch house in the early dawn stretched a brown sheet of water across the pasture all the way to the broken bank of Cottonwood Creek, more than a mile away.

When I was twelve, December rains again soaked the valley. Melted snow rushed down from the mountains. *The Madera Tribune* ran this front-page headline.

Worst Flood in Madera's History
Scores Left Homeless

I rode with a farmer through the night in a truck on flooded country roads to check on stranded neighbors. The National Guard was out. I'd been hunting jackrabbits when the rain started and by the time I got back to my pickup it was stuck. Four days later on Christmas Day, a foreman and I brought supplies into a workers' camp. "Can I have them rabbits?" the camp cook asked about the half-dozen soaked rabbit carcasses in the bed of the truck. After four days in chilly winter rain, they became Christmas dinner.

A few years and floods later, I published my first short story in my high school magazine, "The Flood," about a fictional Basque sheepherder named Fermin Erro, who'd lost his band of sheep in a Cottonwood Creek torrent.

The cycle recently changed. The rainy season stopped longer than usual. Snow in the Sierra Nevada vanished. Basque sheepmen became the anguished faces and voices for a valley without floods, without rain, without water. Sheepman Martin Etchamendy appeared in a video with a widely appropriated title: *California: Paradise Burning*. Born in the Basque country, Etchamendy speaks with a strong accent. "We need water, water, water, water," he says in the video. Behind him sheep stand in a barren dirt field. "It's stopped raining and we don't know what to do."

Despite his sickness and the crushing drought, Mitch as usual found bright spots in the gloom. "I hit a huge lick in the stock market," he said. To defer income he partnered with a Bakersfield feed-yard cattleman to buy eleven thousand small Holstein bulls. "We raise them up to fourteen hundred pounds." He was selling them at the moment and making a profit. "The market turned good for them."

Mitch's almonds also did well. Grapes were problematic because the wineries had inventory from two years of big crops. Last year Fred Franzia bought all the Lasgoitys' grapes, but this year he told them, "My tanks are full."

"They've also been importing a lot of wine the last two years," Rosemary said. "I don't think Fred is, but cheaper imports are also affecting him. The Gomberg Report said his shipments are down. Gallo, too."

Fred did end up buying most of the Lasgoity grapes, including the Cabernet, Ruby Reds, Merlot, and Carignan. A different buyer bought a thousand tons of Zinfandels, but about 120 acres had no buyer and two thousand tons of Lasgoitys' grapes were dumped onto the ground. Another eighty acres of unpicked Barbera were rotting on the vine.

I asked if Franzia was still developing vineyards on the Houldings' land he'd bought on the Westside.

"He's pouring money into it that you wouldn't believe," Mitch said. "First class, too."

We looked at magazine photos I'd brought of the valley's parched Westside, not far from where Franzia was planting.

"This drought can't go on forever," Mitch said. "It's going to rain. I guarantee it."

Photos showed sheep in a barren, desolate landscape near Firebaugh, where the Lasgoitys also own land. The sheep looked especially gaunt because they'd just been sheared. Their hooves kicked up dust from the dry ground.

"It looks like that most of the time," Rosemary said.

She was right. Fifty years ago I took a photo of Firebaugh cattle feeding on cantaloupes scattered in a ranch field of bare dirt. The Westside country in the rain shadow of the Diablo Range is always dry, averaging eight inches of rain in the best of years. Now it was even drier, with less than two inches a year during this drought.

A bit of valley history is important here. This same arid country is what the Basque explorer Gabriel Moraga saw in the fall of 1806. Moraga left Mission San Juan Bautista, crossed Pacheco Pass, and rode into the Westside valley with twenty-four soldiers and a Franciscan priest, who noted in his diary "very unattractive lands" with "alkaline deposits" and a "scarcity of water and grass." Farther south, the land was "worse than bad."

Moraga also discovered signs of flooding, especially along the river, where the diarist noted excellent meadows, fertile lands, and good pasture. Moraga pitched camp by the river he'd named Río San Joaquín in honor of his father, José Joaquín Moraga, who'd first seen the river's estuary in 1776. Forty-two armed Indians approached the younger Moraga, "demonstrating great affability and making us a present of fish." The Yokutsan-speaking Indians told Moraga that the river held an abundance of salmon and beaver and was called Tihshachu, or "salmon-spearing place."

Abundance is a word the Franciscan repeats in his diary about the Indian way of life in this land of drought and flood. North of Firebaugh's future site, Indians led the Basque and his men across the river to become the first-known explorers in what is now Madera County. They entered a village "situated on the other side of the river, hidden behind some willows. It is called Nupchenche and has around 230 people under a chief named Choley." An old woman showered Moraga and his men with grain. Villagers spread out soft rush mats and deer hides to serve "an abundance of dishes and two loaves of very white bread made with a grain resembling our rice" but, as another diarist noted, with "a better flavor."

Moraga visited twenty-five Indian villages, or rancherías, as California Indian communities are still called. At that time, valley Indians controlled their environment by burning grassland to stimulate seed growth. Tule elk and pronghorns provided moderate grazing helpful to native grasses, especially in drought years. During extreme floods, Indians moved to higher ground, but even in that dry season, Moraga's party encountered miles of impenetrable tule-choked marshes. A mid-century Spanish map of California shows the entire valley to be a maze of "Ciénagas o Tulares"—swamps or tule marshes—that gave all the native valley people the generic Spanish name Tuleraños or "Indians of the Tule Marshes."

Twenty-one years later, the American mountain man Jedediah Smith found those marshes and swamps so impassable in winter that he and his men had to build tule rafts and elk-skin canoes while trapping beaver along the San Joaquin River. Smith wrote in his journal that large boats would be navigable up the river from San Francisco Bay all the way to present-day Firebaugh. Near Delano, Yokuts greeted the mountain man, as they had the Basque explorer. "Grass seed was poured on my head," Smith wrote, "until I was nearly covered." After a supper of roasted fish and a grass-seed mush, a dozen Indians danced for the trappers. Farther north along the river, Smith remarked on the absence of many valley Yokuts. They'd been abducted, he said, and marched to the missions in San Jose and Santa Clara.

The valley's extensive marshes and swamps launched a terrible pestilence in 1833 to decimate the remaining valley Yokuts. French Canadian fur trappers for Hudson's Bay Company brought malaria into the mosquito-infested valley wetlands from Fort Vancouver, where trading ships had carried the disease from Hawaii. An epidemic wiped out entire villages. Kit Carson and other trappers and traders noted the disappearance of valley Indians and the appearance of mass graves. When tractors later leveled Firebaugh grasslands that Mitch Lasgoity came to own, workers upturned stone mortars and bones in a mass grave at what seemed the village site Gabriel Moraga had visited in 1806.

Devastating droughts and massive floods continued in tandem throughout the nineteenth century, each worse than the last. Ditches and canals arrived with the Swampland Act of 1850 to drain the tule-soaked marshes and sloughs, mainly for cattle ranches. Wetlands disappeared and the valley became drier. The next year the state officially recorded its first drought. Ten years later the geologist William Henry Brewer described the San Joaquin Valley as a desolate plain, practically a desert, until the Great Flood of 1861, when he wrote, "The great central valley of the state is under water," becoming a vast inland sea nearly the size of Lake Ontario. The following year, however, the Great Flood gave way to the Great Drought, wiping out thousands of cattle not previously drowned in the flood. "Dirt, dirt, dirt—eyes full, face dirty, whole person feeling dirty and gritty," Brewer wrote. "Dust fills the air."

After the Civil War, the valley remained largely a dry, flood-prone wasteland until diverted river water and dry farming began to make it bloom. Along Cottonwood Creek, ex-Confederate plantation owners formed the Alabama Colony and planted twenty-five hundred acres of wheat. Within a few years, grain covered the valley, and California grew more wheat than any other state.

Even a hundred years ago, a sense of desert still prevailed in the valley. "In many places the land would be vineyard and orchard land," William Saroyan wrote about the valley of that time, "but in most places it would be desert land and the weeds would be the strong weeds of the desert." That's when my grandfather grew wheat and barley as a tenant farmer along the San Joaquin River. After the First World War, with the expansion of irrigation and the development of deep-turbine pumps, he moved to the interior valley to plant a vineyard and cotton on his own forty acres. He expanded to cattle and hay along Cottonwood Creek, pumping water from the valley's enormous underground aquifer.

It had taken a long time for the valley aquifer to develop. For sixty million years the San Joaquin Valley was flooded with ocean water. Two million years ago it was an enclosed glacial lake. More recently, about fifteen thousand years ago, the last melting glaciers sent torrents of icy water into the valley. Over thousands of years, future good-tasting water accumulated underground. Floods followed droughts, even megadroughts, to bring more rich topsoil to the fertile land and fresh water into the ancient underground reservoirs. Then began what Marc Reisner in *Cadillac Desert: The American West and Its Disappearing Water* called the "suicidal habit of mining groundwater," the pumping of nonrenewable fossil water. In 1986, Reisner predicted that unless California took drastic conservation measures the shortage of water would become intolerable. By the 1930s, he noted, farmers had already exhausted a hundred centuries' worth of groundwater in a generation and a half. His calls for conservation were ignored. Valley farmers dug new wells or deepened old ones. Rain and floods diminished memories of drought, as they did when the floods of the 1930s hit the valley.

Mitch Lasgoity recalled the flood of 1938, when Cottonwood Creek broke its banks and wiped out the Southern Pacific Railroad tracks south of town. The flooding San Joaquin River washed out a workers' camp near Firebaugh. Eight hundred Dust Bowl migrants were driven through the rain to schools and other shelters in Madera. "That was one of the worst years in California history," Mitch said. "I was eight years old, and my dad had all that sheep range on the Westside." He pointed to the area on a map. "We'd come in a pickup through the water across Firebaugh and all the way to Road 19 before we got out of water. The salmon came up the river in the flood. What was ugly is that when the water went down in June thousands of salmon got stranded and died there. The Flood of 1938 is what hastened the building of Friant Dam."

Friant Dam became part of the biggest irrigation and public works project in the world—the Central Valley Project—launched by the federal government in 1933. At the heart of the Great Depression, during California's worst recorded drought, farms were going under, wells pumped dry. Unless something was done to help farmers, especially small farmers, it was predicted that the underground aquifer wouldn't last another thirty or forty years. At the dedication, the secretary of the interior described how the dam would overcome floods, resist drought, provide recreation, generate cheap power, and enhance American civilization. California's governor added that it would help the arid San Joaquin Valley turn into "a modern Eden."

The enormous gray concrete slab of Friant Dam diverted the San Joaquin River into canals and reduced the main stream to a dribble. Without fish ladders at the dam—it was too high even if ladders had been wanted—fifty thousand salmon and steelhead swimming upriver to spawn hit a dead end.

In the 1960s, the California State Water Project joined the

federal system with two dozen more dams and reservoirs inter-connected with thousands of miles in aqueducts, canals, tunnels, and lateral ditches to send water up and down the state. The project made water run uphill by pumping it over the Tehachapi Mountains to Greater Los Angeles and San Diego. Subdivisions, malls, and industries spread though the dry lands of Southern California. While the Westside desert blossomed into orchards, most of the state's water went to urban users. Thirty percent went to agriculture.

An irony of the water projects is they killed off half the smaller family farms in the valley and helped bigger and richer corporate farmers like Standard Oil, Prudential Insurance, Southern Pacific, Getty, and Shell. "Get big or get out" became the valley apothegm. Mitch and Fred Franzia got big. My family got out. Governor Pat Brown, who shepherded in the state water project, said after his retirement, "This project was a godsend to the big landowners of the state of California." He went on, "I was never convinced that the small farmer could succeed or would be good for the economy of the state."

In his novel *Census*, Jesse Ball writes:

No one but farmers understands fairness.
What is there to understand? I asked.
That there isn't any.

Many farmers sold out to developers. Since 1950, urban development has paved over some thirteen million acres, more than a third of California's farms and ranches. Nevertheless, many valley farmers, like most of our neighbors, hung on. The majority of valley farms remained family farms. Down the road from us, the Morini brothers sustained two families and their mother with a hundred-acre vineyard, plus twenty acres their immigrant father had planted in 1910. With the bulk of the ranch now sold, a grandson still farms the original twenty while holding a full-time job in town. Today, though reduced in number, several Madera farms owned by families of immigrant stock can continue to make a profit off small acreage, especially with the high price of almonds, as long as they have water.

After my visit with Rosemary and Mitch, as the epic drought burned into the summer of its fourth year, a lot of finger pointing went on about the waste of water. "Three main groups are competing for water," the county assessor and my longtime friend Frank April told me as we drove onto my family's old ranchland, now covered with almonds. Disoriented by the monotonous similarity in the rows of trees, I was unable to identify where former fields of cotton, corn, alfalfa, and cattle pasture began and ended.

In Frank's office, we looked at an aerial flyover county map showing hundreds of small parcels of twenty acres or less. Of the 1,507 farms in Madera County, most are small: half are less than sixty acres and 1,095 are smaller than 180 acres. Only 118 are a thousand acres or more. Some small farms get rented to larger ones. The original forty acres once owned by my grandfather are now leased for table grapes to the biggest agribusiness investors in the San Joaquin Valley, Lynda and Stewart Resnick, the Beverly Hills billionaires, whose Paramount Farms morphed into a holding company questionably named The Wonderful Company. On the dry Westside, the Resnicks took control of a government water storage facility and bought up nearby water rights to irrigate 70,000 acres of almonds and pistachios, helping to make them the world's biggest growers of nuts and tree fruit. A columnist in *The Bakersfield Californian* revealed how they also sold public subsidized water for profit to a private 2,000-acre suburban development hundreds of miles away in Madera.

"Water rights are very complex in California," Frank said. "The biggest sellers are agricultural, the biggest buyers are municipalities for residential and commercial use. Environmental interests are in the middle, getting water rights mostly from legislation and court decisions."

Farmers get blamed for using so much water without paying their fair share. The media repeats how it takes a gallon of water to grow one almond. Urban dwellers complain that farmers are exempted from the statewide order for towns and cities to conserve water by twenty-five percent. In the drought's fourth year, valley farmers pointed out how they'd already been completely cut off from federal and state water. You can't reduce zero by twenty-five percent, they said.

"Did you come by the San Luis Reservoir?" a farmer asked me. The Madera Irrigation District had distributed no water to farms for the previous two years of the drought. "It's full, but all the water is going to L.A." Los Angeles is the world's largest desert city after Cairo, but in the third year of the drought it helped California set a record for new swimming pools and was on track the following year to break it.

Many farmers, in turn, blame environmentalists, those labeled Enviro-Nazis and Ecofascists, for pissing away good water down the rivers and doing nothing for the fish they claim to help. Environmentalists want to reintroduce salmon into the San Joaquin River, while detractors claim the stream is too warm. Hundreds of threatened wild Chinook salmon in the Great Valley—more than one-tenth of the wild population—went belly up in the spawning run in Butte Creek because the water got too warm. California salmon all the way to the Oregon border struggled in low, warm water caused by the four driest years in the state's history.

—⁓—

On a Saturday in June 2015, I drove into Madera, where the digital thermometer at my old elementary school registered 105 degrees. Wildfires raged in the dry foothills, closing roads and forcing evacuations. The city council a few days earlier, under pressure from complainers, increased outdoor watering to twice a week, risking fines or a state takeover if the city didn't meet its mandatory reduction. With no surface water, farmers let millions of acres go unplanted, costing agriculture billions of dollars. A front-page newspaper photo showed Cha Lee Xiong on his small twenty-acre farm, hunkered down in a barren field with dirt in his cupped hands after his well went dry.

On the other hand, *The Fresno Bee* announced, "Drought a Boom for Valley Businesses." Artificial lawns were in demand. Sales of low-flow showerheads doubled. Hardware stores sold gallons of lawn paint. Landscape rocks and drought-tolerant plants replaced lawns. More than thirty years earlier, my father had moved into town and in a moment of perspicacity transformed his front yard into a rock garden of desert plants. I drove by his old house to find that new homeowners had removed the rock garden and planted grass, now turning brown.

"We've got a problem," Frank April's brother, Ray, told a group of us that night at Gabriela's Restaurant.

The problem extended beyond the lack of water. The valley had the dirtiest air in the country—Los Angeles was second—and the drought made it worse. Valley air had become an allergen. Dried-up wells in some places left drinking water contaminated with nitrates. People with stomach sickness and breathing problems showed up at clinics with coughs, asthma, bronchitis, pulmonary obstruction, skin rashes, and urinary tract infections, especially among the poor. Hot dry winds stirred up fungus spores from the dirt, causing a silent epidemic of sometimes deadly valley fever, mostly among the have-nots. California poverty was statistically burgeoning. Valley towns ranked among the nation's poorest.

"How long can this go on?" Ray April asked. "I don't see a water bill because I rent. I turn on the faucet in my apartment and water comes out, but the pressure in my shower is way down. I just don't use much water. People are stepping up. I think everyone realizes we've got a real problem."

Ray felt tremendous gratitude for local water. "Madera water is the best I've ever tasted anywhere I've ever been," he said. "Traveling in Europe or anywhere around the country—Portland, Colorado—I think Madera water's the best."

My wife, Holly, pointed to her glass on the restaurant table. "Is this what you consider a sample of good Madera water?"

"Yes," Ray said, "Madera city water."

"Well, it is good," Holly said.

Ray, like his brother, is a former high school and college wrestler. Now a retired elementary school teacher, he does private tutoring and plays duplicate bridge four to five days a week. He doesn't have a TV. Tuesdays and Thursdays are for reading. We enjoy literary conversations when I visit the valley. Ray recently went to a bookstore to pick up copies of *The Mayor of Casterbridge* and *The King of Lies*, but mostly he reads and rereads John Milton's *Paradise Lost*.

"The poem is just astounding," he said. "I can't get enough of it. All I want is the work itself and a lot of quiet time. You get the proper sense of it going slowly, line by line, and taking notes, the language is so rich. When I finish I go back to the beginning and start over. If all you get in Milton is the literal story, you miss so much. You constantly have to reach for the figurative, transcendent reality. I'm amazed it's not taught everywhere.

"If all the information contained in just Book One of *Paradise Lost*—798 lines of epic poetry—were common knowledge, if people thoroughly understood it, we would live in a totally different world. In a Miltonic society, the vast inequality between the haves and the have-nots that we see in the world today wouldn't be tolerated. And it would not have to be *not* tolerated because it wouldn't be perpetuated in the first place."

And would this vision extend to the drought? "Yes, because if you have a vision of God as not just a patriarchal, top-down, hierarchical figure but as an animating figure, the spirit animating us all, including nature, then you have a totally different view of things." The result would be a transcendent vision of nature and a sense of care and gratitude.

"In the past," Ray continued, "poets like Blake, Wordsworth, Keats, Shelley were aesthetic revolutionaries, because they knew from their own experience of studying Milton the transformative effect of reading on the human spirit. Great poets always understood that. Now you have math and science, and it's like poetry is banished from society. If people would just sit down and read the poem. Read it and absorb it. They'll get a sense of gratitude for the poet, for the poetry, for the whole story. It's a surefire antidote to despair."

Ray recalled his early sense of gratitude for water. "We grew up out in the country, we had a pump and a well and a storage tank, and when I drank the water in our house, wow, it was good. Really good." He remembered as a kid drinking water out in Herndon not that far away, and thinking, *Gee-whiz, what's wrong with this water?* "It really made me appreciate what I had," he said.

Both city and country water comes from the underground aquifer containing glacial melt from the last Ice Age. This is the water that farmers are pumping out of the ground in order to survive. Without rain to fill reservoirs or mountain snow to swell rivers, pumping is the dominant source of valley water. The aquifer isn't a big underground bowl but several aquifers and layers of clay, gravel, and sand, with varying stretches of water, some fresh, some tainted, some brackish.

"The city has probably ten or twelve wells, in different locations," Frank, said, "and by law the city will put a bunch of stuff in the water, chlorine, fluoride. But I still think—this is not a scientific opinion I'm giving you here, this is anecdotal—I think people out in the country, not in the city limits, with their own wells and pumps still like their water better than treated water."

I agreed that I'd loved drinking the water gushing up from underground at my family's ranch. We all had our favorite pumps on the ranch. On hot summer days we'd unscrew the plug from the discharge pipe and chug sweet, cold fossil water from the glacial age. I've never tasted better.

During two summers when I was in college, I worked for the DuBose & Moosios Pump Company and drove their big rig to ranches on the Westside to install deep-turbine pumps in newly dug wells or to lower piping and turbines into the dropping water table. Some of that good-tasting water may have then carried agricultural poisons, especially when drunk from ditches as I sometimes did. Fifteen years after DDT and other pesticides were banned, twenty-four test wells on a hundred-mile stretch through Madera turned up poisonous residues.

One of the ways to deal with the valley's disastrous drought is to move. Fred Massetti, my cousin by marriage, and his wife, Diane, had just returned from Idaho looking for a possible new place to live. "California is drying up," Fred told me over breakfast at Farnesi's Restaurant. "All the farmers are going out of business. It's bad. Now they're regulating the water. In Boise, eight out of the ten people we talked to have migrated from California. My brother-in-law has his farm up for sale."

I have a hard time seeing Fred leave the valley, where he was born and raised. He owns land in the hills where he recently used witching rods to locate a site for a new well. "The well driller then walked around the same area with his sticks and—bam!— they crossed." In two days Fred had a new well at the site.

At an older, undeveloped well in the hills, he then installed a storage tank and a pump mounted with four solar panels. "When the sun shines," he said, "I've got water coming in." Now with sufficient water he can fence the perimeter of his property and rent it for cattle grazing.

The next morning Holly and I headed up into the foothill cattle country. Along the rolling road where once stretched blond wheat fields and dry farms, I was shocked to see green permanent crops—vineyards and new orchards of almonds, figs, pistachios, and citrus—all the way from town into the hills. Here farmers have switched to the new technology of more efficient drip irrigation. Furrows of exposed irrigation water don't evaporate in the sun as they once did. Instead, miles of narrow black hoses with pinprick openings drip water for crops.

The problem is that while efficient drip systems conserve water they also allow planting and irrigation on uneven land, such as in hill country, so more land is being planted and irrigated than formerly possible.

The orchards disappeared when we reached the cattle ranch of Clay and Dusty Daulton. The original Henry Clay Daulton was a Kentuckian who first came to California during the Gold Rush and later returned when hired as assistant captain of a Missouri wagon train. His grandson built the house where Clay and Dusty now live. Stone from the Daulton foothill copper mine frames a large open fireplace in the living room. Clay's great-grandmother Adelaide planted the trees in the yard and drove cattle into the mountains every year.

Both Clay and Dusty wear blue jeans and rancher shirts, looking ready to go to work. Big-boned, balding, and surprisingly soft-spoken, Clay exhibits an imposing presence when he gently leans forward from his great height as though to hear better or maybe keep from bumping his head on the ceiling.

Clay and Dusty have a few of their own cows but mostly they pasture cattle for others during the winter. "We don't lease our land," Clay said. "We don't own the cattle. The owners pay us on the gain. If the cows don't gain, we don't get paid."

Last season because of the drought he had to cut the number of cattle by two-thirds, running only 550 steers, along with 650 horses and mules.

"We keep the horses and mules for Yosemite Park," Dusty said. "At least last year we did. We don't know anymore."

Clay pointed out the window. "You look out there and you're looking at a lot of dirt. You should be looking at a lot of grass."

"What are you going to do this year," I asked.

"Pray," Clay said.

I laughed uneasily, along with Holly and Dusty.

"Well, you understand," Clay said to me. "You grew up on a ranch."

Clay said in the last twenty-five to thirty years he'd spent a lot of time on what he calls "managed grazing" of his ten thousand acres, drying up different fields, rotating them, fostering wild oats, and developing different species and varieties of grass for better gains. Both Clay and Dusty are California-certified naturalists.

"All of this requires a huge investment in water facilities," he said, "because you can't throw fifteen hundred or even five hundred cattle on one water trough." Clay has several wells on the ranch—he drilled two new ones last year—and twelve springs, all running, and he's been installing windmills, solar pumps, and miles of pipeline with solar boosters. Contrary to what you might expect, as you move higher into the hills the wells are shallower than in the valley because the aquifer basin slopes upward at the edges.

"Water begins every year in some wells at twelve feet, twenty-four, maybe thirty-two feet," Clay said. "Every year they start the same. On this ranch the water's renewed. It always comes back. I have to emphasize that. I'm not depleting anything, but I'm not irrigating anything. They have a serious problem in the valley, and most farmers want to face it, but they don't know how. They depend on pumping groundwater. They used to flood-irrigate until the water went down. Now they use drip systems, but that's irrigation technology, not groundwater technology."

Today the overpumping of valley groundwater has actually increased. Thousands of wells have gone dry, the water table keeps dropping, roads buckle and bridges crack as the ground sinks. Out on the Westside, where the explorer Gabriel Moraga traveled, the ground is thirty feet lower than in 1806. With the loss of government-controlled surface water, a frenzy of well drilling erupted in the valley.

In the New West as in the Old West, as Marc Reisner wrote, "Reason is the first casualty during a drought." Denial grows rampant. *Recharge* is now a favorite word today in relation to aquifers, as though they're batteries, and a good soaking rain were the source of energy to recharge them.

The problem is that the water table in parts of the valley has dropped so low that no amount of rain will restore it. In the past two years, the water level in some Westside wells has dropped nearly 200 feet. A friend of Clay's from high school is

Ken Schmidt, now a leading Western states hydrologist. "He knows everything there is to know about groundwater," Clay said. "He told me that when a foot of water falls up here in the foothills, only about an inch of it gets into the ground. I later saw him at a party and asked if that was also true for the valley, and he said, no, he didn't think so. A little might get into the ground in places like Cottonwood Creek and sandy areas; otherwise, none of it gets back into the ground. It's not going to recharge at all. Down in the valley it's a mess. It's going to change the whole economy of California." That's because, as Reisner warned years ago, "a lot of the water being pumped out of the ground is as nonrenewable as oil."

Most predictions about the coming years are just as dire, despite all the elevated talk about 2016 "Godzilla" El Niño and its drought-breaking storms. Winter rains that year finally pummeled parts of the parched state. Knowledgeable Californians didn't dance in the vineyards because even if it had rained harder than in fifty years, which it didn't, the drought still wouldn't be over.

Rainfall on Clay's ranch later approached a normal measurement of eight inches as the drought entered its fifth year. The ground was so dry, though, only one of his five ponds filled. By May of 2016, ninety percent of the state remained in drought. Forty years earlier, in 1976, I was living in San Francisco during the third-driest year in the state's history, followed by the driest. I recall dust storms, water rationing, and predictions of statewide doom. Then the rains started. El Niño and five rainy years clobbered California with floods and mudslides. The drought was forgotten.

The same thing happened a hundred years earlier when Clay's 300-pound great-great-uncle sat in a rocking chair at his Wide Awake Ranch with his feet in a tub of cold water, smoking a pipe and playing solitaire, until a drought sent his sheep ranch belly up and he went bankrupt. "That was the Drought of 1877," Clay said, a drought not as long but more disastrous to valley ranchers than the current one. "When you put droughts in perspective," Clay said, "there have been worse." In 1877, the north fork of the San Joaquin River dried up in places. Kern River went completely dry. Thousands of rotting sheep and cattle carcasses covered the valley. Then came the Great Flood of 1878.

The history of floods and drought in the valley suggests that global warming didn't cause the current drought—most scientists agree that it didn't—but human-caused global warming has exacerbated this one into the longest and the driest. California will become wetter in future years, say the experts, but also warmer, meaning less snowpack in the Sierra, the most important source of California surface water. Farmers will be dependent on underground water, whatever's left of it.

California has imposed mandatory restrictions on pumping underground water, but they won't fully kick in until 2040. Nobody knows if groundwater will last that long. Depleted aquifers, acute pollution, poisoned soil, and a sinking valley floor portend a new era in the valley, as Clay conjectures. *Disaster* may be too strong a word, at the moment. *Diminishment* isn't.

Ninety-four-year-old Short Watson agreed with Clay when Holly and I picked him up at an assisted-living suburban house, called Fresno Guest Home, where he lived with five others. "It's looking pretty rough, I'll tell you," Short said, "and it's going to get worse." Once 240 pounds, Short looked to be shrinking into the essence of himself, the skin on his face tightening, leaving him in profile with an eagle's beak and eye. Out in the front yard of the house, the lawn was totally brown.

We drove up into the hills to gamble at Table Mountain Casino, near Friant Dam. The other casino in the hills, run by the Picayune Rancheria of Chukchansi Indians, remained shut down nine months after fifteen men with drawn guns had invaded the casino in a battle between tribal factions over control of the tribe. More than a thousand casino employees remained out of work. Thirty reservation families said they had no water because wells shared with the casino had gone dry. While tribal factions in the Picayune Rancheria fought each other, the Chukchansi tribe with its Wall Street backers, Brigade Capital Management, sued Governor Jerry Brown to prevent North Fork Rancheria of Mono Indians from building an off-reservation casino near Madera.

The Table Mountain Rancheria had joined the fight against the North Fork Mono, while outcast members of their own tribe simultaneously picketed the casino, but the gambling halls were open. Short pulled himself onto a high stool at a blackjack table, tossed out from his wallet five one-hundred-dollar bills, arranged the chips he bought into stacks, and turned off his hearing aid. The Asian dealer smiled at him as she slid red-topped cards from a shoe.

I wandered off to play elsewhere and thought I'd done pretty well with winnings of $147, but after an hour and fifteen minutes when Holly and I returned to fetch Short he cashed out chips for $1,050.

"I usually quit after I double," he said.

"Do you ever lose and pull out your wallet for more money?" He nodded yes.

We drove up to Friant Dam and looked out over Millerton Lake. "It's pretty low," Short said. He pointed to waterlines on the hills. "It should be way up there. You can see the line. It's about sixty percent off. Look at the sandbars. A couple of years ago they wanted to build another dam above this one, but they don't need it. This one can hold what water there is."

As we drove through the dry yellow hills, he talked about the drought in the valley. "The water table's gone way down," he said, echoing Clay. "I've never seen it so low. Some of the wells are over a thousand feet. On the Westside they go down fifteen hundred, two thousand feet. They go so low it costs too much to pump." At three thousand feet, some wells have run out of fresh water and hit layers of salt water and salt-saturated sand that continue descending for another five miles.

"I remember years back," Short said "you could drive a pipe with a point on it ten or fifteen feet and get water with a hand pump. On your ranch at two hundred feet I put in a well and got two thousand gallons a minute with a seventy-five-horse pump. The pipelines couldn't take all the water."

Water, water everywhere, that's what I remember from those years. As a boy on my grandfather's home ranch, I recall a huge fire hose hooked up to the turbine pump to wet down the yard on summer evenings. On the ranch, we drove water trucks up and down the dirt roads to settle the dust and prevent the spread of red spider and other mites onto crops. All summer I wore knee-high rubber irrigation boots while setting siphon pipes on irrigation ditches and sloshing through furrows of water. The earth under my boots vibrated from underground water running through concrete pipelines, or at least it felt that way. The air hummed with the whine of deep-turbine pumps. And in some winters and early springs, I watched floodwaters spread across pastures and fields.

"There were creeks all through that country at one time," Short said. "Just west of the Bank Ranch"—named by my grandfather for the real owner—"on Houghton's twenty acres, they plowed up a lot of Indian grinding bowls. History says Indians used to camp along a creek there."

In addition to pumped groundwater, the Madera Irrigation

District supplied ranches with surface water. We called it "ditch water," and ditchtenders controlled allotments at headgates. Water flowed down an open-air dirt canal in front of our house. In those years, some farmers stole water by lifting or lowering boards in the headgates. I recall sitting in a pickup all night guarding a Bank Ranch headgate, while reading with a flashlight, because someone had been stealing water allotted to us.

"I only had a problem once," Short said, "there at the home ranch west of your house. I was laying out in the field one night on a windrow waiting for the dew to come in so I could bale. About midnight, I heard a Jeep start up and I saw my neighbor at the west headgate put more boards in and take my water away. I let it go, but a long time later I told him I saw him do it."

Short went on. "He had only gravity and no pumps. I had both. I could push ditch water anywhere on the ranch, except up-hill onto that eighteen acres of South America." All ranch fields in those years had names, and Cottonwood Creek divided the fields named South America and North America.

In the hills, we crossed the bridge over Cottonwood Creek. It was totally dry. I asked Short, "Do you think we'll ever again see floods in the valley from Cottonwood Creek?"

"More likely floods of people, a lot leaving."

"What will happen to the valley?"

"It'll go back to desert," Short said, "the way it was a hundred years ago."

Short died before winter storms pounded California in 2017 with what was called a "seemingly endless barrage of rain and snow." A Christmas card from a Los Angeles friend announced, "Rain has arrived. Water tables to go up in the Central Valley." Millerton Lake was three-quarters full. Jim Unti texted me to say that Friant Dam was releasing water into the San Joaquin River. There was also water running through Madera in the Fresno River and even some in Cottonwood Creek. "No big problem I know of," he wrote. "Things in control. No Wild West days."

Farther north, two hundred thousand people fled their homes as water crashed over the emergency spillway of Oroville Dam for the first time in history. The Sierra snowpack approached a record high.

On April 7, 2017, after five years of punishing California, the drought was declared over. Surfers rejoiced to have showers once more flowing on beaches. Farmers weren't so optimistic. The problem remained: no matter how wet the year, the state everywhere was using too much water. More water gets pumped out of the ground than gets back in. Another disaster for valley farmers is that overpumping during the drought caused the ground to sink an additional three feet, permanently crushing space for underground water storage. The governor declared a state of drought emergency to remain in the southern San Joaquin Valley.

Jim told me over dinner at a Fresno Thai restaurant, "In twenty years, if you come back to the valley it won't be here. Part is the farmers' own fault. Well, it was here for a hundred years . . . ." His voice drifted off.

I learned that my cousin Fred and his wife, Diane, had bought a condo in Boise. Her brother had sold his Madera farm and told his son he had a choice: He could manage buildings in Boise. If he wanted to farm, he could grow almonds in Australia.

Irene Waltz

Albert Wilburn

Louis Owens

I I

Western Voices
in the Great Valley

Valley Tolerance

Dr. Albert Wilburn recalls his San Joaquin Valley boyhood as a time of tolerance. "I was called nigger one time," he told me, "and that was in the second grade at Washington Elementary, and he didn't even call me that." Albert and a white kid named Tyrone Atkins were fighting for a swing in the schoolyard. "I was bigger and got the swing. I don't know what his parents had told him, or where he heard the word, but he walked off and called me, 'You niggerow,' and I thought, *What is that?* If after a fight he'd called me nigger I'd understand, or if he'd called me Negro or colored that would be all right, but niggerow? That confused me."

Albert has a baritone voice and laugh matching his broad shoulders and hefty chest. He conceded that Tyrone was probably confused, too. He probably didn't know what to say.

"It didn't come out right," Frank said.

My friend Frank April and I were visiting Albert in his suburban Fresno home a few months after he'd attended his fiftieth Madera High School reunion. He claimed to be six feet, "maybe a little over," he admitted after I protested that he looked taller since he towered over Frank and me. He weighed 235 pounds. "I'm fat now," he said, though he was only five or ten pounds over his weight as a college football player. His relaxed manner and warm voice evoked a physician's gentle bedside manner rather than his former ferocity on the playing field.

"After I left here and went away to Stanford and into the world I realized how tolerant people had been in Madera," he told us. "At the class reunion I was one of the MCs, and I talked about tolerance here. This was the sixties. I was aware of what was going on in the South—the girls were killed in Birmingham and King made his dream speech in '63, the year I graduated, there were sit-ins at lunch counters—all that stuff was going on. We knew about it and talked about it as a family, but I hadn't dealt with any kind of racial prejudice in Madera. I knew about it because my parents lived it."

Red River County in East Texas is where Albert was born, the fourth of five children, and where his parents owned a farm with chickens, dairy cows, four mules, a big vegetable garden, sorghum, corn, and a main cash crop of cotton. They sold eggs in the tiny town of Acworth. Albert was six when events propelled the family to leave Texas for California. "All kinds of crap was happening in the South in those days," he said. Tensions increased when a neighboring white farmer kept claiming damages for the Wilburn cows getting into his cornfield. Every time Albert's dad fixed the fence the cows were back in the field the next day, and they realized the farmer was letting them in. At the time, Albert's brother, who was nine years older, had gone through the eighth grade twice because there were no unsegregated high schools in the area. A hailstorm also had flattened the family's cotton crop when it was a foot high. "My father had borrowed the money to buy the seed," Albert said, "but now he couldn't pay the banker back. My mother was worried about the farmer next door. All these things were coming together to push us out of Texas."

His father went to West Texas with Albert's thirteen-year-old brother to pick cotton in order to pay back the bank loan. "My father could pick five hundred pounds of cotton a day, and my brother could just about match it," Albert said. "That's a lot of cotton." After paying off the loan, they left for Madera, where some relatives had moved eight or nine years earlier. "It was time to go for educational reasons, social reasons, and financial reasons," Albert said. "Blacks were just becoming aware that this was not the way it had to be."

In Madera, off Roosevelt Street, "we lived in a one-room shack behind my cousins that winter in 1951." That summer they bought an acre of land in the country and moved a house to it, where Albert's parents spent the rest of their lives.

"I had a lot of fights in the first grade," Albert said. He didn't see them as racial. "My biggest fight was with a couple of black dudes. Weldon Lane and Benjamin Fuller jumped me walking down the road. I went home crying. In school somebody pushed me off a swing and my sister had to jump in front of the battle. Mexicans, whites, blacks picked on me. I was the new kid with a funny accent."

Back in Texas, all eight grades were in one classroom and he'd been able to sit wherever he wanted, but in Madera the teacher wouldn't let him sit in the desk next to a new friend. "That threw me off," Albert said. "It wasn't important, but I didn't adjust. It was an odd year. I've thought about it frequently. All I remember about that year is that I was worried about the tension. I didn't get it together and I flunked the first grade."

His mother, who like his father, stressed the importance of education, thought it was her fault. That summer his sister worked with Albert on his reading. "I had Dick and Jane memorized," he said. He moved to a new school and except for missing two weeks in the third grade because of measles and chicken pox he was never absent another day and had no difficulties.

Sports in grammar school weren't organized in those years. Except for flag football in junior high with St. Joachim's School and a basketball game with Chowchilla, no games were structured except Little League Baseball in the summer. "You played for Rotary," Albert told Frank. "You had the good team." That's when Frank's father was the coach. "Your father was a great guy. You had all the Paynes and Tates and farm boys from Dixieland. You guys kicked our butts. My first year on Cal Spray we were one and fourteen."

Albert didn't play tackle football until high school. In his sophomore year he received the award for the most improved player on the championship "B" team, and the next year he lettered in football, basketball, baseball, and track. As a senior, he played on the varsity basketball team that won the valley championship for the first time in twenty-nine years.

"I loved school," Albert said. "I got along with all my teachers. I never did not do the homework. I was compulsive about that kind of stuff." He got straight A's. "My parents had told me many times that many people may try to pull you down because you're black, so you've got to work twice as hard. I knew that if I worked hard, I could get good grades. In biology it was just how hard you worked. Did you memorize the stuff? That had nothing to do with intelligence. That was just work."

He went on. "I knew there were racial problems in Madera. My father worked for the NAACP in town, and he'd been pushing for equality." Albert was aware of a division between white and black sections. "I knew the black part of town, where my cousins lived, did not have sidewalks and gutters, they did not have a developed park. I was aware of all that, and I did think there certainly was some racial overlay to it—that was structural—but for me personally I never felt that a teacher was putting me down or holding me back because of the racial thing."

He also felt no discrimination or racial tension among his friends. Diversity was a given. He had friends, he said, who were Italian, Armenian, Native American, Mexican, Russian, Yugoslavian, Catholic, Protestant. "In high school there were so many different ethnicities. Madera is one of the most ethnically diverse areas in the country, in the world. You absorbed it like osmosis because it was around you, and you tolerated it because these were your friends. We played sports together. You grew up with this knowledge of diversity, with seeing and practicing tolerance."

He'd gotten along with white kids since elementary school. "James Monroe Grammar School was full of Okie kids," Albert said, "poor whites, poor blacks, poor Puerto Ricans, and poor Mexicans. It was Okie territory." Two of his grammar school friends were Artie and Richard. "They're my friends to this day," Albert said, "and they're about as Okie as you can get." All the kids from James Monroe, St. Joachim's, Dixieland, Dairyland, Ripperdan, and elsewhere got dumped into one high school.

"We knew the Epsteins," Albert said; "they were Jewish, or we thought they were Jewish, but it didn't factor into doing anything differently with them."

A lot of kids didn't quite know what being Jewish meant other than that it was another religion or race or ethnicity among many.

"Jewish was kind of a vague thing," Frank said.

When I'd once asked Frank's classmate Jerry Weinberger whether he'd experienced discrimination as a Jewish kid in Madera, he said, "Hell no. There weren't enough of us. To have discrimination you need a group."

Jerry did recall in grammar school seeing his father hunched over in a chair staring at the TV screen during the McCarthy hearings. As a young doctor intent on improving the world, Jerry's father had joined the New York Communist Party and had worked as a volunteer physician in the Soviet Union for a period, something Jerry didn't learn until much later in life, along with the news that his father had sought out the valley as a remote hinterland where he might not be discovered as a former Communist.

At the fiftieth high school class reunion, Albert talked with Roger Mah, whose father owned a clothing store in town when they were growing up. Roger, now a psychiatrist, told Albert, "When I got to Berkeley I was aware there were a lot of Asians there, and when somebody walked up to me and wanted to talk about discrimination, I said, 'Discrimination?'"

"It was a new concept to him," Albert said.

There was separation in high school, Albert admitted, with the black kids hanging out mostly with black kids, and white kids mostly with whites. "I was able to move between those lines pretty well," he said. Except for being called "niggerow" in the second grade, "I didn't have to deal with that kind of racism," he said. "I don't think any of the black kids did." In contrast, "in the South at that time there was all this emotional turmoil. We didn't have to fight to go to school. We didn't have to fight to walk on the campus or to be on the same team."

I interrupted Albert to say, "You better give me something negative or my friends back east won't believe your story."

He laughed. "They didn't grow up in the valley."

As a matter of fact, one of my friends who grew up in the Boston area later responded to my account of Albert's experience as "being a little Pollyannaish about racial and ethnic tolerance." During a reading in the valley, I reported my friend's claim that I'd "made Madera out to be a multicultural utopia."

Albert, who was in the audience that night, responded, "I'm not naïve. I was born in Texas, and my parents grew up in Texas. My father told me stories about what was going on, about the black man shot in front of a white man's house. I also knew there was a racial divide in Madera, a racial difference, but it wasn't like the South. Compared to Texas, Madera *was* utopia." He told the group how his family had moved to California because his father couldn't see his children not having an education. "All my siblings went to college. I had to work hard, but I knew I was graded just like everyone else."

He repeated what he'd told Frank and me about his awareness of what was going on in the rest of the country, the freedom rides, the lunch-counter sit-ins, the Chicago boycott of segregationist schools, the Birmingham church bombing and deaths, and Martin Luther King's "I Have a Dream" speech, all in 1963, the year Albert graduated from Madera High.

He didn't mention that in that same year he was class valedictorian, student body president, and the Northern California Scholarship Federation Student of the Year.

"One of the things I realized," he told Frank and me in his Fresno home, "was how things were different once I left this area with all these people mingling, and accepting each other, and working together. It all came naturally. When I got to Stanford you assumed that everyone there was halfway intelligent and aware."

As a college freshman, Albert arrived on campus early in the day. After he'd unpacked in his dorm, his parents left at midday and he strolled around campus. Like all freshmen, he didn't know who his roommate was going to be. He was assigned to a dorm and his roommate was picked for him.

When he returned to his dorm, he saw his future roommate sitting on his bed, looking as though he were halfway crying, his eyes all red. "His parents were sitting there looking intently at him," Albert said, "and I thought, *Well, this is a goodbye thing, this is very emotional, they're saying goodbye to their son, so I'm going to leave.*"

When he later returned to the dorm and the boy's parents had gone, Albert's new roommate "went into this whole litany of all the things we were going to do: we were going to keep the room clean, we were going to pick up after ourselves, there's not going to be any dirt here, the bed's going to be neat, there's not going to be any trash around. I said, 'Okay, I like things to be clean, too. That's fine.'"

Months later, his roommate showed Albert a paper he'd written for an English class assignment about the most upsetting, cataclysmic event of his life. "He wrote about me being his roommate," Albert said. "He wasn't from Mississippi; he was from a Mormon family in Portland, but apparently that conversation I'd peeked in on was after his parents had tried to get their son's roommate changed. They didn't want him rooming with a black kid." Their request had been refused.

"We got along fine," Albert said. The irony of the story is that later in the term Albert and his roommate were both studying in their room around eight or nine at night when the resident faculty member of the dorm came in and gently commented on the condition of their room. "My bed was made, my books were neat," Albert said. His roommate's side of the room was a mess, his bed unmade, his books scattered. The dorm prefect said, "Lyle, your side is kind of unkempt. Albert's is kind of neat."

Stanford had recruited Albert to play football. "As far as I know," he said, "I was the first black athlete recruited for Stanford." No black athletes were on the football team at the time, none even on the track or basketball teams. In Albert's freshman class of twelve hundred, he was one of twelve black students.

The Stanford varsity coach, John Ralston, and the freshman team coach, Bill Walsh of later San Francisco 49ers fame, had come to Madera to meet Albert and his parents. "They were trying to get their defense better," Albert said. Bill Walsh told Albert, "I need somebody who can run and catch people." They knew, Albert said, "if you're going to compete with USC and

UCLA and the University of Washington, you better get all the good athletes you can from wherever the hell you can and whatever color they are."

Albert played defensive end, which in those days was equivalent to today's outside linebacker. In his senior year, he was the team captain and Stanford's athlete of the year.

He majored in biology partly because when he was in the seventh grade a teacher had helped him earn some money by having him chop wood at her house. After she'd paid him for splitting wood and was driving him home, she asked, "What are you going to do, Al? What do you want to be?" Albert told her he wasn't sure. "Maybe teach," he said, and she responded, "You ought to think about going into a career like medicine or law."

Albert's mother was a maid at Dearborn Hospital, where a doctor who'd gone to Stanford, named Dr. Swift, became the family doctor, friend, and mentor. Albert thought about medicine more and more, and in high school his most influential teacher was his biology teacher, Mr. Mastin. Although UCLA, Berkeley, and other colleges recruited him, he focused on Stanford, and later went to UCLA Medical School.

After working in public health and later maintaining a private practice in Los Angeles for a dozen years, Albert moved with his wife and family back to the valley to be closer to his parents, who needed medical care. Since moving from Texas, his father had worked in construction until he was crippled by a falling boulder when he was fifty-eight and building the earthen Hidden Lake Dam in the foothills northeast of town.

While helping to take care of his parents, who still lived in their country house, Albert worked at Kaiser Hospital in Fresno as the medical staff president and the first chief of hospital-based services. His mother died at eighty-four and his father at ninety-three.

"One of the things my father did after he got settled in Madera," Albert said, "is he used to go to the courthouse park on Saturday afternoons and just sit in the park. That was his recreation. To go sit in the park after he'd worked all week. I asked him, 'Why are you sitting in the park?' and he responded, '*Because I can.*'"

He went on to tell Albert, "Nobody asks me to leave the park, and I can drink out of the water fountain when I get thirsty, and I can go to the bathroom when I want to."

"And that floored me," Albert said. "It just kicked me back. He was going in there because it was a free place to go."

Albert recognized in high school how radically his boyhood experience differed from his father's. "I realized how tolerant Madera was," he said. "You could walk across the campus and you breathed the tolerance in the air. You got it osmotically. It was just there. You could sense it. It was palpable."

Black Ranch Girl

Nancy Turner Gray grew up on a Madera ranch and attended high school with Albert Wilburn, but didn't share his view of valley tolerance. Nancy and I sat outside one warm January morning at a Starbucks table in Fresno's Fig Garden Village on Shaw Avenue, trying to talk amid the roar of passing cars that urban Californians accept as a staple of contemporary life. Dressed in a camel-colored pantsuit and a loosely knotted scarf, Nancy maintained the steady gaze and calm demeanor of a former social worker and parole agent accustomed to sizing up people as she spoke about her childhood. "Madera was a very racist place," she told me, "and still is, I think, in a lot of ways, but during the time I was growing up it was very racist."

Blacks and whites were separated, she said. "A lot of the blacks and whites came from the South—my father came from Alabama, my mother was from Oklahoma—and a lot of the whites came from the same areas and carried those values with them."

All her teachers were white. "In elementary school, junior high, and high school we never had black teachers," she said. "Not even a janitor, come to think of it.

"In high school, a cousin of mine tried out for cheerleader, and she was told her legs were too dark and she could not be on the cheerleading squad. This was in the sixties."

Nancy was a freshman at Madera High when senior Albert

Wilburn was the school's valedictorian and first black student body president. "One of the things that set Albert apart," Nancy said, "was—not that he wasn't intelligent—but he played sports and was a big thing on the football team. In most small towns, football or any kind of sport can put you on the map. If he'd been a little nerdy-looking somebody who didn't play sports, I don't think he would've been as distinguished."

Nancy's friend Kay, a former court clerk who worked with her as a member of the Juvenile Justice Commission, joined us at the table. Kay was my country neighbor and childhood friend and also Albert Wilburn's high school classmate.

"All the black girls liked Albert," Nancy said.

"All the white girls liked Albert, too," Kay added.

"The factor of who he was," Nancy said, "being on the football team and valedictorian, that thrust him into a lot of white circles."

We talked about dating at the time. Blacks and whites didn't go out with each other. "That was totally unheard of," Nancy said. "If they did, nobody knew about it. Now you don't even turn your head. In fact, I wasn't allowed to go to a lot of the dances because of religious stuff, but I don't know that a lot of the black kids went to social things, like Christmas formals and proms. Albert went, of course, and at lunchtime we all sat around wondering: Who would he take?" After the prom, she and her friends investigated. "Who did he take?" they asked. "What did she wear?" Even Albert, she said, "with his being around white culture, he knew better than to take a white girl to the prom."

Racism became more of a problem after Nancy left Madera. "I probably had more racist things happen in college than in high school," she said. "In high school, I was in the college prep classes. We were the ones going to college. Albert Wilburn's brother was always in my classes."

While attending Fresno City College she tried to get a job as a substitute teacher in Madera. She'd acquired enough units to be qualified. "I'd graduated from high school, I was going to college and working on my AA, and the lady wouldn't even give me an application. She said, 'I'm not taking your application. You're not qualified, and we're not hiring you.'"

Nancy earned a degree in social work from Fresno State College, married, and returned to Fresno State to get a master's degree while going through a divorce, and then worked two part-time jobs until she was appointed to a mental health agency in Visalia for four years, followed by a year as a social worker in Fresno and then as a state licensing agent for day care centers and foster homes. She later became a parole agent until she retired as an agency supervisor.

"I enjoyed being an agent on the street more than a supervisor," she said. "At the time, parole agents were respected. I remember going to a home and a mother—or a family member—started going off on me and the parolee said, 'Don't you talk to my parole agent that way. You don't disrespect her.' Now that's not likely to happen today."

As she grew older she came to realize how subtle and insidious racism could be. "California thinks it's so above racism," she said, "but I think California is worse than in the South, because in the South you know where it's coming from. White people in the South will tell you they don't like you or they don't want you in their house, or whatever, and they're open with it. California people won't say that but they treat you different, so the racism to me is worse here than in the South—in the sixties and now."

Nancy's son, who was born in the valley, currently lives in New York City and loves it. "I don't think he'll ever move back to California. He really enjoys it there. When he comes home he doesn't even bring a coat because our cold isn't like their cold."

Kay mentioned that Nancy recently made an astonishing discovery about her son's New York girlfriend. She happened to be close to Albert Wilburn's daughter, who lives in Virginia. "Who would think that?" Nancy said. "I just met her and found out she's good friends with Albert's daughter, not just acquaintances."

Kay had given me a front-page article from *The Madera Tribune* about her high school reunion, announcing that distinguished alumnus Dr. Albert Wilburn was grand marshal of the homecoming parade. Kay had worked with him on the class reunion committee.

I showed Nancy a section of an inside-page article about Albert's talk at the reunion dinner and dance. Nancy read it. In the article, Madera historian and journalist Bill Coate wrote:

> Wilburn pointed out that students of all colors and races, coming from varied economic backgrounds in Madera "lived diversity."
>
> "We assumed tolerance," said Wilburn. "It came to us through osmosis and was as natural as drinking water and breathing air," he said.
>
> "We became one together; let's continue to live that diversity," Wilburn concluded.

When she finished reading, Nancy nodded and said, "I think that pretty well describes it."

I asked if her agreement contradicted what she'd said earlier about racism.

"No," she replied, "I think there was tolerance because we didn't know any better." She went to the same schools as Albert. "We were in classes with a lot of mixed races, a diverse population," she said. "In junior high and high school we all came together. I always said the doctors' kids went to school with the winos' kids. You had to be together."

Albert and her views coincided in recognizing an overlay of racism existing simultaneously with tolerance in the schools. "There was racism, but we weren't aware of it," she said.

"Here's a real clear example. In elementary school I was friends with a little white Okie girl—she didn't have as much as I had—and with a Japanese girl. All three of us were best buds in the first and second grade. We used to go over to each other's houses until one day the little white girl told us we couldn't come over to her house, me and the Japanese girl. So we were like, 'How come we can't go over to your house?' and she just said that her mother didn't want us guys over to her house anymore."

Nancy complained to her mother that she didn't understand why she couldn't go over to Linda's house. Linda and Deborah Tanaka—her father was a phlebotomist at Dearborn Hospital—still came to Nancy's house, and all three of them continued to go over to Deborah's but they couldn't go to Linda's. "My mother knew why, but I didn't," Nancy said.

"I forgot about the whole incident until I saw Linda at a class reunion." She came up to Nancy and said, "You don't know who I am, do you?" Their reintroduction "brought back all those memories. I wondered if she understood why her mother had stopped us from going over to her house because Deborah was Japanese and I was black. That was the real reason. We exchanged phone numbers—she lives in Gilroy—and I said I ought to call her and develop a conversation and ask her about it, but then I thought, *Nah, forget it*. Her mother probably didn't tell her either; she just said they can't come over anymore. Back then kids didn't ask parents why. When they told you something, you just believed, at least black kids did."

Black kids also had to contend with the black community as well as with parents. "I grew up in the Ebenezer Apostolic Church on Magnolia Avenue," she said. "If someone from your church saw you doing something not right, they'd tell your parents and you'd get in trouble both with the person who saw you *and* with your parents."

There was a strong black community in those days, with black churches, black leaders, black businesses. "A lot of older black people owned their own homes. Now the area is dispersed with more Mexicans. Madera is now seventy-five percent Hispanic, if not more. You'd think you're in Guadalajara." Back then, "There was Young's Market, a little hole in the wall run by an older black lady. There was another store—and I cringe to say it now—but we called it the Jap Store. It was a Japanese-owned store—Washington Market—but we always called it the Jap Store."

Nancy's father supplied both stores with fruits and vegetables—watermelons, cantaloupes, corn, black-eyed peas. He also sold directly to customers at his own farmer's market. "One of the girls at school told me, 'Will you please tell your daddy to stop growing black-eyed peas so my mama can stop buying them?'" The girl had plenty of peas to eat because her mother bought them from Nancy's father in fifty-pound sacks.

Nancy's dad had come from Alabama and sharecropped for a white family until he saved enough money for a down payment on an eighty-acre ranch just outside the city limits, where he raised cotton, grapes, and peaches as well as garden vegetables. "I was the youngest of eight and the only one to get a degree in my family," Nancy said. "My father made us all work in the fields, picking cotton and cutting grapes. I decided I didn't want to do that. It was too hot and sweaty. That made me want to do something else. I said I'm going to go to school and get me a job inside because I didn't like being out there in the hot sun."

Nancy didn't understand why she had to work in the fields at all. Since her father was hiring field hands, she figured she should be a little bit above doing fieldwork. She asked her father,

"You got people working for you, why do I have to get out there and cut grapes and pick cotton?" And he replied, "Because I'm teaching you how to work," and she thought, *That's the dumbest thing I ever heard because I already know how to work.*

"As I got older I understood that he was teaching me responsibility, accountability, getting to work on time—all the work ethics kids now don't have because their hard work is working at fast-food franchises. They don't know what it's like working in the fields—real hard, hard work.

"We had families working in my father's fields to buy their kids clothes for school." She and her friends had to do the same if they wanted spending money. "The fair was always in September," she said, "and I remember if you wanted to go to the fair then you had to work to get money. That was just accepted. It was almost a social thing because all my friends were out there in the cotton fields, too, working, laughing. Everybody was working. It wasn't odd at the time."

Other memories underscored some strands of racial tolerance in the valley at that time. She recalls that the white kids who got along with everybody in school and didn't express any kind of racism were the same way years later at class reunions, like the school drum major, who was a dentist's son, still outgoing and handsome. "We all liked him. He was handsome then and he's handsome now. Kids who were racist and snobbish in school, ten or fifteen years later they were still racist and snobbish."

Nancy's experience of growing up on a ranch at the edge of town differed from many of her town friends. "On the street where we lived, there weren't any other blacks. We were friends with all our white neighbors. We would go to their houses, and they would come to ours.

"At that time, the culture was to treat people with respect who worked hard. My father was a hard worker. He was able to manage an eighty-acre ranch and raise eight children along with my mother without knowing how to read and write. He never went to school because he was the oldest and had to work, but when he died and we sold his place it was pretty much paid for."

Her father could sign his name, Nancy said, and when he went to buy things people would fill out his checks for him. No one tried to cheat him because they knew him. He'd been there a long time, and they knew how hard he worked.

"One other thing pretty significant was my mother died when I was sixteen." Her mother was fifty when she died. All of Nancy's older brothers and sisters had left home, and Nancy was then put on her father's checking account. At sixteen she continued working through the California Youth Authority to provide a foster home for delinquent boys, as her mother had done.

"We had a parole agent, who was so impressed with the home we had and how things were going when my mother was alive. I became a foster mother as a teenager, a surrogate mother at sixteen and seventeen." This same parole agent, who happened to be white, Nancy said, "got me wanting to be a social worker."

When her mother was dying of kidney disease, Nancy walked from school to see her in the Madera Sanitarium. "Had she been rich and white she probably would've been on dialysis. This was before dialysis became common. She was fifty when she died, and fifty became very significant for my sisters and me." As that birthday approached, Nancy told her sister, "I'm staying up past midnight because I'm going to make sure I'm fifty."

Now sixty-five, Nancy reminisced about how despite the discrimination she experienced elsewhere, she was like her classmate Al Wilburn in feeling supported by her teachers. She recalled the daily walks she took to see her mother in the hospital. "One of the things I remember kindly about Madera High," she said, "was the teachers allowed me to go visit her during the lunch hour, and I remember I was late coming back and a teacher said, 'I understand what's happening with your mother. If you're late for class I understand.' "

Chicano Vet

"You know," seventy-one-year-old Joe Alvarez told me in a gravelly voice, "being born here in Madera, in the sixties there was nothing racial." It was late January, during the fifth year of the drought. The air felt summery. Joe sat in a lawn chair in his front yard, facing the mid-afternoon sun. He had gnarled hands, short-cropped hair, intense dark eyes, and the compact body of a former athlete. Like his football teammate Al Wilburn, he didn't experience discrimination until he left his hometown. "Here in Madera," he said, "I couldn't see anything racial. I mean, it was there, but it was never pointed at me. Then I joined the Navy."

Joe enlisted right after high school and was sent to boot camp in San Diego. That was in 1961. "Then that's all I faced was racial discrimination because the guys I'm with are all from the South—Alabama, Texas, Oklahoma, Georgia, North Carolina, Kentucky, Tennessee—and they called me all kinds of names: *Wetback. Spic. Alien. Greaser.* I couldn't believe it. I was born in Madera and go to San Diego and get stationed with Okie boys and they treat me like crap, call me names, spit on me. We couldn't fight the racial because there were fifty in the company and forty-five were from the South."

Along with Joe, there was one black kid, an Indian guy they left alone because he was six-four, another kid from Texas who told everyone he was a Spaniard, and a Jewish kid who got kicked when he carried the flag while marching between rows of recruits. "Oh, that Jewish boy," Joe said, "they kicked him and that poor guy was crying when he got to the end of the line."

After boot camp, Joe shipped out to Hawaii and had to do mess duty on the base. "The guy in charge of me was an Okie boy, so I had to do extra duty every day." When others got off at four, Joe had to clean tables, sweep floors, or peel potatoes. He saw guys in the kitchen breaking eggs for omelets in the morning—five hundred eggs into big metal containers used in bakeries. "I'd be peeling my potatoes, and when those guys finished with the eggs they'd piss in them. Agh! Two guys would piss in the eggs. I couldn't say nothing because it would be those two guys and all their friends against me." And the guy in charge was from Mississippi. Joe ate cereal for breakfast and lunch. "I never ate scrambled eggs. I don't eat 'em today unless I do them myself.

"Those Okie boys put all this nasty stuff in my head. They used to tell me, 'If you come to our town the cops will stop you and throw you in jail because you're a Mexican.'"

It did no good to say he was a Californian. He was told, "I don't see no horns on you, so you must be a queer." Because, of course, only queers and cows are born in California.

"I hated that," Joe said. "I had no desire to go out of California. I still don't."

Joe's parents had come to California from Mexico, his father as a fieldworker and his mother as a house cleaner from Guadalajara. His father died when Joe was five, and a couple of years later his mother married a VA nurse. "I didn't get along with my stepdad at all. Terrible growing up around him. He was an alcoholic and an abuser. He'd come home on weekends and beat my mom up."

After fifteen years of cleaning houses, Joe's mother worked at the local olive-canning plant for ten years, and then another ten years at the winery.

"I remember asking my mom what's for dinner," Joe said, "and she'd say rice, beans, and potatoes, and I'd say, 'Ah, not again,' but after the military I never complained about food."

In the Navy he lost his name and was known as Jesse. "Uncle Sam said 'Joe' didn't exist." Because his birth certificate read José de Jesús Alvarez, he was told José didn't count because of the "de" in his name. He had to be Jesse. His I.D. noted him with "no middle name" as "Jesse NMN Alvarez."

"That bothered me. It took me a long time to get used to it."

In Hawaii, he served on the USS Elkhorn, a Patapsco-class gasoline tanker with seventy-eight on board under a Japanese American commander, and later in Alameda on the USS Cockrell, a destroyer used as a naval reserve training ship with about seventy on board. He showed me a photo of his first ship and crew. "Look at all those Okie boys," he said. "We all got along pretty good. I learned my lesson and stayed away from people. I'm still that way now. I don't hang out with people."

In Alameda, when guys left ship and went into town for a drink, Joe wouldn't sit at the bar itself because a guy would knock you in back of the head. In contrast, he said, "Whenever I walked down the street in my uniform, all the civilians were respectful, even on the bad side of town. In Oakland I walked across the freeway and all the way down 98th Avenue to see my uncle and there was no back crap."

In the Navy, Joe suffered hearing loss and severe ringing in his ears from firing large naval guns off ships. During exercises in Hawaii, he said, "We fired six rounds of three-inch-fifties off the tanker twice a week, and were given cotton to protect our ears. In Alameda, we fired ten rounds of five-inch-thirty-eights off the destroyer once a week and were again given only cotton." He asked for earplugs but was told they weren't authorized.

"I was thinking of writing Senator John McCain about my

hearing. He's my last resort. McCain's a veteran. He would understand about those guns."

From Hawaii he sailed to Japan, the Philippines, and Hong Kong. "One thing I liked was to steer the ship." He used a compass and didn't go off course a single degree. "I was good at steering." And he loved the sunrises and sunsets at sea. "Beautiful to see the big sun coming up and going down into the ocean. That's the only thing I miss about the Navy: the sunrises and the sunsets."

One night, in Hong Kong, he and some shipmates were told about a bar that required them to take a ferryboat, but they boarded the wrong ferry and ended up in Communist China.

"We went from 1963 to 1863. No lights. Everything was candles." He and his shipmates didn't know where they were. In darkness they walked half a block and met a guy with an ox and a cow on ropes who made a shooing motion with his hands signaling them to get out of there. "Back on ship we learned we'd been in Communist China. We were lucky. The government wouldn't have done anything to get us out of there.

"That's one of those things I won't forget," Joe said "that and being involved in rough seas, in fifty-foot waves, and swimming in the middle of the ocean."

The ocean swim took place while sailing to Japan during a man-overboard drill. A dummy was tossed into the water, but it took rookie officers an hour to get the ship close enough to pick it up. Finally the order came: "Swimmer in. Go get the dummy."

"I'm the swimmer," Joe said. "I jumped overboard in a life-jacket and swam about fifty yards and grabbed the dummy. When I looked up at the ship I seen this guy pointing an M1. I thought he was going to shoot. That's the impression the white boys gave me, that they were going to shoot me in the middle of the Pacific Ocean. It scared the hell out of me, more than when I went into

Communist China." In reality, his shipmates were looking for sharks with M1s poised to protect him. "Because of what they'd put into my mind, I first thought they were going to shoot me," Joe said, "then I thought about sharks."

He finished his stint in the Navy as a Seaman E-3. "I didn't want to move up the chain because I'd have to be in charge of the Okie boys and they'd disrespect me. I didn't want to put up with that."

"But," I said to Joe, "you went to high school with a bunch of Okie boys."

"Got along with all of them," he replied. "Well, you know, playing football, playing sports, you're popular with everybody."

At St. Joachim's School, Joe was the quarterback of our make-shift, self-organized tackle football team. He experienced no prejudice in grammar school from his classmates or the nuns. "None at all," he said. "Nothing." The first time he felt discrim-inated against was in high school but not from his classmates. "The coaches wouldn't let me play baseball. Their reasoning was that they had too many kids, but I was better at baseball than I was at football. I would see guys playing baseball who weren't half as good as I was."

He played football for the Madera Coyotes as a five-foot-four, 121-pound halfback. "They had a hard time getting me," Joe said, "because I was quick. Third down, nine to go, and I'd get the first down. I always got the first downs. I'd get the ball and run ten, fifteen, maybe twenty yards. Nance would fight for every yard he got, but he got all the credit, all the glory."

He was talking about his teammate Kent Nance, who in his senior year was named a high-school All-American, the only player from California that year selected for the first-string na-tional team. Nance was also named Northern California Player of the Year. In nine games he scored thirty-two touchdowns, eight in one game. He later scored the only touchdown for the North team to win the California North-South All-Star Game in Los Angeles Coliseum.

"Nance was a great player," Joe said; "he was a hitter, a tiger. He was strong and could carry a defender. Plus he had the grades. I didn't have the grades so I couldn't go to college."

Nance, who was a Mormon, turned down bids from Notre Dame, USC, UCLA, and Navy to play college ball for Brigham Young University, where he blew out his knee in his first varsity game. After several operations, he again played in his senior year, mainly as a defensive back because he couldn't make his cuts anymore.

"I'd get the majority of the yardage," Joe said, "and Nance would get the touchdowns." On the high school squad of thirty-nine players, Joe was one of five Chicanos. The other running back, Charley Jackson, was also from our grammar school and was one of six black players on the team. Japanese American Katsu Shitanisi, the previous year's quarterback, had graduated. "If I'd been a little taller and a little smarter I could've really accomplished something," Joe said. "But they should've given me some kind of credit."

The high school yearbook did give Joe credit. In the game against the Tulare Indians, the yearbook noted how "Nance and Alvarez moved the ball to the 10," and "Alvarez ran for 14 yards, then 25 more in a perfectly executed reverse."

Against the Fresno Warriors, the yearbook reported that "Alvarez covered 74 yards for a touchdown," and later "Alvarez made another touchdown."

Against the Merced Bears, "Alvarez started a drive which led to a Nance touchdown after a 23-yard run."

At the fiftieth high school reunion, Joe had words with Nance how back in high school he'd resented his getting all the glory. "But it dawned on me that it's a team sport," so he added, "what you did was all right with me. I was there to help you—I pitched in. I'm a team player."

Nance was surprised about Joe's feelings back in high school but was glad to hear that Joe recognized football as a team sport.

"You can't do it without ten other guys," Joe told me. "I was good at football but I give the credit to my linemen. If they hadn't blocked for me, I would've had a hard time getting first downs. If Mike Vizcarra wasn't blocking for me I wouldn't have got that extra yard."

Mike Vizcarra, our grammar school classmate, worked with Joe in the fields during the summer, picking peaches and nectarines or cutting grapes. During the fall on weekends and school vacations, it was cotton for Joe. "In high school when I'd go to apply for a job in town, they'd tell me they didn't need anybody. I'd go back in a week or so and there'd be some white guys they hired." So he worked in the fields.

Once while picking fruit in a Planada orchard, on the other side of Chowchilla between Merced and Madera, Joe said, "We started throwing nectarines at each other and the foreman kicked us out. It was around ten o'clock so we went to Millerton Lake and horsed around till four o'clock, and on the way home we stopped in a field and rolled around to look dirty and then went home."

One of the boys that day was our schoolmate Jimmy Gonzalez, later killed in Vietnam. In contrast, our classmate Mike Vizcarra, who'd been the instigator of the nectarine fight, went on to become a doctor. What made the difference for Mike? "Going to school," Joe said. "He realized he couldn't do nothing else unless he went to school.

"You know," he continued, "it's a bitch. I went into the military and then to Fresno City College and got all A's and B's. In grammar school I got nothing but D's and F's. I found three report cards my mother kept"—they were from our third-grade class with Sister Alphonsus—"and they were full of D's and F's. If I could maintain an A and B average in college, why couldn't I do that in grammar school instead of maintaining an F average? All I had to do was pay attention. In high school I was into sports, just getting by. In college I paid attention."

Joe finished his time in the Navy in 1965, the first year U.S. combat troops arrived in Vietnam, and he returned to Madera to work at Mission Bell Winery. A lot of Okie boys were there, but, Joe said, "They were cool." He was later working the graveyard shift as the line captain of the bottling machines when he started night school, taking criminology classes in the evening from 7:00 to 10:00 p.m. and then working from 11:00 p.m. to 7:00 a.m. in the morning. He wanted to be a detective.

As he was telling me this story, his thirty-seven-year-old son pulled up to the house in Joe's canary-yellow Mustang to deliver a fire-starter log to his father. "He's my friend from grammar school," Joe told his son. "He wrote the book," meaning my novel *Jesse's Ghost*. Then he added, "His dad used to be in the FBI."

"In the eighth grade we used to talk about your dad being in the FBI," Joe added. "That was a big deal. He got me steered in the direction of wanting to be a cop. When we were out at your ranch he showed me his badge. That was big, big, big."

Things didn't work out for Joe's becoming a detective. "I spent five years going to City College to get my degree. When I got my A.S. and went to apply at the Fresno police station, they said I was too old. I was thirty-three. They said the cutoff was thirty-two." He looked out toward the southwestern horizon, which was turning pink. "I would've made a good cop." He added, "That was around the time that Sandee died."

Cassandra Moss, nicknamed Sandee, was Joe's high school sweetheart. They started sneaking out on dates in their sophomore year. One of the three fistfights Joe had in high school was with Sandee's brother, an Okie boy who didn't want him dating his sister. In June, right after graduation, Joe and Sandee got married and two months later Joe joined the Navy. When they separated ten years later, they had two daughters and a son.

When I asked how Sandee had died so young—she was around thirty-three—Joe pointed his index finger to his head and cocked his thumb like a pistol hammer.

"She called and wanted to talk to me," Joe said. "We were separated, she was seeing some guy from Utah and was pregnant. She felt she'd got herself into a mess she couldn't get herself out of. I told her the only thing I can say is to have an abortion, but she said she wouldn't. She called the next day for me to go be with the kids because she was going to kill herself. 'Don't do that,' I begged her, and told her I would try to raise the baby as my own. Too late. On Route 145, past the Santa Fe railroad tracks on the way to Bass Lake, there are some new houses on the left where they found her." She'd gotten a .38-caliber pistol from a guy in Madera.

For the next nine years Joe was a single father. After twenty-one years at the winery, "I lost my job because I started drinking. The company didn't offer me help—psychologically. I got three kids I'm raising by myself. They're going through a traumatic event. So am I."

He went to work for Sunsweet Dryers for five years and then Vendo, the soda-machine manufacturer. That was his last job. "I had a stroke," Joe said, "and they retired me."

He doesn't drink or smoke anymore. He doesn't buy anything he doesn't need and is happy to sit in his yard and listen to music. "If the VA would take care of my hearing," he said, "everything would be cool. I'd be set for life."

He'd petitioned the Veterans Administration in 1967 about the debilitative effects he was experiencing from firing high-caliber naval guns with only cotton in his ears for protection. "I was turned away and told I'd had the proper equipment." He figured he didn't get help because he wasn't a combat veteran.

Forty-four years later, his brother, who was a Vietnam vet, urged him to try again because the government was taking better care of veterans. His disability was accepted, he was given hearing aids that proved ineffective, the ringing in his ears remained severe, and he was awarded $250 a month retroactively, based on the time between his petition and treatment, for a total of $1,250. When he pointed out that he'd first petitioned the VA in 1967, not 2011, he was told the records were lost.

"That's why I'm thinking of writing John McCain," Joe said. "I just hope he can see what I've been going through. I didn't fight a war with bullets, but I fought a war of verbal abuse. If I had to be away from my family for four years and put up with all that racist bullshit to where it stopped me from wanting to go out of the state of California, I think they owe me something."

Despite Joe's experience in the military, his son also joined up. "He did four years in the Air Force. I made him join the Air Force because he was hanging around with the wrong crowd. Now I'm trying to talk my grandson into going into the military because he's not working. He's just wasting his time. I tell him if you're going to give up your freedom, give it to the government because at least you'll have freedom of movement. In jail, you won't. And you'll have a chance to see how other people live, and how great it is to have freedom."

The low western sky glowed as the sun dropped in what was approaching a San Joaquin Valley record of eleven consecutive January days with temperatures above seventy degrees. The horizon wasn't visible from Joe's yard. Pollution hid the coastal mountains. Still, as I told Joe, "You get good views of sunsets from here."

"Yeah," Joe said, though his tone was reluctant. "Not as I used to see them out on the ocean. Those were beautiful. Sunrises and sunsets. When you look out at sea, you can see twenty miles to the horizon." His chest rumbled with a gravelly chuckle. "So when the sun goes down you can see it twenty miles away, because that's as far as you can see the horizon."

After I left and was back in my motel room, my cell phone rang. It was Joe. "I've been thinking," he said, "I can say I did three things no one else did." At least nobody else could say they did all three: "I've been to Communist China, I've been involved in fifty-foot waves, and I swam in the middle of the ocean."

New Woman Warrior

One October night at the Denver airport, I walked across the tarmac to a lonesome-looking SkyWest CRJ-100 for the final leg of a long trip from New York's Hudson Valley to California. In the small, dark regional jet, with two seats on each side, I looked up when I heard a voice, "Boy, it's hot in here." A young Asian woman in the aisle was slipping off her jacket. I stood up so she could take the window seat next to me. Air began circulating through the cabin. Passengers in the twelve rows of seats buckled up. We sped down the runway and took off into the night for a two-and-a-half hour flight into the heart of the San Joaquin Valley.

"You should write about me," my new seatmate told me, after we were airborne and had established our purposes for flying to the valley, hers to return home after a company meeting in Denver, and mine to give readings from a new novel and gather material for another book. Her name was Heather. She was thirty-two. In the flickering darkness, her smooth skin gave her an aura of unblemished youth and innocence, and her voice sounded even younger, with the chipper lilts of a teenager. "I've been through a lot," she said. "I've lived quite a life I would say."

Most of that life, she told me, was lived in California, but she shared little experience with other Asian women from California. "Like Amy Tan and that *Joy Luck Club,*" she said. "I have no understanding of that. I mean, I have an understanding in that I know what she's talking about—that Chinese American heritage—but I don't feel the way she does."

"Why not?" I asked.

"I grew up in the valley."

Heather felt that the Sacramento and San Joaquin Valleys made her a completely different person. "My mom was Korean so you'd think I'd feel more the way she does. My mom tried to teach me some of the Korean ways but it didn't have any impact on me."

This "mom" was her third mother. Her actual mother as well as her first adoptive mom was also Korean. "I was born in Korea and immediately adopted out. Mom got pregnant and back then in the seventies they take you away to a farm and you disappear for nine months and then you come back." She didn't know if her mother was married or unmarried. "There's no history of my parents," she said.

Her adoptive parents in Korea were childless, but a year after adopting Heather, who was then known as Hong Joo Mee, a son was born. "You hear about that happening a lot," Heather said, how a woman gets pregnant after adopting a child. "My brother loved me dearly. He absolutely loved me." Her adoptive father owned a little grocery store where Heather liked to eat hot buns stuffed with meat or sweets. "I remember that vividly," she said. When she was four, her adoptive father separated Heather from her brother because he and his wife were getting a divorce. "He was going to get rid of us," she said. He sent Heather to the mountains to live with his parents.

"My grandpa was a drunk. I remember him being an alcoholic. In the evenings he would always be lit up." He told Heather how when she got older she would take care of him. "I remember at that age thinking I'm not going to take care of you. I have a future ahead of me. Can you imagine? In Korea that was very unladylike." Her laughter was like a teenager's giggle, expressing a genuine delight in a memory that tickled her.

She maintained her independence with her grandmother as well. "In Korea there's a nightlife," she said. Her grandmother sold coffee and pastries in the evening. Heather recalls asking her for money to buy ramen. Heather liked opening the packages and eating the crunchy noodles uncooked, but her grandmother refused. "I was stubborn and tenacious until she gave in to me."

Although winter brought lots of snow to the mountains where they lived, Heather still played outside, either with neighborhood friends or alone with rocks and snow. In the spring, she caught bees and dragonflies and made nail polish from the petals of flowers. "I remember being outdoorsy at a young age," until one day her adoptive father came to fetch her because her grandparents told him they couldn't care for her anymore. "She's a handful," they told him. "We're getting too old."

"My adoptive dad took me on a train ride, gave me a lot of change, and left me at an orphanage." She was five and a half. "The women at the orphanage were stinking mean, and that's why I don't have many women relationships today." She was then sent to a foster home. "As soon as the agency knows you're going to be adopted out, they put you in foster care." It took a year and a half for her U.S. adoption process to go through. Meanwhile, the lady in the foster home was also mean. "I didn't like her at all." She was making fun of Heather's purse one day at the doctor's office and Heather tried to run away. "In Korea the streets are wide" Heather said, starting to laugh, "one street is double of Shaw in Fresno, and here I'm running away from her and she's trying to catch me." And Heather did get caught.

"In that culture the people are cold. As far as feelings go, Asians are pretty strict. They're more cold than Americans.

We're more in tune with our feelings here. They keep their feelings inside. I'm like that. I've gotten better because of my dad."

This dad was an Okie in the Sacramento Valley, who with his second wife adopted Heather when she was seven. Her mother, also in her second marriage, was Korean. Heather became a Korean Okie. "My parents offered me the best life they could," Heather said. "They were extremely frugal. They pushed education. They knew it was valuable and important for me to get educated."

Her father worked as a service man for a vending machine company in Marysville and then Yuba City. Her mother, who was actually half-Chinese and half-Korean, came from a rich family who lost everything in the Korean War. She'd been pushed into marrying a G.I., who was also an Okie, and moved with him to the States. "Korean people want you to send back money all the time. My mom couldn't because she was trying to make a living. So they disowned her. That's how cold Asian people are." Her mother, divorced from the G.I., worked for dog groomers in Marysville, an Okie couple who virtually adopted her and came to be Heather's informal grandparents. "I had an Okie grandpa and grandma," she said. "I grew up in that Okie culture." Meanwhile, Heather's mom groomed poodles and later worked in a Yuba City food-canning factory.

"My mom and I didn't have the best relationship when I was growing up. I would say it was borderline abusive because she beat the crap out of me all the time. She broke brushes on my head. I had no sense of identity—of who I was—it was always what she wanted. I used to stay up late at night figuring out ways to get the hell out of there. Once my mom and I got into it but I defended myself, and she called the cops on me. I hated my circumstances. That was the relationship I wanted to get out of. So I did."

She ran away twice but didn't get much farther than a nearby friend's house before her mother came to get her. At fourteen she escaped to Sacramento, where her friend Lisa, who was half-Mexican and half-Caucasian, lived with her mother, a drug addict. "My parents put out a milk carton thing, and they found me." Her mother tried taking her to counseling, but the counselor basically said, "If I had a mom like you, I'd be way worse than your daughter is."

"I'd never really seen my mom cry," Heather said, "but that day driving home she broke down in the middle of the street and told me, 'You're a bitch.'"

Her dad had three children by his first wife, all much older than Heather and involved in drugs. "I wasn't close to any of them and don't consider them my brothers or sisters." Her father's son had groped her when she was younger, feeling her up, but she didn't tell anyone.

She'd met a boy in Sacramento when she'd run away. "This boy and I started to talk to each other." Her parents allowed her to continue traveling back and forth to see the boy named Jimmy, who was Asian and four years older, until her mother decided Heather must either marry him or never see him again. "She felt if I did get married I would be safe," Heather said, "and for her being safe was more important than taking a chance I'd run away again. As an adult I look back and say she just didn't want to deal with the issue, or the problem, because after our first counseling session she never returned me to counseling."

Heather was fifteen when her mother drove her and Jimmy to Reno to get married. They moved in with his parents in the community of Antelope, north of Sacramento, where thousands of other Mien families had migrated into the Great Valley after the Vietnam War. "Because this guy was Asian I saw an identity I didn't have. I didn't see many

Asians when I was growing up, In Yuba City I grew up with more Anglo-Americans and with Hispanics. In Marysville, it was strictly Caucasian; all my family was Caucasian and all my neighbors were Caucasian." She remembered a vivid moment after being with a blonde girl in school and asking her mother, "How come I don't have blonde hair? What's wrong with me?" and "my mom said, " 'Oh, you're the prettiest girl out there, blah, blah, blah, it's okay, we're different.'"

Heather said, "I really didn't have any issues at school. I fit in quickly. I remember little boys making fun of me for slanted eyes and a flat nose, the whole Asian thing, but that happens even now. My children share stories. I didn't have any real problems. I blended in quickly and made friends quickly."

Heather had stopped speaking Korean at seven when her mother told her, "I don't ever want to hear you speaking Korean again." Her mother wanted her to be fluent in English without an accent. When Heather was twelve her mom tried to reintroduce her to the language and culture in Korean school, but it didn't take. "I had no interest," Heather said.

After she married, Asians surrounded her, but unlike the people she'd known in Korea, these were "poor Asians, one hundred and fifty units of nothing but Mien people. Their culture is very primitive." Her husband's parents were on welfare. "That's what they did. They had nine children and were making tons of money off welfare. Down the road they ended up owning a strawberry field, so they got into farming, but when I was with them they were on welfare."

Pregnant at sixteen, Heather had a baby just before turning seventeen. She and Jimmy moved into their own apartment. "My mom helped me furnish it. It was really a nice apartment. My mom also helped me buy my first car." Heather went to an urban league high school with a day care center for her daughter. An older African American woman there was a published poet. "She was very articulate and inspired me, just hearing her visions and her speaking about going to college and setting goals for yourself."

Jimmy worked for a store delivering furniture as well as at other minimum-wage jobs. "I'm married to this guy," Heather said, "and he's abusive, he's drunk—he drinks all the time. I dropped out of school again. It wasn't fun. He hit me a couple of times. He didn't like beat me all the time, not to that extent, but we'd get into a conversation and he'd hit me or push me. No one asks for it, right? But I fight back. I don't hold my tongue."

While trying to leave him two or three times, she'd grown closer to her mother in Yuba City. "I felt I could open up to her so I moved back home." She worked full-time during the day on an assembly line, testing Hewlett-Packard printers. She'd finished high school, and at night she went to community college. Her relationship with her mother soured again.

"When my mom is mad at me she refuses to talk." Her mother's silence became constant. "So if she didn't want to talk to me, I didn't give a hoot. I didn't want to continue living there. I knew internally I had to figure out a way to be on my own, but I didn't know how, so instead I leaned on another boy, a Caucasian guy at work. He was in love with me, he was too in love with me, I needed space." No relationship developed. "We didn't do anything. He might've kissed me or something."

She then met another fellow worker. "This other guy was a Hmong, another Asian guy." Like the Mien, thousands of Hmong had moved into the Great Valley after the Vietnam War, the latest Asian immigration that began during the Gold Rush with the Chinese, who in the 1880s formed half the valley's farmworkers until the Chinese Exclusion Act, followed by the arrival of Japanese in the 1890s, who worked in the fields when agriculture shifted from wheat to orchards, vineyards, and vegetables. Suspension of Japanese immigration brought Sikhs from India in the 1900s, former Punjabi farmers who irrigated my grandfather's ranch because supposedly only a Sikh can make water run uphill. In the 1910s, Mexican immigrants flooded into the valley during Mexico's Revolution, increasing in the 1920s. Seasonal Filipino workers spread through the fields by the end of the decade. American-born white ranch workers formed the largest group of farm laborers at that time and increased with the Okie migration in the 1930s, joined by African Americans from the South, leading to the "repatriation" of some 150,000 Mexicans to their homeland. Mexicans were brought back as braceros in the 1940s. To fill the shortage from men at war, Madera ranchers even paid 250 German prisoners of war in a camp near Chowchilla to pick cotton. In the mid-1960s, the Bracero Program ended, farm mechanization increased, Filipinos initiated the table-grape strike, and the Vietnam War cranked up, leading to refugees emigrating from Southeast Asia into the valley.

—m—

Heather's new boyfriend was from Fresno, where more than thirty thousand Hmong live in the city. In surrounding San Joaquin Valley fields, many Hmong, like earlier Asian immigrants and recent Mien, moved into farming, renting small plots to grow specialty crops like strawberries and cherry tomatoes, while continuing to make the valley the most multiracial and multiethnic rural area in the U.S.

Rather than speaking in general about the hostility and difficulties many Hmong had encountered as new immigrants, Heather spoke personally about her own negative feelings toward her new boyfriend. "I didn't like him," Heather said. "He irritated me. I don't know how we ended up together, but I knew he kind of liked me. He courted me. I needed an escape. I needed a way out. So in a sense I was using him, huh? You put two and two together now. He helped me move out.

"Long story short," Heather said: she married him. His parents still lived in Fresno and they moved into their house so she could attend Fresno State College. "I had the strongest desire to go to school. I loved school, especially my psychology and business courses."

She didn't really love her husband but she learned to love him in a certain way. "Emotionally there was no connection," she said. At one point she was ready to leave and had all her stuff packed. "And then I was watching Oprah Winfrey and there was an episode about women like me, always bickering. I bickered at him all the time. Then I realized *I* needed to change. So I stayed with him. I finished college and we bought our first house. Everything was going fine."

Heather's first job after college was as assistant manager at Fastenal, an industrial supply company. Six months later the company opened a store with her as its branch manager in Hanford. Her husband was in construction, and they had plenty of money, making even more when they sold their old house and bought a new one, a twenty-six-hundred-square-foot home with a swimming pool. Just as an older African American woman at Sacramento Urban League High School had inspired her to go to college, a Hispanic woman, a twelve-years-older friend from Fresno State, helped her think about her marriage.

"She helped me open up a lot of things emotionally. Do I really love this person? I used to be fine with our relationship. I didn't complain about him. We tried going to a counselor and when he asked what was wrong, I said, 'I don't know what's wrong. I don't know why I'm here. I'm just not in love.'"

As far as their sexual relationship went, Heather said, "When we did have sex it was good sex because he always wanted to. But for me I was tired and didn't want to, so we negotiated. I'd say I'm busy, duh, duh, duh, and he'd say let's make it two or three times a week. Okay, that's fine. So I kept my end of the bargain."

They had two children together, a boy and a girl, but after seven years, they separated. She was twenty-six. "I'm with Jake now," Heather said. "He's a Caucasian guy, an Okie, he's twelve years older." She'd gotten together with him a year after her previous marriage had dissolved when she was twenty-seven. "He and I had a baby." She was then twenty-nine with four children. "Four kids with three different guys," she said. About the possibility of more children, she said, "No more. I'm done. I've got great kids, though." Her voice grew warm and enthusiastic. "They're good kids. I must've done something right, huh?"

On her older daughter's recent birthday, Heather posted a note on Facebook, "WOW!! Can I say WOW again! You're 18 years old. From the moment you were born, I knew what love was really about. I loved you more than anything. The bond I felt was unbreakable…I will be here for you always and forever…"

The next month on Heather's birthday her daughter posted: "Happy birthday to the number one person in my life. I am truly blessed to have you as my mother. You've taught me so many things and have always stuck by my side through everything. I can only hope to be as great of a mom as you've been to me. Love you Momma."

When she was thirty, Heather moved with her family to Tulare to be closer to Jake's job as the maintenance and repair supervisor for Ruiz Foods. As an account manager for Grainger Industrial Supply, she could work from home, if she needed to. When I met her, she was returning from a Grainger company meeting in Denver. As she neared the end of her life story on the flight, she told me she was ready to make a move in her work.

Her job put her on the road a lot up and down the valley, and she was looking for an opportunity to be an entrepreneur. That was her goal.

As the commuter jet began its descent toward the Fresno-Yosemite Airport, I asked about writing down the details of her story. "You can write about me all you want," she said. It wasn't even necessary to change her name. I said I probably would change some of the names. She said she would come to my reading at Fresno State and afterward as well as at a later time we could talk, if I needed to ask her any questions, which is what we did to fill in the details of the story she'd sketched during the flight.

When we later met at The Cheesecake Factory in Fresno for lunch, along noisy Shaw Avenue, a street half the width of those she recalled in Korea, her biographical account was almost uncannily word for word the same as she'd narrated on the airplane.

It was two years later, she was thirty-four, and she'd left Grainger to start an industrial cleaning company with Jake. She now had up to ten people working for her on new construction sites and industrial buildings in the valley. "Because of my jobs," she said, "I run into a lot of old-school types of guys. This is a very good ol' boy network here in the Central Valley. I understand these guys. I grew up with them."

As far as her being treated prejudicially in her work, she said, "Never. Sometimes guys are taken back visually, perhaps, by looking at me and seeing only slant eyes and a flat nose, but once a conversation has been struck I'm able to express myself and sometimes, if I need to, I explain myself, and they see where I'm coming from. I'm a woman who speaks my mind, so if I want something I'm very explicit about it."

She recalled how a man at her previous company couldn't understand how she was the account manager when he had twenty more years of experience. "How did you work that deal?" he asked. Heather told him, "I negotiated." She added to me, "I'm not afraid to ask for things I think I deserve. Externally I'm Asian, but internally I'm Caucasian. My brain thinks more like a Caucasian." She recalls when she was at a social gathering with her ex-husband's friends and relatives, a Hmong woman asked her what she was doing there. "You're so different from us," the woman said. "I knew I was very different," Heather said. She was a Californian, a Central Valley girl.

"I'm not prejudiced, but we're all judgmental. I don't have many Asian friends. They have to be very Americanized for me. I like American culture."

She said she'd considered moving back into corporate America to work for Nalco, an Ecolab subsidiary that offers industries and institutions products to reduce energy and enhance air quality, but she'd changed her mind and now wants to build her company. While Jake is comfortable managing a crew, she prefers one-on-one sales situations with managers and owners. She works well in this way because she understands valley culture and fits into it.

"It's because of the way I was raised," she said. "My dad was really Okie. His family migrated from Oklahoma and he grew up in Waterford-Modesto." His brother—Heather's uncle— "was a college grad and his daughter had a child with an African American guy and that gentleman was never allowed into my uncle's house. That kind of gives you an idea of what I was brought up with. That's the valley." She repeated what she'd told me on the plane trip: Her mother had been abusive but not her dad. Her dad had two older daughters and a son by his first marriage. "I was sexually abused by his son," she told me again.

As on the plane, she gave an involuntary shudder and expelled her breath in a monosyllabic utterance of disgust, sounding something like "Ugh." She was disinclined to say much more about it. There hadn't been intercourse, but she'd been pawed, fondled. "I never told my parents. They'd asked, because his daughter had told my dad something." But Heather didn't speak about it.

She reflected on the source of her stoicism. "All my life I've been through so many changes, I had to learn to overcome so many adversities—look at all the things from a young age—so perhaps when things happen to me today I'm not as affected as some might be." She was that way as a child in Korea, intensified by the Okie culture she grew up in.

"I do CASA," she added in clarification, "as an advocate for foster children, and here's what I learned through that experience." After six weeks of training as a CASA volunteer—a Court-Appointed Special Advocate—Heather attended a meeting with other volunteers and foster children and young adults ranging from five to twenty-five, who talked about their experience in the foster system and what it meant to them.

"It was pretty amazing," Heather said. "The children could speak their feelings. I could never understand my feelings the way they understood their feelings. I went, 'Huh? How could they know that?' Because they could say something like, 'I was that way because I didn't want anyone close to me,' or 'I was this way because duh, duh, duh, duh….' I could never say that. I can look back now after watching them and recall things and put a clearer picture on them, but I never had feelings like that. I just knew to be resilient."

A Valley Indian's Search for Roots

Irene Waltz felt rootless when she was a little girl growing up as a California Indian in the San Joaquin Valley. "I felt alone," she told me. "There were no other natives in Madera besides my family. If there were, I didn't know them." Her four brothers and sisters assimilated better than she did. "They made a lot of friends. My younger sister connected with Hispanic people. I wasn't Hispanic. I didn't look white even though my father was. I didn't have best friends. I had no friends. I didn't go hang out at someone's house. I was the tan kid who didn't fit in. It was really a weird time."

Irene's childhood reflected the obliteration of Indian life in the San Joaquin Valley, leaving the region an ethnographic blank spot as extreme as any in California history.

"People knew I was Indian," Irene said, "but it wasn't talked about. I never felt discriminated against or made fun of." In elementary and middle schools named after George Washington and Thomas Jefferson, as well as at Madera High School, during discussions of American history, she said, "I felt indifferent to what was being taught about how Indians murdered and butchered everybody."

Only at home did she feel linked to her Indian heritage through her grandfather's brother and sister, who lived with her family. As children, her great-aunt and great-uncle had been sent away from their mountain home to the Sherman Indian School in Riverside, the state's first off-reservation boarding school for assimilating Native Americans into mainstream society. There they mixed with Indian children from other tribes, all forbidden to speak their native languages while being taught useful trade and agricultural skills. Her great-uncle later served in the Navy during the Second World War—he was at Pearl Harbor when it was bombed—and her aunt worked first as a home caretaker and then in Madera's juvenile detention center.

"They both came to live with us," Irene said. "I'm sure being uprooted from their homeland and sent to Indian school was a breaking point for them. They'd tried to fit in but never did. They both chose not to have children because their way of life was done, their culture was done. I have no cousins, I have no uncles, I have no aunts. My grandfather was the only one to have a child—my mother."

Irene's mother was born in the mountains, where her father was a logger and lived on a 600-acre Indian land allotment at Bailey Flats along the Chowchilla River. "My mother learned some of the language and culture," Irene said, "but it was pretty much gone. Her mother died when she was a couple of months old." Irene's father was of German American heritage and in the U.S. Air Force, first in Egypt and then at the Madera Air Force Station, before working as a truck driver for the Noble Meat Company. "He was on the road and wasn't home much," Irene said, "but he would drive my mother and me into the mountains to visit my grandfather. My mother would always tell me, 'You have to be careful because these natives in the mountains will try to kill you. You have medicine in your family,'" which Irene came to understand as shamans with special spiritual powers. She later found documents with testimony from other natives characterizing some members of her family as "medicine men," others as "witches." "I grew up with a sense of something different about me."

Isolated at school and wary in the mountains, she felt most centered with her great-aunt, who helped raise her. "I would go into her bedroom at night, and she would talk to me about cultural things, spiritual things, how life had changed, but it didn't readily come out. She had a hard time talking about those things. As the years went by, she grew more into herself."

Irene happened to wander into the kitchen when her great-aunt and great-uncle were washing dishes and speaking Chukchansi. They told her to go out. "That's how they were taught," Irene said. "They weren't supposed to be speaking their language." Her great-uncle was fluent in Chukchansi, Miwok, French, Spanish, and English. "I don't know where he learned them," Irene said. "I couldn't have conversations about a lot of stuff. They were very private people. They weren't forthcoming." In intangible ways she felt rooted to them, but it was only later that she learned more about her heritage.

At Fresno State College, during the initial decade of the American Indian Movement, Irene met other Native Americans, one from out of state and several California Monos, like Gaylen Lee, who went on to write a memoir about his North Fork Mono family. "It was the first time I had a sense of belonging," she said. She was reading a book for a class by a University of California anthropologist when she saw an acknowledgment to Bessie Jacobs. *Holy crap*, she thought, *that's my great-aunt. That's the guy who came to my house.* When Irene was ten years old, a man from Berkeley had shown up to talk to her great-aunt about native life and lore, but Irene had no idea who he was. Her great-aunt told him stories and introduced him to people in the mountains, who also helped him document information about Chukchansi history, ceremonies, and language.

The Chukchansi were one of some fifty Yokutsan-speaking groups of different dialects who once lived in the San Joaquin Valley and the Sierra foothills. When talking historically about California Indians, the notion of "tribe" is less useful to our understanding than a division into "languages." Linguists have classified all the diverse languages of Europe into just three families—Indo-European, Finno-Ugric, and Basque—while in America, north of the Rio Grande, over fifty language families flourished, with more than three hundred mutually unintelligible languages and many more dialects. California was the most linguistically diverse and densely populated area in the country, organized into villages of varying languages and dialects. The villages were called *rancherías* in Spanish times, a tradition continued today in the naming of many federally recognized California tribes and reservations.

Irene is a member of the Picayune Rancheria of Chukchansi Indians, but she's a descendant from native speakers of Chukchansi, Miwok, Tallenchi, Chowchilla, Casson, and a mixed Yosemite band, making her a veritable United Nations of central California native heritages, several now extinct.

"The Cassons are gone," Irene said. "The Tallenchis are gone, their culture gone. You'll see natives in other states that maintained more of their culture. Ours was decimated. There was nothing left. It's very different with the Hopi because they have strong traditions that still go on. And with the Navajo, there are thousands of them. With our tribe it's difficult to bring back the culture. There are some who know a few basic things, about acorns and so forth, but the elders don't want to talk about it. Those times are over. You see Hollywood movies and they don't show what happened to the natives in Yosemite or what went on here in the valley."

Irene and I were talking in her Madera suburban home at

the end of September 2016. In that same month 210 years earlier, September 1806, Gabriel Moraga rode into the valley to be
greeted and fed by hundreds of Indians in twenty-five rancherías.
The Basque explorer was under orders to look for places to es-
tablish a chain of valley missions parallel to those on the coast,
a project that never materialized.

Many valley Indians were later abducted and taken to the
coastal missions. Franciscan missionaries kept careful records, so we know that the coastal missions, founded by the
now canonized St. Junípero Serra, accounted for the baptism
of 81,586 Indians and the burial of some 62,600, dead mostly
from malnutrition, overwork, and disease. My own candidate
for sainthood—or at least beatification—is Padre Antonio de la
Concepción Horra of Mission San Miguel, who wrote a com-
plaint to the viceroy of New Spain about the California missions.
"The ultimate treatment shown to the Indians is the most cruel
I have ever read in history," he wrote. "For the slightest things
they receive heavy floggings, are shackled and put in stocks, and
treated with so much cruelty that they are kept whole days without a drink of water." Father Antonio was then himself shackled, declared insane, placed under armed guard, and shipped
out of California.

In 1833, the same year that Mexico shut down the missions
and released Indians, malaria swept through the San Joaquin
Valley's mosquito-infested wetlands and killed between twenty
thousand and fifty thousand Indians. Kit Carson saw entire
rancherías replaced with mass graves and cremation pyres.
Skulls and dead bodies lay under trees. Along with earlier ep-
idemics of smallpox, measles, and other European diseases,
malaria left much of the valley depopulated. I recall as a kid a
local amateur historian named Guy Crow, who came out to our
ranch to talk with me about the Indians who once lived along

Cottonwood Creek, where our tractors had disked up several stone mortars for grinding acorns and seeds.

I told Irene that I'd finished reading a recent book by Benjamin Madley, *An American Genocide: The United States and the California Indian Catastrophe, 1846–1873*, describing horrific events during the first years of U.S. occupation. When the United States seized California from Mexico in 1846, an estimated 160,000 Indians had already died during Spanish, Mexican, and Russian colonialism. Madley reports that massacres under Mexican rule were relatively unusual, although California landowner Captain Salvador Vallejo led attacks against two Indian rancherías and "shot or cut down" 320 men, women, and children.

Those Indians who avoided bullets, disease, or starvation became an integral part of California colonial life, especially as laborers on large Mexican ranchos. Salvador Vallejo himself, the owner of a thirty-thousand-acre Napa Valley rancho, summarized dependence on Indian labor: "They tilled our soil, pastured our cattle, sheared our sheep, cut our lumber, built our houses, paddled our boats, made tiles for our houses, ground our grain, killed our cattle, and dressed their hides for market plus made our unburnt bricks; while indian women made excellent servants, took good care of our children, made every one of our meals." Indian women, as Madley reports, also became wives, consorts, rape victims, and sexual slaves.

In 1846, after John C. Frémont raised the Stars and Stripes above Sutter's Fort, where he imprisoned Captain Salvador Vallejo and his brother General Mariano Vallejo, he left a guard of fifty Indian soldiers. Hundreds of uniformed California Indians fought for the U.S. Army in the campaign against Mexico. After gold was discovered near Sutter's Mill, tens of thousands of miners rushed into the mountains and the real slaughter of California Indians began.

"My great-grandfather was run out of Yosemite by the Mariposa Battalion when he was eight years old," Irene said.

That was in 1851, when the *Sacramento Transcript* warned, "Savages...infest a great part of the richest mines....Thus we are cut off perhaps from thousands of square miles of the richest mines." That year California's governor in his annual message to the legislature announced, "a war of extermination will continue to be waged between the races until the Indian race shall become extinct." Federal treaty-makers and other opponents of native annihilation faced a brutal choice as printed in the San Francisco *Daily Alta California*: "KILL, MURDER, EXTERMINATE, OR DOMESTICATE AND IMPROVE THEM." The second option meant treaties and reservations.

During the Gold Rush, James Savage was a bearded, blue-eyed mountain man and Indian trader with shoulder-length blond hair who fought Indians and made treaties with them. He set up trading posts near Yosemite, on Mariposa Creek, and on the Fresno River in what is now Madera County. He wore a coarse red shirt, often without trousers, spoke Chowchilla, Miwok, and Chukchansi, and married five Indian women. He set fire to oil floating in a bowl of water to impress Indians with his magical power, if he wished, to burn up all the rivers. As many as five hundred Indians panned gold for him, and he traded goods from San Francisco. An ounce of gold could buy a pound of bacon or five pounds of flour. A mountain Chowchilla leader told a federal Indian agent (in translation), "My people did not permit any stranger to pass our country, or stop in it, except Mr. Savage—he made us many presents. If you will make us presents, too, you may remain in our country a while."

Vigilante attacks and indiscriminate killing of Indians in mining districts generated what was called at the time an "Indian panic." If a starving Indian stole a cow, vigilantes massacred and torched an entire ranchería. To defend themselves, Indians banded together. After three white men were killed at Savage's trading post near Coarsegold, vigilantes attacked an Oakhurst encampment of some four hundred Chowchillas, Chukchansis, and Kechayis, killing forty to sixty and burning the ranchería. Typical of the time, only two white vigilantes were killed and four wounded.

California's governor ordered a state militia called the Mariposa Battalion, commanded by the troop-elected Major James D. Savage, to relocate Indians by treaty or by force to reservations in the San Joaquin Valley. An editorial in the *Daily Alta California* advised, "We must now kill these mountain thieves and murderers into submission, or annihilate them." In contrast, *The Stockton Times* urged treaties because the "Indians have been shamefully maltreated and imposed upon."

Major Savage and federal commissioners signed a treaty with sixteen bands. The battalion pursued those Indians who fled into a spectacular valley that Savage's men voted to name Yosemite, a misnomer for the native inhabitants, a mixed polyglot band of self-described Ahwahneechees, including Irene's great-grandfather. After capture, the group's leader, Tenaya, was told that the battalion had named a Yosemite lake in his honor. He replied, "It already has a name."

Irene's great-grandfather in the Yosemite band was later known as John Jacobs. "I don't know who his father was," Irene said. "I just knew they were run out. I have a newspaper article about when his mother passed away"—she was a full-blooded Chukchansi—"it was the last time a traditional Indian ceremonial funeral dance took place in Bailey Flats." On the other side of her family, her great-grandfather was an Indian named Savage Lewis because his grandfather, who was white, was James Savage's friend and adjutant in the Mariposa Battalion.

"So you have ancestors on both sides," I said.

"Yes," Irene said. That's not uncommon. Irene discovered that one of her ancestors, a Tallenchi shaman named Choketi, signed the Camp Barbour Treaty of Peace and Friendship on the San Joaquin River that sent her Chowchilla ancestors to the reservation ten miles northeast of Madera. Savage Lewis's white grandfather and Irene's great-great-great-grandfather ran the reservation. "Until it fizzled," Irene said. It lasted only six years because none of the eighteen treaties signed in 1851 was ratified. Many Californians shared the objection voiced in *The Los Angeles Star* against placing "upon our most fertile soil the most degraded race of aborigines upon the North American continent." The U.S. Senate not only repudiated all eighteen treaties but also locked them under an injunction of secrecy lasting more than fifty years.

To convey the genocidal atrocities perpetrated by California vigilantes, federally funded state militia, and the U.S. Army, Madley cranks up his metaphors. What he calls a "well-oiled killing machine," created an "inferno of violence" and a "firestorm of mass murder." Accounts of the time spoke of a "saturnalia of blood" and a "war of extermination." In two hundred pages of appendixes, Madley documents that California Indians killed some 1,377 non-Indians between 1846 and 1873, while "at least 9,492 to 16,094 California Indians, and probably many more" died by shootings, stabbings, hangings, beheadings, and beatings—the most lethal and sustained killing of Indians anywhere in the United States or its colonial antecedents. In the twenty years between 1846 and 1866, disease, famine, massacre, and murder reduced the largest number of Indians in the country from an estimated 150,000 to 33,860, as counted by the California superintendent of Indian affairs.

In 1906, the special agent for California Indians reported to Congress "an Indian population in California of a little more than

16,500." The accompanying census for nonreservation Indians in Madera County listed Irene's great-grandfathers, "John Jacobs & wife 2 children 1 ward in Bailey Flat," and "James Savage Lewis & wife 7 children owning land in Spring Valley District."

Today, according to the last 2010 census, 352,427 Californians identify themselves as Native American, the most of any state. An estimated 150,000 are of California Indian ancestry. California also has over a hundred federally recognized rancherias and tribes, again the most of any state.

After graduating from college with a degree in finance, Irene served twice as treasurer and twice on the tribal council of the Picayune Rancheria of Chukchansi Indians. She married right after college and went to work in Madera for Canandaigua Winery, where she worked with Jim Unti and Sal Arriola. Although they both left the winery after it became Constellation, Irene remains their friend and continues after thirty-eight years as the winery's manager of grape grower contracts. "You better tell Sal to watch out," she told me after she learned that I would soon be seeing him. "Trump is going to want to send him back to Mexico."

Irene's first husband died in a car accident, and she divorced her second. She has a son and two daughters. Even though the material culture of her ancestors is gone, she feels she internalized an Indian sense of herself. "When I was raised with my great-aunt—maybe not intentionally or knowingly—I absorbed the spiritualness of the culture. I think a lot of natives do that now."

She remembers as a child having premonitory dreams she associated with her mother's account of shamanism in her family. Her mother would ask if the dreams were in black and white, or in color, as well as other details, to determine if they were true. If true, her grandfathers' spirits were talking to her through dreams, telling her something was going to happen, and it would.

"I call them dreams," Irene said, "but they were more like semi-awake visions where I actually experienced something. I had one about my father dying. I dreamed he was gone." Her family came into her bedroom to wake her and tell her that her father had just died. He was forty-two.

She also had a recurring dream for many years where she lay in bed, partly awake, unable to breathe, her body broken but without pain, surrounded by her family. "I wasn't asleep. I was living it. It was a vision."

Two weeks after having the dream again, when she was forty-nine, Irene was on her Harley-Davidson in the mountains near Bass Lake with thirty other motorcyclists on a fundraising ride for the Valley Children's Hospital. A thirteen-ton Forest Service dump truck came too fast around the curve ahead of her and went into a side skid. "When that was happening, I locked my brakes and prayed to my grandfathers. That's what I do when I need help. It's just what I believe." The out-of-control truck crashed into her.

"I was on life support for three weeks. I had twenty-one major fractures. I broke my jaw, my nose, both wrists, my eye ruptured out, I had a punctured left lung, eight broken ribs, a fractured sacrum, my pelvis broke in half, every bone in my left foot was crushed except my big toe. She paused and said, "I broke a lot of stuff." She punctuated her understatement with a quick pullulating laugh, as she often did whenever we talked. I was reminded of the kind of joyful, cascading laughter I heard among the Chamula, Zinacanteco, and Lacandón Indians I spent much time with in Chiapas, a laughter I interpreted, whether rightly or wrongly, as a life-enhancing and energy-renewing spit in the face of fate for its vicissitudes.

With her bold brown eyes, blacker than black hair, and a strong, lived-in brown face, it was hard for me to see a shy, isolated child in this dynamic fifty-nine-year-old woman. She spoke without self-pity. Her upbeat mood seemingly altered only once as a tear streaked down her right cheek. She wiped it away and explained, "Don't mind this. My eye waters because I have a prosthetic eye."

In the hospital, on life support, "I was asleep for a week," she said, "but I lived that very experience as I'd dreamed it. I was in that bed and my family was there. I felt at that moment what I had felt all those years before. It's the weirdest thing. I knew I was not going to die. I had no fear. Now that dream is gone. I've never dreamed it again."

On the sixth day in the hospital she was in trouble. "I was very hurt," she said. "I had fluid developing in my lungs." Though semiconscious she heard a tapping sound in her brain and was later told a bird strangely appeared and started pecking on the third-floor window of her room. "To me it was somebody telling me to get up and go out of there. That's how I internalized it." The pecking went on for a couple of days, then the bird vanished. "It was like a kick in the butt. *I got to get going,* I thought. I knew I was not alone." Four months later she returned to work. Doctors told her she should be dead. She got back on a motorcycle, first with a friend and then alone. Last year she ran eight miles. "My grandfathers got me through it," she said.

Every winter since the accident and after the grape harvest, Irene has had surgeries, more than thirty of them in the past ten years. Bones are rebroken and reset. Her latest eye surgery was four months ago in Beverly Hills. She also recently had an inter-proxil bone transplant. "This bone was completely gone," she said, rubbing the skin between her mouth and nose. "They took a piece of bone from my hip and put it here in my upper lip. Now it's fine."

Meditation practices coalesced with her spiritual tribal heritage to help her through excruciating pain during rehabilitation. She would mentally say, *Come to me*, as a way of staying ahead of pain and separating herself from it, at least briefly. "People think I'm crazy, but it works for me. I'm definitely not the same person as I was before the accident," she says. "I've learned to embrace difficulty for what's important."

Tribal conflicts over casinos are a difficulty she's embraced, though, as she says, "They're not a lot of fun. Native Americans have been given an opportunity for economic growth to invest finances for the benefit of the tribe, for education, elder care, housing, and so on. But you get too many people involved who are greedy and it makes for bad medicine all around. It's just a shame."

When Irene was tribal treasurer, she helped raise funds to build the Chukchansi Gold Resort and Casino. "I personally got on a jet with three others and went from corporate boardroom to boardroom and raised $115 million in one week." For years rival families had battled over tribal funds with some gaining control of the council and disenrolling other members, a seesawing power struggle that accelerated after the casino was built in 2003. Eleven years later Irene got a call that took her up to the casino. A tribal faction of fifteen men with guns invaded the casino to seize financial records of rival Indians in control. The feds shut down the casino for fourteen months.

"It's all about greed and money," Irene said. "The way our constitution is written too many people in a family can get control and kick out anybody they want. They can interpret the laws as they see fit and there's nothing you can do about it. It's horrible. It's just devastating."

Disenrollment as a way of stripping Indians of tribal affiliation and benefits, along with barring other Indians from new membership, also occurred among Chukchansi at the nearby Table Mountain Rancheria, where a couple of years ago I encountered picketing Indians at its casino. The U.S. courts don't interfere in the sovereign right of a tribe to determine its membership.

Now the two Chukchansi rancherias have joined in a lawsuit to stop the North Fork Rancheria of Mono Indians from building an off-reservation casino in the valley just outside Madera. "I tell my tribe it's going to happen," Irene said. "Embrace it. Open the door."

She's distressed about so much fighting over casinos rather than redressing problems that could help tribal people in need. She's certified in Indian law, and through the Indian Self-Determination and Education Assistance Act she received certification in tribal funding from the Bureau of Indian Affairs. "I've taken a plethora of courses to help my tribe," she said. "I've been fortunate because I have a wonderful job and don't need money. It doesn't influence my thinking in what I say at meetings. Others are afraid. If you speak out, your family is targeted, and you'll be kicked out. It cripples the tribe."

In 2018, the tribal council appointed Irene as chair of its constitutional reform committee. "We have two years to work out a reform the tribe can vote on," she said. "We can't fail."

As we talked in her Madera home, two fat binders sat on the table filled with documents of her family heritage. Two Chukchansi families formerly in control of the council tried to remove her from the tribe. "I went into my disenrollment meetings—I had more than one—and I had people yelling in my face." Because she didn't grow up in the mountains she was called a Flat-Lander. "They'd sit there and say we don't know who you are. What do you mean you don't know who I am? My great-grandma is your great-grandma's sister, and you're telling me you don't know who I am? Mandy Lane is named after my great-great-grandma." That was Mandy Joaquín, married to Savage Lewis. "Go into the cemetery," Irene would say. "My grandma's buried there. I got ancestral uncles, aunts, and cousins there, and you—some of you—you don't have family buried there. Who are you to tell me I don't belong? Maybe you don't belong." Irene started to laugh. "I'm not going away and they know it. They might try, but I got roots here."

Native American Okie

Louis Owens was a celebrated Native American novelist and critic when he was a writer in residence at Vassar College in Poughkeepsie, New York, where I was teaching. The day after his arrival he told me how strange he felt as a Westerner on this eastern campus, even stranger than when he was abroad with his wife as a Fulbright lecturer. "Polly and I have traveled all over Europe," he said, "but this place feels more foreign to me than any country I've been in."

A few days later, Louis, who was eyeing potential colleges for his daughter, commented on the enthusiastic way some Vassar students in an American culture seminar had lunged from their couches to examine a book of George Caleb Bingham paintings I'd placed on the table. "I like how they did that," he said. "I think this would be a great place for Elizabeth."

No one who saw him move through classes on that eastern campus would suspect the sense of displacement he'd given voice to. He seemed so comfortable, such a capable manager of the routines and responsibilities his post required—he'd learned to adjust quickly to that foreign world, to feel lost and at home at the same time, an uneasy condition he experienced on college campuses in both the East and the West.

In the West, his many deep friendships enabled people at his memorial service at the New Mexico Sandia Ranger Station to make these kinds of statements: "I was Louis's favorite student"—pause—"Oh, I know he made everyone feel that way," a sentiment echoed by a fly-fishing buddy of twenty years who announced, "I was Louis's favorite old man."

Louis also had a profound effect on those he met briefly and who knew him scarcely at all. In the East, he displayed his memorable power as a teacher in the attention he gave to individual students' stories and in the honesty he brought to classroom discussions.

When a student asked him about the prejudice he might have experienced as a child, Louis said in his thoughtful, deliberate way, "I really wasn't discriminated against for being Native American. You can look at my features and see why—not the way some of my relatives were. But I did know another kind of discrimination." He gazed at the student as though remembering something painful. "We were always the poorest family in every town we lived in, and that was a great embarrassment to me."

Louis knew the wound of shame that poverty in our culture can burn into a person's heart—a felt knowledge that formed the baseline of both his great compassion and his unrest. I don't think I'm speaking from hindsight here. I was as shocked as anybody when I heard of Louis's death, quickly thinking of a dozen friends and acquaintances who were more likely suicides than Louis, so talented, handsome, vital, and productive. Still, I'd often recalled as a revelatory moment that day in the American culture seminar when he spoke of his childhood poverty. It connected the various things he wrote about as a novelist and scholar. As Polly Owens later told me, "I don't think he was so much a Steinbeck or a Native American scholar as a scholar of poverty."

He experienced extreme poverty when he was a kid. Before he was seven, he'd twice moved with his family back and forth between California, where he was born, and Mississippi, where his father's parents were sharecroppers. He recalled eating chocolate cake on his fifth birthday in an A-frame canvas tent with a wooden floor in a San Joaquin Valley migrant camp when his father worked in the fields on the outskirts of Delano. During what he called his "wandering time in California," his family headed farther south into the valley and camped near the Shafter potato sheds before moving to a county housing project in Paso Robles. Back in Mississippi, when he was six, he lived in a rural tin-roof shack with two rooms and no electricity or running water. A barrel on the front porch collected rainwater. In the evening, his father disappeared into the darkness to hunt coons and poach alligators. Louis remembered dinners of stringy possum meat with hominy and cornbread. At seven, he moved again with his family and settled in the Salinas Valley, where his father worked as a ranch hand. Louis hunted and fished with his father and older brother. "That's how we survived," he said.

One of his best friends, Glen Martin, a fellow writer and environmentalist, recalled going to Louis's boyhood home along the Salinas River. "It was a shack of tar paper and cardboard, with linoleum laid right on the dirt, an abode he shared with his parents and eight siblings." Martin described how he joined Louis along the river bottom to shoot rabbits that Louis's mother immediately fried up in Crisco for the family dinner. "His childhood was as wretched, as poverty-stricken, as the Joads' in *The Grapes of Wrath*," Martin wrote. "It was, in short, no coincidence that he first made his name as a Steinbeck scholar."

Like the Joads, the Owens family would've been considered Okies in those years, and like so many earlier Dust Bowl refugees from Oklahoma, Texas, Arkansas, and Missouri, they were mixed-bloods. Louis's father was part Choctaw, and his mother, who was born in Oklahoma, was part Cherokee. She'd left what she called the "Nation" in Oklahoma with her mother and sister to join other "Defense

Okies" working in the California shipyards during the Second World War. She and Louis's father had third-grade educations.

Photos we've all seen from the 1930s with their emblematic images of broken-down trucks and jalopies on California roads, barefoot children, and dirt-floor tents remind us of the uneasy physical suffering and the emotional and psychological stigma Dust Bowl newcomers in the West endured as social outsiders. The worried Okie woman with her three children in Dorothea Lange's famous photo "MigrantMother" is Florence Thompson, reportedly a full-blooded Cherokee. The San Joaquin Valley singer, Merle Haggard, born in Bakersfield of parents who emigrated from near Muskogee, Oklahoma, wrote a series of Dust Bowl ballads, beginning with "Hungry Eyes."

> A canvas-covered cabin, in a crowded labor camp
> Stands out in this memory I revive....
> And us kids were just too young to realize
> That another class of people put us somewhere just below.
> One more reason for my mama's hungry eyes.

—◊—

By 1950, Okie migrants constituted thirteen percent of California's population and nearly a quarter of the San Joaquin Valley. In the next decade, the songs of valley-born Merle Haggard helped transform the word Okie from a generic term of derision and shame to a shout of pride, but Okie pride wasn't widespread when Louis was a kid. His experience was closer to that of the self-described Okie novelist Ken Kesey, author of *One Flew Over the Cuckoo's Nest* and *Sometimes a Great Notion*, who grew up as the son of parents from Texas and Arkansas and moved with them from Colorado to Oregon before he himself eventually reached California. Kesey, who was twelve when Louis was born, wrote in a poem:

Let me tell you what being an Oakie means:

Being an Oakie means being the first of your whole fam-
    ily to finish high school let alone go on to college…

Being an Oakie means getting rooted out of an area and
    having to hustle for a toehold in some new area…

Being an Oakie means running the risk of striving out
    from under a layer of heartless sonsofbitches only
    to discover you have become a redneck of bitterness
    worse than those you strove against…

—⚭—

As an Okie kid, Louis began working in the fields at nine years old, hoeing beans, and by the time he was thirteen and fourteen he'd spent several summers bent over weeding and thinning sugar beets with *el cortito,* the short-handled hoe. He and his brother had connections because their father was a ranch hand and farm laborer. "As a favor to our dad," Louis wrote, "the ranchers would hire us to build a fence or work cattle or inoculate turkeys and the farmers would hire us in the fields along with the braceros, knowing we'd work just as hard and just as long."

Louis spent part of a summer in a former San Joaquin Valley bracero camp with some high school buddies—"I at least knew what field labor was," he wrote; "my high school buddies did not." They joined "two or three hundred black guys from the meanest, hardest, nastiest inner cities in California" to pick to-matoes in the fields near Merced. The entire crew was composed of "black, white, and other," Louis said, and "being part Choctaw and Cherokee did not exempt me from whiteness."

Louis and his older brother were the only members of his family to finish high school, and Louis alone went to college, drifting to Cuesta Junior College, where with the encourage-ment of two English teachers he worked on the school paper and eventually became its editor. When he was accepted at the University of California at Santa Barbara he couldn't believe he'd received a scholarship and threw away the financial-aid form, thinking it was some sort of trick. He'd grown up with his family hiding from creditors, and his father's total income that year as a ranch hand and truck driver was three thousand dollars.

While his brother served three tours of duty in Vietnam, Louis dropped out of college three times. For seven years during and after college he worked as a seasonal wilderness ranger and fire-fighter on a hotshot crew. A photo shows him furiously at work with a two-man whipsaw on his way to winning first prize during the firefighting skills competition at the National Forest Olympics. He fought fires in Washington, Arizona, and California. He climbed granite walls as a sawyer with the Prescott Hotshots, purportedly the only technical rock-climbing fire crew in America at the time.

When he finished college and went to grad school, Louis wrote his dissertation on John Steinbeck, which became his first book. He advanced from graduate student to full professor in eight years, the shortest time in the history of the University of California. He taught at the University of California at Santa Cruz and at Davis as well as at California State University at Northridge and the University of New Mexico. He published critical studies, essays, memoirs, and fiction that established him as an award-winning Native American scholar and novelist. "I have lived," he wrote, "in a world incalculably different from everyone else in my family."

When I first met him at an academic conference, he was forty-one and hadn't yet published any novels. He came up after a reading I gave and pointed to the blurb emblazoned on a pa-perback edition of my first novel and said, "That's me." It was an excerpt from a review he'd written for the *Los Angeles Times*, but his name wasn't credited on the excerpt, though the pub-lisher had seen fit to feature his words in large type on the back of the book. His was the most insightful review I received about the Native American aspect of my novel. Louis was disgruntled about a grudging review someone at the conference had written for an eastern newspaper, in which the significance of the Indian experience in the novel was overlooked. Louis felt that mainstream culture only wanted stereotypes of Western experience, and after he later published one novel with a New York publisher he told me, "I'll never do that again," and he didn't. He thought New York publishers and Hollywood filmmakers maintained a nearly impregnable fortress against realistic portrayals of the West. He also felt that writers who came West with an eastern bias were generally more accepted in academia than those who'd grown up in the West. "Steinbeck," he later wrote, "was a Westerner, even worse, a Californian, and thus he remains second-rate in the halls of academe." Louis always conceived of himself as a California writer. After living in New Mexico off and on for more than fifteen years, he considered himself an expat-California writer.

Stereotypes of American Indian life and culture, he maintained, were also in demand in the dominant culture. As one of his fictional characters said, "White people want to know all the mystical secrets. All the Indian hocus-pocus." Not just white people but Indians themselves, as his books showed, could both fabricate and fall for the hocus-pocus and what Louis called "ethnostalgia." He punctured silly identity politics and posturing about authenticity by some Native American writers. In *Mixedblood Messages: Literature, Film, Family, Place*, he wrote, "I am not a real Indian because I'm not enrolled and did not grow up on a reservation," as some relatives had in his family's past. Other relatives had no birth certificates, let alone enrollment cards. He understood the complexities of his Native American heritage and learned "to inhabit a hybrid, unpapered Choctaw-Cherokee-Welsh-Irish-Cajun mixed space." He went on to described himself without a hyphen: "I conceive of myself today not as 'Indian,' but as mixedblood, a person of complex roots and histories," as just about all his fellow writers of Native American literature are to one degree or another.

Fame came to Louis in a rush. In the decade after I met him he published five novels and three collections of essays and memoirs for a career total of ten books. The awards and honors rolled in. He came to Vassar as its writer in residence and was looking forward to doing the same at Harvard. We'd stayed in occasional touch for fourteen years and in July of 2002 he planned to visit Holly and me in Colorado, bringing two rods to fish the Blanco River. He was an expert fly fisherman and tied his own flies. We were going to talk about a new novel he was working on. The draft he'd sent me opened with a fishing scene. First, though, he had to travel to Western Washington University to give a talk. "Let me know if Vassar wants to hire me," he wrote on the Fourth of July. His fifty-fourth birthday passed on July 18. Nine days later I received an email from his wife, Polly: "I am sorry to tell you that Louis died on Thursday. A memorial service will be held Monday at 10 at the Sandia Ranger Station in Tijeras."

Scheduled to fly out of Albuquerque, Louis had driven onto the third level of the airport garage around 5:00 a.m., found a parking spot, and with a 9mm semiautomatic Glock pistol shot himself in the chest. A passenger in the garage heard the shot and called the police. The driver's door of Louis's red Toyota pickup was found open and he was slumped onto the ground. In the truck was the manuscript of the talk he was to deliver and a note asking that his wife be called. He was taken to the University of New Mexico hospital where he died the next afternoon, thirty hours after shooting himself.

Holly and I jumped the dogs into the back of the pickup and headed down to Tijeras, New Mexico. "I've never seen a larger group of people so grief-stricken, many of whom didn't even know each other," said Jack Hicks, who'd come from Davis for his longtime friend, colleague, and former student's unexpected memorial. "When I heard of his death, I felt poleaxed," his life-long friend Glen Martin later wrote, expressing pretty much everyone's view. "His suicide is inexplicable."

No one knew why. Rumors flew. He'd been sick with pancreatitis and having tests. He'd been depressed. His marriage was troubled, all midlife problems, as Glen wrote, but "nothing that would seem to demand a bullet."

Logical speculation seldom unravels a suicide. All or none of these reasons might apply. Being loaded up on Vicodin and antidepressants, as he was, could've been enough to tip him. Often a suicide just wants the pain to stop, and Louis was in great pain, both physically and emotionally. "For anyone who knew him well," Glen said, "his real legacy is not his admirable body of work, but enduring pain."

Anger accompanied grief for those in mourning. "I'll always love him," Glen wrote, "and I'll never forgive him for what he did." Polly and Louis had been married for twenty-seven years. She and their two teenage daughters sat stoically on folding chairs in the bright New Mexico sunlight, facing a framed photo of a smiling Louis, as one after another of us spoke. "I'm certain it's a cliché but I felt as though I had been drugged," Polly wrote me later, "and so the event passed in a haze." Poised and gracious during our conversation at the memorial reception, she calmly said, "Louis was very impulsive," then all at once her eyes grew wet, and anger gave bite to her voice, as she pointed across the room to her seventeen- and nineteen-year-old daughters, and said, "But how could he do that to them?"

A dozen years later, I was talking with another of Louis's closest friends, the writer and scholar Gerald Vizenor, an enrolled Ojibwe and son of an Anishinaabe father and a Swedish American mother. At the memorial service, grief-stricken, he didn't speak, but he'd told a reporter, "Louis was a man with a worried heart, but it was that kind of worry that gave him such generous character." Now, more than a decade later, Gerald told me he'd learned to be angry. He was very angry at Louis and could say, "Fuck you, you fucker." Otherwise, he said, "You feel guilt. But you can't feel guilt."

Gerald turned his penetrating blue eyes on me and spoke forcibly, "He didn't kill himself because he was mixed-blood. He might have done it out of vanity. He was narcissistic. He shot himself in the side, not the head or under the jaw."

We talked about the complications of his life, the affairs. "There were lots of women," Gerald said. "He'd go off with someone but couldn't leave Polly."

At Tijeras, a woman who'd worked in the forest service asked Gerald if he was going to write about Louis. When Gerald said no, she replied, "Good. Then I can. He was my first lover."

I spoke with that same woman, who said her initial response to Louis's suicide had been to be "angry as hell that he bottled so much in and wouldn't let his friends help him. He told me he didn't think he'd live a long life." She went on to say that Louis planned to leave his marriage after both daughters were in college. She seemed shaken by his other relationships she was discovering.

A rumor was that Louis had just learned of a colleague about to publish a novel based on their affair in which she mentioned Louis's daughters by name, shocking news of great shame to him, I was told. The book appeared eleven months later without the names.

A mystery of friendship to me is how maybe a half-dozen times or so in my experience the instant connection I've felt with someone on a first meeting evolved into a lifelong friendship.

That happened for me with Louis, though he aborted the lifelong part. To this day I feel waves of sadness on occasions of missing him that surprise me with their intensity, followed by the rage others talked about. *He shouldn't have done it. Maybe he didn't want to die. He was an expert hunter and knew how to shoot to kill. If only he'd survived, like most failed suicides he wouldn't have tried again. It was just a damn big mistake.*

We went for long drives in the country during the conference when we first met and spent every day together when he was at Vassar. We talked about literature and writing but it was mainly rural California that connected us. Although from extremely different families, we were both valley ranch boys. We talked about his father. Louis had called him and was worried that his dad, who was still a ranch hand, hadn't had his prostate checked because he had to bring in the irrigation pipes. We both understood that's what a ranch worker did in response to the obligations imposed by a view of time as cyclical—he got the pipes in when it was time to do so. Clarence Bowlin in my hometown of Madera shared a similar code of life and work in an interview unearthed by historian Bill Coate. Clarence was an Okie migrant who worked in the fields, farmed, and ran Bowlin's Cash Store in a section of Madera called "Little Okie." He said, "As far as I'm concerned, the word 'Okie' has no stigma attached to it. Being an Okie means if I tell somebody I'll do something, I'll do exactly that. And if it is impossible to do it, I'll go tell him. If I owe a man ten cents, I want him to have it. If he owes me ten cents, I want it."

Roxanne Dunbar-Ortiz, author of *Red Dirt: Growing Up Okie,* also defined the role of work in a way both Louis and his father would understand. "Like most Okie men I know—the ones who migrated and the ones still back there—work defines life, character, personality, worthiness." Work was the flipside of fighting; both reflected toughness. In *American Exodus: The Dust*

Bowl Migration and Okie Culture, James N. Gregory devoted a section to the "The Cult of Toughness," showing how the values of toughness and courage, the ability to work and to fight, "to suffer from a bruise" without flinching or showing weakness reflected "a preoccupation with toughness that became one of the cornerstones of the Okie subculture." In California, a prowess in fistfighting became a badge of group pride. At Depression-era migrant camps in Shafter, where Louis later lived as a kid, up to five hundred people gathered to see boys of all ages and even girls in weekly boxing matches.

Louis's father would work hard, tough it out, bring in the irrigation pipes, and then go fishing. Indeed, at the memorial, someone's remark about a man's need to go fishing brought the only hearty laugh from Louis's stoical father.

Louis and I had often talked about hunting and hiking and fishing in the valleys and mountains. "California in my childhood was a truly golden land," he wrote, "where in the Salinas Valley we hunted quail and rabbits and deer out the back door." He said he remembered that place with a feeling he could only define as love. He even recalled the months in a Paso Robles housing project as a happy time. He loved the solitude of the mountains. When he was a wilderness ranger in the high country of the North Cascades, packed with ten feet of snow, he wandered "alone above the timberline for days and weeks at a time in the most beautiful place in the world."

He also experienced California as "a place of angry poverty, racism, and field labor that even at age nine I knew was too mean and hard." He'd encountered California's "vast meanness," as he called it, firsthand, mainly as a child of poor fieldworkers, and found it "difficult to reconcile the plait of immense wealth and shameful poverty in California." The ambiguity of the words *shameful poverty* points two ways here:

toward the shame of allowing such disparity in a society where people in million-dollar homes behind locked gates can drive their children in BMWs to exclusive schools past farmworkers' shacks, and also toward the shame poor people feel because of a social code blaming fault for everything on the individual.

So much of who Louis was could be traced to the paradoxes of his early years, when wounded by poverty he could still be proud and happy. "No one but a Choctaw could be as beautiful as my father's mother," he wrote, "or as great a hunter as my father, and though in California I was embarrassed by our poverty and bad grammar, I was none the less comfortable with who we were."

Glen Martin wrote about Louis, "He had worked hard through his adult years, and remained poor for many of them." I keep going back to Glen's comments because he knew Louis since boyhood, ran high school track with him, roomed with him in junior college and college, hiked and camped with him, and worked with him in the forest service. He wrote about Louis as a physically and emotionally strong young man, even when poor, a man of complexity, charm, humor, and yet when all the accolades, awards, prizes, professorships, critical praise, money, and seminars on his novels flowed in, Glen wrote, they left him "somehow befuddled," "feckless," "susceptible to despair and temptation," in short, "they served to wound, not heal him."

The immense gap between Louis's early years and his later fame as a writer and university professor was shared by one of his fictional characters, also a professor. When the professor talked about a Robert Frost poem as a "powerful sonnet," he heard his own words as though on a stage, and the absurdity of them struck him with such force that he almost laughed and imagined how his father or uncle would hear such words. "Some day, he knew, the university would find him out, would recognize him as an imposter and have him removed. The ones who really belonged there, by birthright and Yale, would know they'd been correct all along." The professor also felt uncomfortable with stereotypical roles expected of him as a Native American.

Where could such a professor feel comfortably at home? In the fall after his appointment as a full professor, Louis returned to the mountains by himself to retrace old routes in the Northwest Cascades and to pursue a vague idea for another book. Alone for thirteen days, after following coyote tracks across a treacherous glacier, he stared out in a fierce wind at what seemed thousands of miles of peaks while an eagle circled overhead. "I had never felt so at home in my life," Louis wrote, "and the book I had imagined writing seemed unimportant."

At the memorial I talked about Louis's initial response to Vassar as a foreign country but how readily he took charge in his readings, class visits, and attention to the work of individual students, much as the California writer, Jim Houston, remembered him doing years earlier in a roomful of college students or at a bookstore full of eager readers. "He had those real dramatic looks," Houston told a reporter, "and he would come up to a microphone and take command of a room in a kind of animal way. He had a presence. He's standing up there and you pay attention."

I didn't talk about the valley culture Louis grew up in and its primary division between the tough and the soft, where work and sexual relationships with women defined manhood, and where feelings were something a man kept bottled up. I did talk about the moment he told my students about his family's poverty. Louis's affinity for Steinbeck becomes apparent, I think, in their shared love of the natural world and in Steinbeck's response when pressed to describe his "philosophy." "I don't like people to be hurt or hungry or unnecessarily sad," Steinbeck said. "It's just about as simple as that." Louis's sympathy for the underdog showed up in his work even when he wasn't writing directly about the marginalized or excluded. Sensitivity to the aftershocks of poverty informed both his writing and his compassionate interaction with others.

Some time after the memorial Polly wrote me about my comments on Louis's family being the poorest in town. That's when she described him as a scholar of poverty. "That sense of differentness and inferiority is something that tied all the different areas of Louis's writing together," she said. "I think it's also what ultimately killed him. He was always trying to escape that past but never could."

I'm reminded of what the novelist Arnold Bennett told Somerset Maugham, "If you've ever really been poor you remain poor at heart all your life."

We're all enough the products of our therapeutic age to know that of the inner human hurts we live with, the wound of shame is the worst, more so than that of fear, guilt, or anxiety, all of which are bad enough. Yet the shame—he'd called it "embarrassment" in class that day—he carried with him from childhood poverty generated a wound, sensitive to reopenings, as well as a compassionate capacity because it allowed him to connect with others at their own points of vulnerability. Louis was a master of praise—to students, colleagues, and friends. His method was hyperbole, though persuasive because it was inventively fresh and honestly felt. He always left our self-esteem enriched.

Louis sent a former student of mine an email, offering advice about her grad school plans and various programs in Native American Studies. The email, encouraging and vibrantly alive, was written the day before he died. I don't know what happened the next morning in the moment his shame apparently caught up with him, and unable to give himself the compassion he gave to others, he shot that child from his heart, impoverishing all of us.

Darrell Winfield on his ranch

III

Marlboro Country

Rebellion in Marlboro Country

The $20,000 reward poster in the Nevada desert store looked like something out of the Old West: the sketch showed a buckaroo in an outdated cowboy hat wanted for murdering two wildlife lawmen in a remote canyon where he worked as a lone trapper.

Thirty-five years later, that showdown between the outlaw Claude Dallas and two Idaho game wardens in 1981 eerily resonated with ongoing battles between government enforcers and self-styled cowboy patriots in cattle country. In June 2016, standoffs between federal officers and armed cattlemen on federal land in Nevada and Oregon led to the shooting of a militant protester in a white cowboy hat. This is the West today: Marlboro Country in conflict with itself, the Old West versus the New West, emblematic of colliding American views riving much of the nation. A Wyoming ranch woman told me, "Claude Dallas is still huge out here." On a mythic hill in some Westerners' imaginations strides this now legendary gunslinger, an outlaw model for today's angry anti-government protests against regulations, federal land ownership, and gun control.

When I saw the reward poster in the summer of 1981, Claude Dallas had been on the run for five months. He was thirty-one, reportedly armed and dangerous, hiding somewhere in Nevada between the Black Rock Desert and the Bloody Run Hills, a desolate country of sagebrush and salt flats I was about to backpack across on a camping and research trip with my friend and writer Jack Vernon. The killing of two Idaho conservation officers shocked most Westerners but not all. Dallas became lionized as the free-spirited last of a breed, a rugged, self-reliant mountain man and former buckaroo, whose story evolved in magazines, cowboy ballads, a TV movie, and two nonfiction books.

Photos of Dallas at twenty-one turned up in a National Geographic book, *The American Cowboy in Life and Legend*, taken on the cattle range during his initial season as a Nevada buckaroo. In the first and best nonfiction book about him, *Outlaw: The True Story of Claude Dallas*, Colorado writer Jeff Long deftly balances life and legend when describing a William Albert Allard photo of Dallas with four other cowboys riding abreast in ankle-length slickers. "Except for the peach fuzz and wire-rims, he was the Marlboro Man."

To invoke the mythic Marlboro Man at the time required no additional commentary about the legendary, freedom-loving, self-sufficient cowboy who tamed the West. Dallas cowboyed for the Quarter Circle A Ranch out of Paradise Valley in Nevada. "I'll tell you what about a lot of people in Paradise," an Owyhee County Sheriff told Jeff Long. "When you shake their hand, you don't need a contract afterwards. Their word's good." Those aren't Hollywood handshakes. That was honor in the Old West and in Paradise Valley today. Now those Paradise denizens face bureaucrats with legal documents sputtering acronyms that take away Western freedoms and livelihoods. Proliferating federal regulations and environmental restrictions increasingly shut down the West to grazing, logging, drilling, and mining. Regulations stifle Western individualists like the lone trapper Dallas represented.

The populist Sagebrush Rebellion surged through the West in the 1970s and 1980s with its rallying cry to return public land to the states. The enemy was the federal government that already owned over half the land in the West, including more than four-fifths of Nevada. Ronald Reagan doffed a silverbelly Marlboro Man Stetson and announced on the campaign trail, "I happen to be one who cheers and supports the Sagebrush Rebellion. Count me in as a rebel." The following year Dallas shot down the two wild game officers and emerged as the militant symbol of the battle between government managers and anti-government users of public land that continues today.

After fifteen months on the run, Dallas was captured while hiding in a friend's trailer outside Paradise Valley. At his trial, he admitted to quick-drawing a .357-magnum pistol from a hip holster to gun down the wardens. With a lever-action .22 rifle he then shot both men on the ground, execution style, one bullet each in the skull. He claimed self-defense. Acquitted of first-degree murder and convicted of manslaughter, he was released on bail. When he returned to court for the judge's sentence, he wore a cowboy shirt and a Marlboro Man sheepskin coat, popular in ranch country at the time. Sent to prison for thirty years with a possibility for early parole, he escaped three years later. *People* magazine featured a photo of him as a cowboy on horseback riding full-page toward the viewer in an article titled "An Angry Rebel's Paradise Lost." The last sentence of the article warned: "Taken alive once, he may not be taken again."

Dallas was arrested a year later without incident at a 7-Eleven in Riverside, California. Brought to trial, he was acquitted of escape. A loophole in the law allowed the jury to find an inmate "not guilty" if he fled because he felt his life threatened, though he was obligated to notify authorities once he reached safety. Dallas claimed he'd never felt safe. During his year on the loose, he fled to Mexico, grew a mustache, and had cosmetic surgery to look more like the Marlboro Man he aspired to be.

These bizarre and true events inspired more than one person in the West to tell me, "You should write about him." It turned out that Dallas had done ranch work for my cousins' relatives in Nevada. When he was supposedly hiding out as a wilderness survivalist on the desert, he actually traveled around the West in buses and ended up with two brothers working for a logger in Fort Bragg, California. There my brother-in-law, a marine biologist for California Fish and Game, received warnings Dallas was in the area and dangerous. To him, Dallas's actions threatened anyone who tried to protect the natural world and its animals. While I could understand what Dallas as the mythic outlaw represented to many other Westerners, even some in my own family, I had no interest in writing a novel based on the actual killer, who was no mythic hero, and who'd already been well described in nonfiction works.

Dallas was a seventeen-year-old kid from Ohio when he headed West right after graduating from high school, with dreams of becoming a buckaroo and mountain man. He ended up in California, feeding dairy cows in the Santa Clara Valley, where his half-sister lived. He headed for the Great Valley but didn't find the West he was looking for. In a San Joaquin Valley orange grove he heard about a large Oregon cattle ranch near the Malheur National Wildlife Refuge. He worked on that spread for a season fixing fence, and the next season he was put on a six-man buckaroo crew. He was then nineteen, a little late to learn the ropes in ranch country, but he'd worked tenaciously as a fencer and did the same as a yearning cowboy, though it didn't come easy to him. A fellow buckaroo who became his friend said Dallas never understood horses and was rough on them. At the same time, he tested his own mental and physical toughness by hiking and camping out in harsh weather.

He left Oregon and rode horseback down to a central Nevada ranch after receiving and ignoring a notice from his Ohio draft board to report for induction. Heading north, he found what he was looking for, an old-style buckaroo outfit working the open range out of a cook wagon, the Quarter Circle A, part of a two-million-acre corporate ranch with headquarters in Kansas. He rode into Paradise Valley on a buckskin while leading a pack-horse, dressed in old-style chaps, boots, and spurs, as if fashioned to pose for cowboy artist Charlie Russell. His old-fashioned hat with a handling dent in the round crown rather than a crease looked much like a replica of the artist's own Boss of the Plains hat Dallas saw on a cowboy pilgrimage to the Charlie Russell Museum in Montana.

Playing cowboy with a serious history buff's intensity, coupled with his willingness to work, a shy closed-lip smile, a soft-mannered drawl, and a polite altar-boy demeanor—he grew up Catholic—earned Dallas acceptance in Paradise Valley. He voraciously read and reread Louis L'Amour novels just as when a boy he'd devoured Zane Grey Westerns. He didn't cuss or smoke or dip or chew. He drank tea and grapefruit juice. He might join buckaroos at times in Winnemucca's Gem Bar but not in the cathouses along the river. A ranch woman in my cousins' family, who at the time was a Gem bartender, said, "Claude was humble." He was pretty much a loner. He also packed a pistol in a thigh holster, like a movie gunslinger. Fritz Buckingham, who at ninety was worrying about his eyesight but still riding his bicycle daily to the Paradise Valley post office, told me Dallas was the only person in town to wear a gun everywhere, even when he picked up his mail.

A Nevada family friend and rancher wrote in an email, "I know Claude well. He first came to the ranch when he was running from the law for draft dodging. He worked as a cowboy for around a year, then traded horses and left horseback going north. The next time I saw him he rode into the Eureka rodeo grounds while we were practicing and rode one of our horses with his slick fork saddle. He then went to work for the Fish Creek Ranch as a buckaroo. He was famous for having a horse in his string that later became the bucking horse of the year for the NRF." That's the National Rodeo Finals.

At the end of 1973, at age twenty-three, Dallas was arrested for draft evasion and sent back to Ohio for trial. The abolishment of the draft earlier that year and a technicality about his notification allowed the charge to be dropped. The rancher went on: "After amnesty was granted, he came back to the ranch and camped out. He ranched and trapped bobcats and coyotes. I was with him when the NDOW biologist gave him the only citation he got."

Dallas had other encounters, if not citations, with the Nevada Department of Wildlife, formerly called the Department of Fish & Game—one time his traps and guns were confiscated, another time a friend was cited for mountain lion pelts Dallas had poached. He shot out-of-season deer for a bar owner who sold the venison to Mexican migrant workers. A photo shows him holding the severed head of a poached bighorn sheep. No longer a buckaroo—all the old cow outfits were going belly up—Dallas worked as a farm laborer, tractor driver, irrigator, and harvester, while trapping in the winter.

Dallas was known as a "trash trapper," using illegal bait of exposed venison, rabbit paws, or sagehen wings. He didn't ID his traps or use spacers to protect eagles and hawks. He insisted on teaching himself the craft, and many fellow trappers didn't think he was very good at it. The professional trapper and hunting guide Tony Diebold took me out one afternoon and showed me how to set a line, how to read the country in terms of the way scent traveled, how to find draws and overhangs along game trails bobcats were likely to travel, and how to rake away human odor. He took offense at the way Dallas botched the skinning of a poached mountain lion, not even knowing how to split the tail. It was said that Diebold could set a half-dozen traps in the time Dallas set one.

After his arrest for draft evasion, Dallas trained himself as a combat shooter. He studied manuals and practiced fast-draw, police-style techniques with speed-loaders. He owned an M16 military assault rifle, like those some of his classmates used in Vietnam, along with sixteen other guns, five thousand rounds of ammunition, a bullet-proof vest, a gas mask, and tank helmet. He now carried one pistol in a shoulder holster and another belted at his hip with a forward-tilted FBI-cant. He accelerated his poaching of wild game. Fur prices for bobcat pelts were peaking toward three hundred dollars apiece. In Nevada's Humboldt County alone, more than two hundred licensed trappers worked seasonally. Dallas considered game laws and seasons inapplicable to him. Freedom meant killing any animal any time he wanted—deer, pronghorns, mountain lions, chukars, coyotes, bobcats, sagehens, foxes, raccoons, bighorns, and wild horses—often to the embarrassment of his ranching friends.

When Dallas headed north for winter trapping in 1980, it was almost a fluke he ended up confronting game wardens in Idaho. For ten years, Nevada had been his base, but his canyon camp was some two miles over the line. At his trial, he claimed he didn't know where the boundary was. Tipped off by cowboys about illegal trappers on the BLM land they leased, two Idaho wardens entered Dallas's camp where they found poached deer and bobcats. Three hours earlier they'd written up two men from Oregon for out-of-season trapping and hanging illegal sagegrouse wings. The poachers signed the tickets. Dallas didn't.

At his trial Dallas claimed he had to knock down deer because he had to live. "Not anyone else that I know lives like I do, or under the conditions that I do," he told the court. "I have no one to fall back on but myself." In his scenario, the conservation officers threatened to arrest him for the bobcats or carry him out dead. The shootings in his telling became an Old West quick-draw showdown, and he won. He fetched a .22 lever-action rifle from his tent and finished off the men on the ground, as he would animals in a trap, shooting one above the left ear, the other in the back of the head. If it weren't for those headshots, the jury foreman later explained, he would've been fully acquitted.

The two dead wardens were born Westerners, one from a small Oregon ranch and timber family. The other, Bill Pogue, grew up in the rural San Joaquin Valley and was a former Marine who fought in the Korean War. The defense portrayed him as an overbearing and bullying game warden. He wore a cowboy Stetson and sometimes, according to a friend, "a Marlboro coat, one of those long-tailed mackinaws like you see in the cigarette ads." One Marlboro Man went after another. In Dallas's account, Pogue was "belligerent and on the fight." His hand kept moving to his pistol. "I thought the man was nuts," Dallas testified. "And I thought he was going to shoot me." Pogue kept "flying hot" and then drew his gun. "I responded in the only way I could have to prevent those men from killing me."

An eyewitness happened to be in Dallas's camp at the time. Jim Stevens, a thirty-seven-year-old potato-and-wheat farmer on leased land outside Paradise Valley, was one of five friends who'd formed a three-vehicle caravan of a Chevy SUV, a pickup, and an old bus to haul Dallas and hundreds of pounds of traps, stretching boards, guns, camping gear, and provisions to his canyon camp the previous month. The pickup pulled a trailer with two mules and sacks of grain to feed them. So much for rugged self-sufficiency.

Within a month, two groups of friends had returned with fresh supplies, and Jim was making the third trip, bringing mail and oranges (fruit was Dallas's first request), homemade pista-chio pudding, and brownies. Dallas lived in a large canvas out-fitter wall tent with a wood-burning cook stove and a kerosene heater. So much for roughing it.

At the trial, Jim said he'd known Dallas for four and a half years and was his pretty good friend. Jim stood outside the tent with the trapper and the two conservation officers after they found the illegal pelts. In the previous month Claude had only managed to trap two cats. Jim said the head warden was stern and forceful but didn't shout or threaten. Both wardens told Dallas they were going to cite him for possession, but Jim claimed he didn't see what happened next. He'd turned away, he said, and was looking across the river when Dallas asked the wardens, "Are you going to take me in?" Then Jim heard Pogue's surprised shout, "Oh, no," in conjunction with a deafening roar of gunfire. When he turned around he saw Dallas in a crouch with his arms extended rapidly firing his pistol. Pogue fell back-ward, smoke rising from his chest as he reached for his gun. The other warden stumbled forward and fell on his face at Jim's side.

Dallas ran into his tent and emerged with a .22 rifle and shot both men in the head but Jim couldn't watch. After hearing the shots, he walked up to Dallas and asked, "Why, Claude? Why?"

"I swore I'd never be arrested again," Dallas replied, "and they had handcuffs on."

I was inspired to write the novel *Wild Game* after imagining how a wildlife biologist might feel when his game-warden friend, killed by a poacher, becomes vilified as an oppressive enforcer of government regulations, while the poacher gains national at-tention as an old-time Western folk hero. The conflict between individualistic Old West values and New West communal con-cerns, both legitimate in their own ways, allowed me to explore what it means to be a man in the West.

I talked to trappers, buckaroos, game wardens, poachers, wildlife biologists, and ranchers in Nevada, California, Idaho, Oregon, and Wyoming. Several embodied the complexities I was writing about. As a deputy sheriff, Noel McElhany had helped to confiscate Dallas's traps, arrest him for draft evasion, and track him when he was a fugitive in camouflage fatigues. Noel also had worked as a buckaroo and mustanger. After his time as a lawman he trapped bobcats and coyotes in season and legally. He laughed off the myth of Ian Tyson's cowboy ballad: "Claude's out in the sage tonight. He may be the last outlaw. Ay, ay, ay."

Myths have tenacity. A screenwriter who'd optioned my novel flew with his family from Los Angeles to Nevada during the 2014 Fourth of July Basque Festival in Elko to do some research for the movie he planned to write and direct. When meeting my cousins' cowboy and rodeo relatives (in their boots and hats)— on whose ranch Dallas had once worked—he talked about the myths of the last cowboy, the last trapper, and what we've lost.

When I mentioned that along with cowboys there were still trappers in Nevada, the screenwriter appeared surprised. When told the number was down, he asked, "Why? Fewer animals?"

"No," a rancher at the table replied, "regulations."

Regulations became what Dallas flouted as unjust impositions on Western freedom and individual enterprise. A less violent defiance put my cousins' Battle Mountain ranching family on the front page of *The New York Times*. Ordered to halt grazing on public land during the drought's fourth year, Eddyann and her husband, Dan, filed lawsuits and helped launch a 3,000-mile horseback protest ride from California to Washington, D.C. They used federal drought subsidies to buy hay for fenced-up cattle on bare dirt near their ranch yard. It wasn't enough. Cows grew gaunt. Some died.

"We're pretty close to extinct," Eddyann told the *Times*, "and they're using the drought as the ax to cut our heads off."

In June, she and Dan, with forty supporters, including two elected county commissioners on horseback, illegally released cattle onto federal land.

"We are not conceding anymore," Eddyann told the Elko newspaper. "We can't and survive. If we quit, our way of life and that of our children will be gone."

My cousin's daughter posted on Facebook:

Stand with Battle Mountain.
Please support our family if you are in the area.
They are fighting a long battle that, in my opinion,
    should not be a battle at all.
They love the land & this is their livelihood.

Dan and Eddyann paid a $106 fine and with two other Battle Mountain ranching families negotiated a new three-year grazing deal with the government. Their twenty-one-year-old son Hank aspires to continue ranching as did his great-great-grandfather, who immigrated to Nevada in 1885. "I always wanted to be a cowboy," he told the *Times*. "But they've been trying to break us for a long time."

I mention the *Times* because to many Westerners, the eastern urban media—newspapers, magazines, internet, radio, and TV—either ignore the rural West or report it negatively. Like a lot of people struggling to make a living in the rural West, they feel left out and looked down on, even vilified, with their voices unheard, their stories untold. From the rural San Joaquin Valley to rural Wyoming I heard the same refrain: "It's like we don't exist. We're invisible." A ranch woman in the Madera hills told me, "If I turn on a morning TV show, I want to write a letter. *Good Morning America* needs a country reporter."

I saw such a country reporter interviewed on TV after the Oregon invasion by what the *Times* described as "a band of armed cowboys from other states who took over the government-run wildlife refuge." The local Harney County reporter said the "Patriots," as they called themselves, represented a widely held view in the area. The militant takeover of a wildlife refuge, forty miles from the ranch where Claude Dallas first worked as a buckaroo, highlighted the drama of an intensifying conflict between an environmentalist, recreational West and a diminished mining, grazing, and logging West. The *Times* reported, "There was a Wild West quality to the episode, with armed men in cowboy hats taking on federal agents in a tussle over public land."

"While we're here," the militants' leader said, "what we're going to be doing is freeing these lands up and getting the ranchers back to ranching, and getting the miners back to mining, and getting the loggers back to logging."

This call to free up lands to the industries of rugged individualists echoed the same Old West whoop of seventy years earlier when the American National Livestock Association protested the formation of the Bureau of Land Management and demanded the turnover of national parks and all other federal lands to the states, "part of an unceasing, many-sided effort," the historian Bernard DeVoto wrote at the time, "to discredit all conservation bureaus of the government, to discredit conservation itself."

The current call to get back to ranching, mining, and logging reflects the rough economic times and angry sense of neglect many feel in the rural West, but the return to old times isn't going to happen, and not just because of regulations.

Federal government subsidies enabled these Old West industries to thrive in the first place. Government-supported railroads in the nineteenth century created the Texas cattle drives, and the cowboys to run them. Mining and logging on public land with minimal taxes encouraged industries crucial to the development of the West. Now the economy has shifted.

Logging mills and mines have shut down. Grazing on public land contributes marginally to the West's income. California has more cattle in feedlots and on private land than Montana, Arizona, and Wyoming put together. Oregon has less than 1.5 percent of all the cattle and calves in the United States, Nevada less than 0.5 percent. Those statistics, though, aren't helpful to a family whose survival depends on cattle or to the former buckaroo and logger now working in the local prison.

The takeover of the Oregon wildlife refuge again found the West in conflict with itself. Some local citizens supported the protesters. Many did not, including the Burns Paiute Indians. A tribal council member said, "We as Harney County residents don't need some clown coming in here to stand up for us."

After forty-one days, the Harney County armed standoff came to an end with one of the occupiers gunned down and another wounded. A protester from Arizona in a white cowboy hat, LaVoy Finicum, shouted at the Oregon State Police, "Go ahead and shoot me! You're gonna have to shoot me!" They did. One of my Nevada cousins emailed my sister: "This is so BAD!!! They have been waiting to shoot these men for a long time. We are so screwed."

Twenty-six of the anti-government protesters were arrested, jailed, and out of the way for the opening of the 2016 annual spring Harney County Migratory Bird Festival. The Wild West lost its showdown to the Environmental & Recreational West. Or so it seemed until the first seven occupiers went to trial. The group's leader, Ammon Bundy, told the jury the purpose of the takeover as he'd conveyed it to his armed followers. "I want to be clear," he said. "I proposed to them we go into the refuge and basically take possession of it and take these lands back to the people." He explained the only reason they carried guns was so they wouldn't be immediately arrested and they could later fire back if the government attacked them. In October 2016, after a five-week trial, all seven defendants were acquitted.

A protester's defense attorney said, "My client was arrested in a government truck, and he was acquitted of taking that truck." Bundy added, "The war has just begun."

The militant leader in the cowboy hat, Ammon Bundy, wasn't a buckaroo. He owned an Arizona maintenance-and-repair service for commercial fleets of diesel trucks. His father, Cliven Bundy, was the Nevada rancher who'd led a weeklong armed standoff against federal law officers over grazing rights. Fees on federal land are one-tenth market value, but for twenty years Bundy refused to pay them, amounting to $1 million, because he claimed the federal government had no right to the land where he ran his cattle without a permit. Republican presidential candidate Ted Cruz from Texas announced during the 2016 presidential primaries that he wanted Cliven Bundy's vote in the Nevada caucuses and would fight day and night against big government to return full control of Nevada's lands to its rightful owners, its citizens. Donald J. Trump said he would stop government agencies from abusing ranchers with regulations. About Bundy, he said, "I like him, his spirit, his spunk." Four years after the dispute with the government over grazing rights turned into an armed standoff, Bundy, his two sons, and a supporter went to trial.

On January 8, 2018, a federal judge in Las Vegas declared a mistrial due to the government prosecutors' "flagrant" and "reckless" withholding of evidence from the defense. To Bundy and his supporters, including some of my family, the prosecution was a persecution, a good reason to continue distrusting the shady government. On Facebook one of my Battle Mountain cousins posted: "Are there other cases where this misconduct has happened? Are there other cases of people being imprisoned unjustly because of it? What is going to be done to ensure it does not happen again?"

Lost in the dispute over ranchers and land rights is that Bundy is no representative cowboy or rancher. Ninety-nine percent of the 16,000 ranchers who graze cattle on public land haven't fallen more than two months behind on their payments. As Miriam Horn points out in her book *Rancher, Farmer, Fisherman: Conservation Heroes of the American Heartland*, "Bundy's million-dollar debt was four times the amount owed by every other rancher in America combined." Nobel economist Paul Krugman wrote that Bundy initially "came across as a straight-talking Marlboro Man," but rather than a rugged individualist he's one of the "welfare queens of the purple sage."

Like Bundy, Claude Dallas was also far from the Marlboro Man he aspired to be because he didn't understand that the true American cowboy isn't the self-sufficient, independent, gunslinging loner so popular in American fiction and film. The cowboy code honors cooperation as well as individual toughness and self-reliance in daily tasks. Unlike Dallas's actions, the most valuable cowboy trait is good judgment, along with enjoyment of hard work, nonchalance about money, indifference to fame, reluctance to whine, and love of the physical world. Too often misunderstood and invoked to justify impulsive violence and overpraise toughness, the cowboy code actually honors comradeship in a world of dangerous work and marginal survival. Even in the Old West, communal values prevailed. The brigades of mountain men trapping from the San Joaquin River to the Rockies and early cowboys on trail drives in California or Texas depended on each other, the natural world they lived in, and the government of their country for protection and economic support. The true story of the American West is not of independence but of interdependence.

A *National Geographic* photo of Dallas as a baby-faced cowboy in wire rims and an old-style buckaroo hat became after his capture the newspaper photo of a prisoner in an orange jumpsuit and belly-chain handcuffs, refashioned through a mustache and cosmetic surgery to look like the Marlboro Man he failed to be.

West of California:
The Marlboro Man

On Monday evening, January 12, 2015, the Marlboro Man died of heart failure at his Wyoming home. It wasn't the first time I'd heard a report of his death. A few months earlier, when I told a friend I was going to the Riverton horse ranch of the Marlboro Man to celebrate his eighty-fifth birthday and his sixty-sixth wedding anniversary, my friend responded, "Oh, how's that possible? The Marlboro Man's dead. He died of lung cancer."

I've heard similar reports for decades, starting not long after Darrell Winfield first appeared as the Marlboro Man in 1968. Several actors, professional models, and a handful of working cowboys have appeared in Marlboro advertising, but according to people in the Philip Morris Company and the Leo Burnett advertising agency, who created Marlboro Country, there was only one real Marlboro Man. "You could look at the different cowboys that we've used and you could argue that they were all the Marlboro man," a company spokesman told *The New York Times* in 1992. "But Darrell is really the Marlboro man."

At six foot one, with a square jaw, straight dry lips, and sky-blue eyes surrounded by razor-thin wrinkles, his features are those of the archetypal cowboy etched in whang leather. His weathered face and trademark mustache, imitated by so many cowboys as to become a commonplace in ranch country, are familiar even to those too young to remember him from TV commercials and billboards because they've seen him online or in museum exhibitions or other countries where cigarette commercials aren't banned.

When he rode across TV screens, accompanied by the musical score from *The Magnificent Seven* intended to excite everyone's Western blood, his unhurried movements and gestures suggested a man perpetually and wondrously relaxed. In *The New York Review of Books*, Texas writer Larry McMurtry called him "a last survival of the Western male in the heroic mode." No one better represented Old West values in the New West than the Marlboro Man. *Come to where the flavor is. Come to Marlboro Country.*

The mendacious nature of advertising is so well understood and the deadly ironies of Marlboro Country are so often cited that today they scarcely muster cynical smiles. Surely this man is anything but what he appears to be. In a time of pervasive inauthenticity, encouraged by TV, movies, magazines, and everything online catering to our most tenacious and self-deceptive fantasies, we can't expect a prominent cowboy model to be much of an actual cowboy.

This time we'd be wrong. Darrell Winfield was a working cowboy and rancher all his life. He grew up in the San Joaquin Valley, learning his trade as a cowboy around Madera, roping in rodeos, and working as a hired hand with cattle and horses. He left the valley when he was thirty-eight and hired out as a working cowboy in Wyoming for another six years before buying a forty-acre ranch. He remained a working cowboy and rancher during his thirty years as the Marlboro Man, when for a two-decade stretch he appeared, with or without his reddish-brown mustache, in eighty-five percent of the company's advertising, making him, according to some calculations, the most photographed face in history.

He also helped create one of the most influential icons in popular culture. A 2006 book, titled *The 101 Most Influential People Who Never Lived*, ranked the Marlboro Man number one among legendary characters like Paul Bunyan, King Arthur, Santa Claus, Helen of Troy, Superman, the Great Gatsby, James Bond, Dracula, Uncle Tom, Dr. Strangelove, and ninety others who've had a greater impact on the world than many living people, for better or worse.

The Marlboro Man is "the strongest male image of modern times," the authors say, while they also point out what we all know: smoking isn't good for you. "Cigarettes are addictive things, and how many folks got hooked? And how many will mosey up the trail to emphysema and cancer? Millions, millions." *Come to Marlboro Country. Come to Cancer Country.*

I first heard of Darrell's death five years after he became the Marlboro Man. It wasn't from cancer. A friend called to say he'd been killed—bucked off a horse and drowned in a creek. Darrell told me on the phone as far as he knew he hadn't yet died, but there was a reason for my friend's concern, fully reported in a 1973 *Texas Monthly* article, predictably titled "The Death of the Marlboro Man." Carl "Bigun" Bradley, the first working cowboy used in Marlboro advertising, starting in 1963, had ridden off on a frisky colt and was found mysteriously drowned in a ranch stock pond, with two blows to his head.

Rumors of Darrell's death in subsequent years came up, a few at a time, like corn in a popper, then more rapidly until a climactic burst in 1992 produced headlines across both land and sea, from the *Los Angeles Times* announcing, "Lung Cancer Ends Life of Former Marlboro Man," to the *Daily Telegraph* of London confirming, "Marlboro Man Killed by Lung Cancer."

This time the dead man was a former rodeo rider, actor, stuntman, and model named Wayne McLaren, whose credits included one TV episode of *Gunsmoke* and two of *Mission: Impossible*, along with a 1976 modeling appearance in a group shot of four card-playing cowboys used in retail-store displays for Marlboro Texan Poker Cards. His claim to be a Marlboro cowboy in the May 1981 *Playboy* turned out to be false. Although he never appeared in any Marlboro magazine ads, billboards, or TV commercials, he became notably the most famous Marlboro Man during his later antismoking campaign and antismoking commercial. After a thirty-year habit of smoking a pack and a half a day, he died of lung cancer at fifty-one.

An online search of Wayne McLaren brings up several photos of Darrell Winfield. One account of McLaren's death appears between two advertising photos of Darrell, lighting up.

"McLaren was not a Marlboro man," a Philip Morris spokes-woman told *The New York Times* after McLaren's death. Nor was he ever a working cowboy.

While visiting Darrell at his ranch on his eightieth birthday, I asked if any of the Marlboro men who'd actually appeared in ads had died of cancer. "Yeah, there was one that died," he said, "twelve years ago or so." Darrell didn't know him personally. "He was way before my time."

He was a film and television actor named David McLean, who appeared in several Marlboro ads and commercials in the early 1960s, when the company still hired professional models rather than cowboys. A lifelong smoker, McLean died in 1995 of lung cancer at the age of seventy-three. His family filed a wrongful death suit against the Philip Morris Company.

"They had a Smoke-Out Day in Jackson," Darrell told me. "I heard my name on the radio. Darrell Winfield. Died. I called the radio station and said, 'Who put that in there?' and they said, 'We can't divulge that kind of information,' and I said: 'Well, I think it would be a good idea because I'm Darrell Winfield.'"

Holly and I were sitting in Darrell's horse barn with a ninety-year-old former cowboy who'd worked for Darrell back in Madera. He advised Darrell how he might've responded to his alleged death: "You know what Mark Twain said when they said that about him dying? He said, 'The stories about my death are greatly exaggerated.'"

After Darrell discovered the name of the woman in Jackson who'd arranged the smoke-out and reported his death to the local newspaper and radio station, he phoned her. She was profusely apologetic.

Darrell, always the prankster, soothingly told her, "You know, it doesn't bother me. Actually you've done me a favor, because I've had a lot of people call to talk to my wife and offer condolences. So I've talked to a lot of people I haven't talked to in twenty years."

He went on. "I told her my dad—he wasn't really crazy, but I told her he was—my dad's eighty years old, and he's senile and crazy. And people call him up to say how sorry they are I'd died, and ten minutes later I walk in. Can you imagine the trauma that old man's going through?"

Darrell went on. "Oh, she was just horrified, and she said: 'Well, what can I do?' and I said: 'I want you to put back in the paper that Darrell Winfield is still alive and still smoking.'"

"She later wrote me a nice letter of apology," Darrell told us, "and just before I hung up she said: 'I want to really thank you for not taking legal action.' And I said: 'Don't thank me yet, I'm still thinking about it.'"

Darrell eventually quit smoking, drinking, and dipping snuff. With a slew of grandchildren and great-grandchildren, he stopped drinking when he was fifty-four. "I decided these kids don't need to see a drunk grandpa," he told me. Quitting tobacco came later, with Copenhagen snuff the hardest to banish.

In January 2014, CNN News Room flashed on the TV screen: "REPORT: 'MARLBORO MAN' DEAD FROM SMOKING ILLNESS." A flurry of reports online, in magazines, and on TV picked up an Associated Press story about TV actor Eric Lawson, who reportedly had portrayed the rugged Marlboro man in cigarette ads in the late 1970s. A smoker since he was fourteen, he died at seventy-two of chronic lung disease. "Marlboro Man Eric Lawson was the real deal," a reporter elaborated. So far no Marlboro ads with Lawson in them have turned up. His wife said she still had one from *Time* magazine, but the photos and videos displayed with the news story were of Darrell and two other Marlboro cowboys.

—m—

I first got to know Darrell Winfield in California's San Joaquin Valley in 1962, in Madera County, six years before he became the Marlboro Man. Back then he loaded his lip with Copenhagen, lighted an unfiltered Pall Mall, and took a swig of beer, wine, brandy, or whiskey—whatever was handy—in a sequence mirroring simultaneity. We all did, and without the influence of advertising. We had barn dances, ate at the Basque Hotel, went to rodeos, and drank beer at the ranch pond on Sunday afternoons.

After years as a salaried cowboy, Darrell had gone into the cattle business with a partner and leased the dormant feedlot my grandfather had built years earlier but abandoned when the bottom fell out of beef prices. I spent summers in those years as a ranch irrigator, a hay hauler, and a deep-turbine pump installer for the DuBose & Moosios Pump Company.

Ads and commercials featuring cowboys wearing silverbelly Stetsons in a fabled American West, freshly minted as "Marlboro Country," began appearing in late 1963, shortly after I met Darrell. During the previous decade, the Leo Burnett Agency had created many macho images of Marlboro men—football players, sailors, pilots, and all sorts of rugged but debonair tough guys with tattoos on their hands, including cowboys—to counter the effeminate stigma of filtered Marlboros, first advertised in 1930 as an "ivory-tipped" woman's cigarette. The cowboy proved the most popular of the Marlboro models. In 1962 Marlboro bought the rights to the *Magnificent Seven* theme song, and the following year Marlboro Country made its national debut. I recall telling Darrell at the time, "You look more like a Marlboro Country cowboy than those guys do." Darrell just laughed. At an end-of-the-summer barbecue, Darrell arrived at our ranch house after shaving off his mustache that morning. As my dad tossed steaks onto the pit he mentioned to me, "You know, that Winfield isn't a half-bad-looking guy without his mustache."

An old Polaroid photo I took in those years, recently put on Facebook by his daughter, illustrates small difference between Darrell on horseback in his San Joaquin Valley days and in later ads for Marlboro Country.

How Darrell came to be the actual symbol of Marlboro Country was mainly accidental. His venture in the cattle business collapsed when the beef prices bottomed out in 1964. Broke, he went back to work as a cowboy, moving his wife, Lennie, and their five children from their house on the San Joaquin River to the Eastside Ranch in Firebaugh, where he became ranch foreman. For the next four years, his friend Sonny Clement, once foreman of my dad's ranch before it was leased out, tried to talk Darrell into joining him on the Wyoming ranch of another Madera cattleman, who ran stock south of Yellowstone and the Grand Tetons.

"Sonny, I cannot move to Wyoming," Darrell told Sonny one night in 1966. I'd happened to join Sonny on his visit from Wyoming as he tried to talk Darrell into moving. "I have a wife and five kids. She doesn't want to leave California. I can't move to Wyoming."

Two years later came the fork in the road. Darrell's boss shot himself, and Darrell considered accepting an offer for ranch work in Australia. "But Grandma didn't want to go," Darrell told me years later about Lennie's response to the road not taken. Australia was out. In the winter of 1968, Darrell took the road to Wyoming.

If California's True West is a palimpsest of the old and new, revealing past and future, Darrell moved farther West, in a sense, to the Quarter Circle 5 Ranch outside Pinedale, Wyoming, in Green River country, where memories of long-ago mountain men rendezvous overlapped with the last of old-style cowboy days. Darrell as cowboss joined Sonny as foreman, running up to six thousand head of cattle in the mountains. Three months later, camera crews from the Leo Burnett Agency arrived at the ranch with some models. In search of Marlboro Country with mountains, trees, and water, they'd been advised by the general manager of the Four Sixes Ranch in Texas to contact the Madera cattleman Jack Schwabacher, who owned a large ranch in the Wyoming mountains.

"The first time I saw Darrell I thought he was the second-meanest-looking guy I'd ever seen," Ken Krom, the creative director of the Leo Burnett Agency, told me, "and that's only because I saw Sonny Clement first. Darrell was heavily bearded, and he and Clement were bundled up, chipping ice to get water flowing. I'd heard about the hospitality of the West, but after they introduced themselves, those guys proved it. We took test shots of Darrell and later some 16mm footage and Philip Morris approved it. We like to keep our pictures pure and have had other cowboys working for us. For one thing, you don't have to tell a cowboy how to sit in a saddle." (It also eliminates the letters the company had received complaining how a model's spurs were upside down or his rope on the wrong side of the saddle.)

No cowboy model completely satisfied the agency until they found Darrell. "Darrell has the kind of face we think depicts the West," Krom said, "and when we first saw him he also had a mustache, something else we'd always wanted. On the first shoot we went out by his barn and let 'em rip until we thought we had the right expression." Beginning with that first photograph in 1968, taken by Jim Braddy and called "The Sheriff" by the agency, Marlboro ads and commercials focused on Darrell. Five years later, Marlboros were the best-selling cigarettes in the world, and Marlboro Country advertising was considered the most successful in history.

Darrell remembered how after Marlboro photographers took test shots of him he received a call asking him to fly to Texas for a shoot, but he didn't go. "At first I thought the whole thing was kind of a joke," he said. "I didn't realize how serious they were about paying me." He also thought some cowboy buddies might be trying to trick him into making a fool of himself by flying off to do something that didn't exist. He told the caller, "We're pretty busy shipping cows. If you boys want to take my picture, you better come out here." They did. "Things worked out. They're a good bunch of guys to work with and they pay good, for no more time than you spend."

When Darrell moved to Wyoming, Sonny told me, "Almost the first thing he did was go into town and take out a loan. I guess he had a lot of bills, too, and this Marlboro deal sort of got him on his feet."

In 1970, I stayed for a few days with Darrell and Lennie and four of their six children in their log-sided house near the Green River. Assigned to write a magazine article about the Marlboro Man as a real cowboy, I arrived at the ranch in October during the fall roundup, and within two hours found myself shakily seated on a horse behind a smelly herd of cattle.

The next morning, shortly after 5 a.m.—still no sign of dawn—Darrell's fifteen-year-old daughter Linda gathered four horses from the pasture, muttering how much she hated to do it on cold mornings. It was only the first week in October, but the air bore needles of winter, the temperature in the middle teens. Hooves clanged on metal as the men prodded the horses into a trailer. Sonny started the GMC truck, and the heater threw its musty smell into the cab, warming the leather chaps and bridles on the floorboard. Darrell took a dip of Copenhagen snuff, tongue-packing the pungent snoose into his lower lip. Lennie had cooked a breakfast of ham, bacon, pancakes, eggs, apple juice, and coffee, along with her homemade butter, bread, and preserves.

"Lennie," Darrell said at the breakfast table in his deadpan voice, "you know I cannot eat without music."

With a full halo of flyaway hair and a round-cheeked smile, Lennie maintained her cheery calm as she put a record on the turntable. Patsy Cline began singing "I Fall to Pieces."

"I can't hear it," Darrell said.

Always the straight woman to Darrell's impish provocations, Lennie turned up the sound.

On the drive up into the hills to the corrals and around curves the white bark of densely packed aspen flashed in the headlights. Darrell cut short speculation about possible snow that morning by saying, "If you listen to what everyone says about the weather, you will go crazy."

At the shipping corrals, a cattle buyer, a state brand inspector, and several cowboys arrived. I rode with others on horseback into the dissolving darkness and sifting snow. The frozen ground sounded like glass breaking as the horses crossed the scrubby sagebrush. Soon their rumps were as white as the snowy sky. Splashing across a creek, the riders spread out and went to work to gather the scattered herd.

The weigh-in went fast, forty minutes to push 895 steers through the scales, fifty at a time. Wearing dark glasses and snapping a stockwhip, the cattle buyer, looking more like an accountant than a cowboy, eyed the whitefaces as they streamed past, eliminating those that didn't suit him. "Here comes that little short one, Darrell, take him out…Get the red one, he's got a blue eye…Looks like back trouble there…Catch this one, he's a little compressed."

"It's just like selling a car," Darrell told me later. "They try to find all the dents."

Some cowboys played blackjack and drank coffee in the shed while Darrell and the buyer separately figured the sales price for the 872 steers accepted, averaging 624.7 pounds, minus three percent allowed for shrinkage on the truck ride to Idaho Falls. The going price was 31½ cents. "You're carrying out the fraction?" the buyer asked, looking over Darrell's shoulder. There was only a dollar difference in the finished calculations. The buyer wrote out a check and the two men shook hands. "I sure do thank you boys for coming," Darrell told the other riders, and the morning roundup was over. When Jack Schwabacher later called from California to ask the results of the morning sale, Darrell told his boss, "It was a fair trade for both parties."

In the truck after the sale, on the long curving dirt road down the mountain to the home ranch for lunch, Linda said, "I'm starving."

"Why you haven't even started to work yet, John," Darrell told his daughter, changing her name, as he often did with friends and family. He called Sonny Clement "Clampetts," another cowboy "Gertrude," and his wife any number of names. We all relaxed, alternatingly taking fresh dips of snoose and lighting cigarettes—Marlboros, this time. Two free cartons arrived for Darrell every week at the ranch; he always gave one to Sonny. In a bar, during an early filming trip, while gawkers admired rugged Marlboro men relaxing after a day's work, Darrell had pulled out a pack of Pall Malls. The Marlboro people weren't pleased. "I guess they were sort of saying, 'Don't bite the hand that feeds you,'" Darrell told me.

The truck lurched down a sloping grade. Sonny pointed to a hillside where a dead Angus lay, another victim of high-altitude "Brisket disease." Each cow was a loss, not only for their boss in Madera, but for Winfield and Clement, whose working relationship with the ranch included a ten-percent interest in the company stock. Sonny said the dead steer added to the largest number of cattle lost in a year's time since his arrival at the ranch.

"It really isn't funny about these cows," Darrell said, "but I have to laugh when Sonny gets excited."

Once, when Sonny Clement did "get excited," Lennie advised him with her ever-present smile that if he did not think about things, he would not worry.

"And if a frog had wings," Sonny answered, "he wouldn't bump his ass."

"Sonny if you go in debt, you go in debt," Lennie said, "but if you worry about it, you'll go in debt and have an ulcer, too."

There is a habit of mind and speech in cattle country. Most of the mornings conversations were marked by bluffs, indirection, and teasing to guard one's emotional privacy and to test another's self-assurance. The result is a gap between speech and feeling that often puzzles urban visitors used to more open, ostensibly sincere social encounters. It's a remnant of that culture that bred the West's preposterous storytellers as well as its tight-lipped, laconic actors, a code reduced to its essence at the card table.

Famed for his skill as a gin rummy player, Darrell competed against high-stakes gamblers his boss flew into the Quarter Circle 5 from California. "They would start at sundown," Sonny Clement told me, "and go until dawn." Subsidized with his boss's money, Sonny said, "Darrell would start with five thousand or whatever. At fifteen or twenty dollars a point, he had the pot at dawn. You don't win all the time, but ninety-nine percent of the time Darrell would win. He's a card counter and doesn't get tired." He also played in town. "That's what got him out of debt was playing gin rummy on the side. He got a salary, but the gin rummy made him a lot of money. Today you wouldn't want to play gin rummy with Winfield, I don't think." He was then eighty-three. "Because he'll take your money."

He would also tease cowboys with bets backing Lennie in foot-races. She could run and she was strong. I heard about those races but never saw one. In California, though, during a late-night dice game at their house, I watched Darrell razz a cowboy into betting on himself in an arm-wrestling competition against Lennie, who'd already gone to bed. "Lennie, get up," Darrell yelled toward the bedroom. As Lennie came into the kitchen, Darrell told the cowboy, "My wife will beat you." Squinting in amusement at the situation and not at all intimidated, Lennie locked hands with the cowboy. Darrell lost the bet but seemed delighted to garner exceptional laughter at the seriousness and potential shame in the cowboy's strained face as he struggled to win.

At another summer night patio party, a California woman assailed Darrell with her religious views. In an effort to shake him of his apparent inability to see a divine order to the universe she pointed toward the sky. "Answer this," she said, "Who put the moon up there?"

Darrell looked at her and sadly replied, "I honestly do not know."

Once in a California bar, so the story goes, an agitated drunk nastily informed Darrell, "You know, Winfield, I can pound the piss out of you."

In a measured voice, Darrell replied, "I honestly believe you can."

Momentarily taken aback, the drunk pursued the issue, "Well I'm going to prove it. Let's go outside. Just you and me. Let's go outside."

"No thanks," Darrell said, now annoyed, "I'm queer for girls."

The drunk then proposed to prove his point, right in the bar, in front of everyone. In response, Darrell thrust his hands, open and parallel, in front of the man's face. "See these hands! They are registered with the police!" After a moment's reflection, the drunk noticed an empty stool at the end of the bar and ordered another drink.

Tall tale or not, the story points to a long-standing cowboy code of teasing or "putting the leggins" on someone to test competence and to keep pride in check. "Ain't no horse can't be rode," the saying goes, "and ain't no man can't be throwed." Those subjected to laughter are expected to laugh at themselves. Darrell and other Marlboro cowboys faced skepticism and testing early on when they arrived on ranches for shoots until the regular ranch hands saw they could ride and rope with the rest of them.

Because words cannot and need not say everything where assumptions and experience are shared, there seemed to be among cowboys during my Wyoming visit no nervous urgency to fill the long pauses and silences that would embarrass city people. One afternoon Darrell offered to sell a neighboring rancher some heifers to supplement the stock in the man's feed pens. "I'd like to, Darrell," the rancher said without inflection. Wind flapped the brim of the old hat that matched his equally battered face. Darrell nodded. The rancher felt no need to add, *but I cain't.*

It's all a pose, you say; you've heard and seen all this before. After all, cowboys and ranchers are aware of how we expect them to act; they too have watched movies and Marlboro commercials. And yet no satisfactory explanations can ignore how naturally the earlier working conditions and insular community of the West bred such a style, how free the people were from the daily bombardments of changing ideology and fact that threatened the urban dweller's sense of self. The realities of violence and death invade ranch life intensely. Feeble but necessary jokes and laughter, staving off darkness, can spread cheer in the gloom.

Before becoming a talent scout, Liz Kennedy Rine worked for Marlboro as a location scout in the early 1980s. Years later, in her home on San Francisco's Nob Hill, she told Jim Carrier of *The Denver Post* how during a shoot in Colorado she rounded up every pregnant mare she could find because the camera crew wanted to film a newborn foal. "They wanted the wobbly legs," she told the reporter, who then described how "practical jokester Darrell Winfield horrified Liz by suggesting that rather than wait for a newborn, 'we'll just break some legs.'"

Now outmoded in many eyes, sometimes crude in its standards of judgment and rough in its methods of testing, the cowboy code grew out of a response to hard, often dangerous work that praised toughness and justified provocations in ways unsuited today for most people's urban lives. Darrell stopped giving interviews and steered clear of journalists—"I usually just tell them I'm not available"—after a 1977 story in *Sports Illustrated*, titled "The Marlboro Man," presented him and other cowboys in a hard-drinking, hard-living rodeo culture, callous to injury and women, especially wives.

The writer described how Darrell and other cowboys at the Pinedale rodeo guffawed when a photographer turned away and covered his eyes, appalled, after a bronc rider was slammed into a fence and flung to the ground with a bone sticking out of his leg. Darrell himself looked "not so much hard-bitten as slightly devastated," the article said, hungover with bloodshot eyes, his lower lip bulging with chaw, "like any ordinary battered, mouth-breathing, half-crippled Old West character." And then there were the jokes about wives. "He didn't understand my sense of humor," Darrell later explained about the *SI* writer. The article described Darrell offering Dr Peppers and beers out of his cooler and saying, "If we run out, we'll send the fat lady down to get more." He concisely summed up his marriage at the time: "Twenty-eight years of mortal hell." When he failed to win prize money in the rodeo team-roping competition, he reportedly said, "It don't matter to me really, except I do need the money. I have an extravagant wife." At least he didn't add, as he sometimes did, "Lennie is hoarse from me choking her last night."

The jokes in print, as the reporter presented them, fell flat. Marlboro executives weren't pleased. Humor, the Argentine writer Jorge Luis Borges cautions us, is most effectively "an oral genre, a sudden spark in conversation, not a written thing." Intonation, timing, and perhaps, most important, the context of shared experience allow sparks to catch fire. That's why usually "you had to be there" when people try to describe or write about their friends' verbal hilarity, and, indeed, those who make us laugh are so often friends, or make us feel so, and friends share a culture. The *Sports Illustrated* reporter did acknowledge that at the Pinedale rodeo, "Everybody around here seems to like Winfield a whole lot."

What the reporter hadn't seen was how hard the men and women worked when they weren't roping steers or barrel racing or joking around at a rodeo. After a morning roundup of nearly a thousand steers in the Wind River Mountains, when I was visiting, Lennie cooked mounds of fried chicken for lunch. In the cold afternoon, the men gathered cattle from a home pasture, working with a pickup and on foot, and separated them according to size and breed. "Watch the horns on that Mexican steer," Sonny yelled to me. "If he turns he won't go very far around you." They doctored sick cows in the cattle squeeze, with Darrell jamming his arm down the cattle throats with a metal rod to dispense pills. In the late afternoon, they picked up some lost steers from a neighboring ranch.

On the way home in a truck loaded with lean cattle—before milking the cow and feeding the horses, pigs, calves, and dogs—the men stopped at the Green River Bar, social center of a tiny community several miles from the ranch. When Darrell and Sonny walked in, heads swiveled. A Marlboro ad of Darrell was taped to the bar mirror. "Well, if it isn't Butch Cassidy and the Sundance Kid," the bartender exclaimed. "You boys been cowboying today?"

"Nope," Darrell said.

"Too damn cold," Sonny added.

A pale, bearded young man from out of town was visiting with an off-duty trucker and his wife, who wore a striped jersey and tight toreador pants. Near the pool table a group of men and women talked. "Yeah, that's him," somebody said.

The trucker's wife had been pointing to the Marlboro ad of Darrell taped to the bar mirror. Soon her young friend was off the stool, explaining to Darrell that he was in the area visiting a relative, the woman at the bar, and back where he came from people didn't believe that they actually knew the fellow in the Marlboro ad, and he certainly would appreciate if Darrell would pose with him for a snapshot.

When Darrell said "Sure," the trucker's wife, suddenly inspired, maintained that not only should she and her husband be included in the picture, but they also should hold the Marlboro ad in front of them as evidence that they and the boy truly were with the Marlboro Man, a real cowboy, out West. They filed from the bar into the late afternoon sunlight. The woman put her arm around Darrell's waist, and Sonny, commissioned the official photographer, clicked the camera at the smiling group while the rest of us looked on. "That's a good one," the bartender said.

No remarks, no jokes accompanied Darrell's acquiescence. Spectators are almost as much a part of a modern cowboy's West as cattle and equally accepted. Three drinks later, possibly disturbed by the contrast between the Marlboro Man and her young relative, the trucker's wife suggested that the boy shave off his pointed beard. Her vehemence intensified as she stared at the scruffy hair on my neck and over the tops of my ears. Given to quick inspirations, she must've decided there was no time like the present for two boys to start looking like cowboys, and after a brief search, a small pair of scissors clanged from her purse to the bar. I had come to Wyoming ignoring advice to "trim around the edges. Those cowboys like to rope guys like you." But neither Darrell nor Sonny had cared enough to say anything about it. When the woman picked up the scissors, looking around for strong-arm supporters, Darrell and Sonny decided it was time to drink up.

"Did you see how she was wanting to cut some hair?" Sonny asked, back in the truck.

"Like they say," Darrell said, "Wyoming is twenty years behind the times."

—⁓—

In 1974, the cattle market crashed, taking with it a way of life. Along with the Quarter Circle 5 and his agreement with Darrell and Sonny, Jack Schwabacher had a partnership with two ranchers. His son Gordon told me, "Because of the partnership, at one point they were running seventeen thousand head of cattle in three states. It was crazy. They went all over to get cattle." Montana, California, Idaho, New Mexico. "They were even getting cattle from the Mexican government in northern Mexico. The market crashed; the partnership crashed." The price for steers dropped from sixty-five cents a pound to thirty-five cents. "A lot of people got their asses handed to them. It never went back to the way it was."

"It was a different era," Gordon's sister, Susie, said. "When you think about it, it's over. Everything is now done on the internet. Now we videotape our cattle. We go to big sales in Oregon, Nevada, Idaho and buy cattle on video."

In the winter of 1974, after the crash and when he was forty-five, Darrell left the Quarter Circle 5 and bought a ranch, the first property of his life, outside Riverton, on the other side of the Wind River Mountains, forty acres, later expanded to eighty, where for the next four decades he worked colts in a training ring and hauled horses in a van to cow outfits and dude ranches. Horses were what he loved to be around, whether in the saddle for Marlboro or at rodeos for team-roping competitions. Horse trading gave him a job similar to what he liked to do with people for fun. "He looks at trading as a poker game," a dude-ranch operator once told a reporter.

The summer after the move to Riverton, I met my brother, Mark, on the ranch, where he'd spent some time working with Darrell. Fresh from the Merced College Horseshoeing Program, Mark was traveling around the West looking for a place to settle as a farrier. We watched Darrell, on foot in the training ring, loop a rope around the neck of a riderless horse and work with it until it loped obediently around the ring. When saddled and mounted by a young cowboy, the horse continued an obedient trot until it suddenly became frisky and started bucking.

"This horse has been rode," Darrell told the cowboy in the saddle. The owner had told Darrell the horse had never been ridden. "Don't say a word about it when he comes to get it."

In the new parlance of ranch country, the young cowboy working for Darrell wasn't a bronc buster; instead, as Darrell told us, "he rides for me." Darrell's job was not to break horses but to "start colts." Cowboys no longer got thrown or bucked off horses. If there was an "accident," a cowboy "came off his horse."

Over four decades, most of Darrell's grandsons rode for him at one time or another. "It could get a little Western around here," Dailen Jones told me one afternoon in 2012. "We take things slower now, though we've had a couple of accidents here lately that weren't real fun. But in this business it happens." Dailen became Darrell's partner in the horse business seven years earlier. He'd been referred to as Linda's boyfriend for thirteen years—she doesn't want to get remarried ("Why wreck a good thing?" she says)—and the two of them were managing the ranch. Another daughter, Nancy, who worked in town at an insurance agency, helped them start colts. An older cowboy, a professional bareback rodeo rider for fifteen years, also rode for them.

"I've learned so much from Darrell," Dailen said. "There's a way he knows how to read a horse and what it's going to do. It's phenomenal to see the experience and knowledge he has of horses. Every day I talk to him I learn something."

About eighty-five horses were on the ranch, many with Darrell's WD brand along with several boarders. Darrell's rule was if you can't improve a horse, sell it; otherwise, improve it and sell it for more. "We also ride horses for other people," Dailen said, "starting colts." Cattle of various breeds were used for training horses or letting the owners of boarding horses practice team roping or cutting herds. There were several long-horns on the ranch as well as some Holsteins slow enough to allow a fresh colt time to think. The ranch had no automatic, electrically controlled water for the horses. Darrell didn't want to be dependent on electricity. It might go out. Everything was old-style. "In winter time, we chip ice," Dailen said. No alcohol was allowed at the horse barn.

Back in 1974, after my brother finished shoeing a WD horse and we were about to leave the ranch, Darrell indirectly suggested to Mark that he might stay on for a while. "We don't make much money," Darrell said, "but we sure have fun." As if to secure his point, he added, "We find something to laugh about every day."

My brother told Darrell he'd like to strike out on his own and settle somewhere as an independent farrier. The decision to be out alone, doing what he wanted, fit with Darrell's sense of a free life. Later that night at dinner, the young cowboy starting colts for him was also moving on and was mulling over various job offers. Darrell's advice: "You don't want some son of a bitch telling you what to do every day."

Years later, when I gave Darrell's eulogy in his Riverton horse barn, I met Ron Crawford, who'd cowboyed at the Quarter Circle 5. "Darrell never gave me a direct order," Ron said. "He would say something like: 'Well, do you think maybe this afternoon you can go over and get that heifer out of that draw?' He knew cattle good, and he knew the cowboy code. He was a real cowboy."

—⁂—

Back as far as he could recall, Darrell said, he always wanted to be a cowboy. He could never see himself living in a city, commuting to a job, or working in a building. "It all depends on what you want to be," he told me, underscoring *be* rather than *do*, an indication of the extent to which he considers his choice of work a way of life. "As long as I can remember that's what I wanted to be. I always wanted to be a cowboy. I remember seeing guys horseback when I was going to grammar school. They'd be driving cattle by the school, and I'd think, *God, that would be nice to be able to do that.*"

He didn't grow up in a cowboy family. "My dad worked on a ranch—there's a picture of me on a horse with him—but he wasn't a cowboy." The old black-and-white photograph—taken in Kansas, Oklahoma, where Darrell was born in 1929—shows a grinning eighteen-month-old child on horseback clutching the saddle horn in front of his father, who's wearing a 1930s newsboy cap. Another photo of his mother with her six children shows a smiling Darrell, at eleven, wearing an adult fedora. That photo was taken in California, where his family moved as part of the Okie migration during the Great Depression. His father first made the trek from Oklahoma to find work in the San Joaquin Valley before fetching the rest of the family in 1935 when Darrell was six. "My uncle had a truck with wood slats and a canvas top," Darrell said about their migration west, "and we'd pull to the side of the road and have campfires." In California, they lived in a tent. "It seemed like two years," Darrell told me, "but it was probably only a year."

His earliest memories in California were of trying to spend as much time as possible on a horse or work mule, although his evolution into a cowboy didn't take place right away. In another photo, at twelve, hatless and in a button-up schoolboy's sweater, Darrell holds the reins of a bridle attached to the head of a horse towering over his shoulder. His dad baled hay, worked in a cotton gin, and also became "partners with a guy on a dairy," Darrell said, "and I had to milk those goddamn cows. Forty of them." Darrell was then fourteen.

At fifteen, in another photo, he stands with his outstretched hand holding a rope halter under the chin of a statuesque quarter horse in profile. He's looking more like a cowboy, wearing a plaid shirt, a classic narrow cowboy belt, and a short-brimmed cowboy hat. Riding and roping still remained mostly pleasant diversions for him. Until his sophomore year in high school he thought he wanted to own a dairy farm but he grew tired of milking cows. At sixteen, he ran away with a carnival to Twentynine Palms in the Mojave Desert. He traveled with the carnival from Bishop to Los Angeles, in charge of the horses, running the pony rides and setting up equipment.

When he returned to the San Joaquin Valley, he was seventeen and "bummed around," meaning he got what jobs he could, breaking horses, as it was called in those days, cleaning chicken pens, and working in a cattle sales yard. He got to know cattle and horses. He met Lennie Louise Spring, whose family had also migrated from Oklahoma to California. "I was between five and six when we came out," Lennie remembers, "and it took a week— but it might've been longer" to drive from Hugo, Oklahoma, to the area outside Hanford, California, where the Winfields had also settled. Her family traveled in a little car with a rumble seat. "The three girls sat in the back, and Mom and Dad were up front with the baby."

Darrell interjected. "You was like *The Grapes of Wrath*."

Lennie's amused response was immediate. "No, we didn't have stuff piled up on the top—we came with suitcases. But I remember we'd stop by the road someplace, where there'd be a little creek, and Mom would clean us. So we'd be clean when we got to California."

I mentioned to her that when she married Darrell he was eighteen but she was only sixteen. "Yes," she said, smiling at the thought, "sixteen going on seventeen. I actually met him when

I was fourteen, but I didn't like him. He kept coming around, though, like a little puppy."

When he was twenty, Darrell left a partnership breaking horses and went to work on a San Joaquin Valley ranch for William Holt Noble. He stayed with Bill Noble for twelve years, first as a cowboy and then as the cowboss, also later running the cattle company's feedlots. "He was very capable," ninety-year-old Floyd Nichols, who'd worked many years for Darrell, told me. Darrell's father had quit haying in Hanford and worked at the feedlot mill, where Darrell became his dad's boss. At work and after work, and also in rodeos, Darrell team-roped as much as he could. "We had two milk cows at the time," Lennie said. "Darrell would come in from work but would hang back until he saw me go milk those cows. Then he'd put the horses in the trailer and go roping."

None of Darrell's three brothers or two sisters worked on ranches. One brother was a cook in Virginia, another a truck driver in Oklahoma. His brother Bud lived most of his life in New York City, serving in the international Bethel headquarters of the Jehovah's Witnesses in Brooklyn, home of *The Watchtower* and *Awake!* Bud wrote in typescript a charming verse account of his experience, 440 quatrains of rhymed couplets, titled "My Thirty Years at Bethel."

"He was different," Darrell said about his brother. "I have to admire him. He lived exactly as he believed. He was not a hypocrite."

Darrell never visited his brother in New York. He did fly to the city once for a Marlboro event and a couple of times to Chicago, home of the ad agency, but he left as quickly as possible and did no sightseeing.

How does a cowboy feel about being a model for someone's idea of what a cowboy should be? "I look at it as a job," Darrell told me. "They tell us they want to make these things authentic so there's not a lot of bull in them. They're the ones with the hard job, trying to satisfy a lot of people who have a lot of different ideas." He typically went on six to eight location shoots a year, usually ranging from one to two weeks, occasionally longer. Some shoots were on the ranch or nearby, but at the peak of his Marlboro work, Lennie said, "He was gone two weeks out of every month." He was paid by the day. Besides appearing in ads and commercials, he picked stock, arranged wranglers, and scouted locations for the agency.

"Those Marlboro people would do anything he wanted," Sonny told me. "It got to where if they went to Arizona, he'd say he wanted to use his own horses and he wanted his kids or grandkids to haul them from Wyoming." Production memos for shoots in Dillon, Montana, and Kaycee, Wyoming, list three of Darrell's grandsons as a wrangler, a prop manager, and a production assistant. His son, Brian, also helped with the horses, props, and wardrobe.

A Marlboro memo of 1997 confirms Darrell's centrality to the company even as it moved from increasingly banned advertising into promotional sales. A nearly two-million-dollar budget and a six-day shoot for a 3DCD production, called *The Storm*, was waiting on Darrell. The internal memo reported: "Darrell is short two men and won't be able to get his horses on the road *until February 3rd*. It will take him *3 days* to trailer his horses to Southern Arizona, and that makes our first shoot day *February 6th*." The shoot was moved from Monument Valley to Arizona because of four feet of snow in the valley. "Also," the memo states, "Darrell Winfield reports that the area won't give us the variety of terrains and sounds that we are looking for—water, forest, etc."

Marlboro photographer Norm Clasen explained in a 1987 interview for *Outdoor Photography*, "We take our own stock with us as much as possible. The cowboys want to know what they are riding." Darrell and the three other cowboys Clasen photographed at the time—Dean Myers, Jerry Dominick, and Jim Dolan—were "really hanging it out there." They might take their horses over a cliff at a dead run or chase a longhorn with fifty steers right behind them. "If their horses stumble, they'll get trampled. There's no trickery involved." Clasen said he sometimes let Darrell shoot a roll on the other cowboys "just for grins," so he got a feeling for what went on behind the camera. "He is not even a trained eye, yet he has taught me to see and feel things about the West that I was never aware of before."

Clasen recalled a memorable shoot of galloping horses, without cowboys, a slide show put to music for the Marlboro Country Music Festival. "Darrell and I ran horses for about a week. It was visually some of the most exciting work because it was all improvising."

In the 1990s, Darrell was photographed in the Moab Desert running seven hundred horses. The agency's creative director Ken Krom told me how one morning before a shoot Darrell rode up and said, "It's a great day to die, Krom."

"That's the sort of thing I was dealing with all the time," Krom said.

Clasen talked about cowboy practical jokes as a way of breaking the tension during stressful shoots. They'll untie a latigo so a stirrup falls when a cowboy tries to mount. Or they'll backcoil his lariat so he can't rope. "It's never ending," the photographer said. "It just goes on and on." He told the story of how his assistant was distraught after losing her wedding ring. The cowboys found it but didn't let on, ribbing her for three days, until Darrell showed up with a box of rings he supposedly acquired by trading with local Indians. He urged her to look in the box for a substitute ring. "Your husband will never know the difference,"

Darrell told her. In the box, of course, lay her wedding ring. "It was one of those shoots," Clasen said, "when everybody needed a little outlet."

Clasen said the cowboys and photographers worked ten- to fourteen-hour days from sunup to sundown, in snow and rain, high in the mountains or in bleak deserts, waking up at 4:00 a.m., sometimes in single-digit temperatures, to get sunrise shots, and knocking off after dark. A five-day shoot might produce twenty-five thousand transparencies. A year could produce a quarter of a million. Without cranes and vehicles in those years, a photographer had to improvise and sometimes shoot from the hip while standing in the stirrups on a galloping horse. "I could tell you stories about how one cowboy saved another off a runaway team of mules, and heroism like that," Clasen said, "and they have to protect me. If a thirteen-hundred-pound horse hits me at a dead run, it's going to upset a real good day."

Thousands of letters came in every week to the Philip Morris Company inquiring about the Marlboro Man. Media requests for interviews got denied by the dozens. The company was secretive to the point of paranoia. It still is. About the anonymity of the Marlboro Man and the company's protection of his identity, Clasen said, "Darrell is probably the most photographed male face in the world, yet nobody knows who he is. He is just the spirit that lives in the West. I've learned more from Darrell Winfield than any man I have met in my life—about respect, about hard work."

In 2007, a wall-sized photograph of Darrell in a dramatic horseback gallop down a steep red-rock hillside appeared in New York's Guggenheim Museum. Neither Darrell nor the photographer was identified on the wall plate or in the catalog, and neither received payment. The photo was part of a series titled "Cowboys," blown-up reproductions from Marlboro ads, which initiated the enormous art-world success of Richard Prince. Called "appropriation art," a reshooting of glossy magazine ads minus the words, Prince's reproductions remained mired in obscurity until he began openly pirating the striking cowboy scenes from Marlboro ads. "This was a famous campaign," Prince has said. "If you're going to steal something, you know, you go to the bank."

Prince set the auction record for photography when one of his photos of a Marlboro Country advertisement sold for $1.2 million. No original vintage photograph by an American master had previously sold for a million dollars. After the Guggenheim show opened, Prince again surpassed the record for the most expensive photograph sold at auction when another reproduction from his Marlboro cowboy series went for $3.4 million.

More than thirty-five years earlier, art designer Tony Palladino had done something similar, though on a smaller scale and unblessed with seven-figure offers, when he illustrated the article I published about Darrell in *Audience* magazine in 1971. Two full-page photos sidled up to the piece, one of "The Sheriff," the first famous ad featuring Darrell, and the other of the same ad "redesigned" with all the advertising copy deleted, the technique Prince employed years later.

Technological advances in large-scale color reproduction allowed Prince to enlarge the original Marlboro photographs, some to wall size, but otherwise, except for the excision of advertising copy and slight cropping, Prince's recycled images and the original photographs are indistinguishable; "there's not a pixel, there's not a grain that's different," Jim Krantz, a Marlboro photographer, told *The New York Times* about a photo he'd taken for a Marlboro ad and Prince's enlarged version of it in the Guggenheim exhibition.

Prince told a *Vanity Fair* editor, "Making art has never been a mystery to me. It's never been something that's very difficult."

Marlboro photos once appeared in even larger form than Prince's until they were banned from billboard advertising. *The New Yorker* asked Prince about the ban when it was announced in 1999. "I'll personally miss them," Prince said about the giant Marlboro billboard ads. "Every time I see one I like, it looks like one of mine, and that makes me feel good."

When reviewing the Guggenheim exhibition for *The New Yorker*, art critic Peter Schjeldahl appreciated the striking beauty of the original images in Prince's reproductions. "His gorgeous prints of the cowboy photographs in Marlboro ads stick us with the fact that those pictures are beautiful. Any opinions we may have about advertising, cigarettes, and the West founder in our visual bliss."

Prince began appropriating Marlboro Man images in the early 1980s, the same time that Sam Shepard cryptically referred to the iconic symbol everyone would recognize. In *Fool for Love*, set in liminal True West California "on the edge of the Mojave Desert," a cowboy tells his lover he's moving to Wyoming, and she sarcastically replies, "I'm not moving to Wyoming. What's up there? Marlboro Men?" The symbolic meaning of her reference needed no more elucidation than it did three decades later in 2017 when several notices of Shepard's death described him without irony among such snippets as the "Marlboro Man of the Movies…With that lanky frame and Okie face" (*Movie Nation*), "a taciturn, Marlboro Man-type demeanor" (CNN), and "his chiseled, Marlboro Man visage and seductive stoicism… Sam Shepard's plays eulogized the American West's pioneering spirit" (*Washington Post*).

In the late 1980s, Marlboro began a $345 million search for a new Marlboro Man. The primary objective of the search was to find someone in his thirties with cowboy skills, who'd never acted or appeared in film or advertising, someone with "substance/character similar to Darrell Winfield." The talent scout Liz Kennedy told Jim Carrier in *The Denver Post* that after a monthlong search and considering thousands of Western faces, she produced forty candidates, and sent ten to the Leo Burnett Agency. All were rejected.

The year 1993 produced the best results in the search for a new face. At that time, Marlboro had what it called three "feature cowboys"—Darrell, Jerry Dominick, and Billy Walck—as opposed to "non-feature cowboys" like wranglers and extras who might incidentally appear in advertising. After a year's talent hunt in fourteen Western states and thirty-two locations, five "non-feature" cowboys were identified and added to the talent pool, but the search, according to a company report, had "yet to find the next Darrell." With $262.5 million spent, the search would continue through employment of talent agencies and casting directors as well as a review of 3,400 previously photographed men.

Ken Krom, as the agency's creative director, told scouts he wanted a man "with the history of the West etched into his face," a cowboy who also had good hands. (A famous ad without any text shows only Darrell's left hand—his roping and writing hand—folded around a buckskin glove with a cigarette between his fingers.) "Darrell's hands have as much character as his face," Krom told me. About turning up another such man, Krom reportedly told a scout, "You're not going to find him."

In 1986, Darrell participated in an oral history project for the National Museum of American History. In response to questions at his Riverton ranch, Darrell said he'd gone to California "as part of the Okie migration," he had no new ideas for Marlboro, and he didn't give younger cowboys much advice about being a Marlboro cowboy. In what might be the only surprising remark in the half-hour, tight-lipped, guarded interview, Darrell said he thought his life would have been basically the same if he hadn't been given the chance to work for Marlboro.

He certainly made a lot more money working for Marlboro than he would've as a ranch cowboy but not as much as you might think, compared to the billions he helped Philip Morris bring in, or even to the millions for costs of shoots the size of small TV productions, such as the filming of commercials shown outside the U.S. Darrell was the highest-paid Marlboro cowboy. He started out with a day rate of less than two hundred dollars and a verbal and handshake agreement, but by 1995 he was being paid $2,500 for a ten-hour day with an annual guarantee of $100,000, which he regularly exceeded, given his additional work as a scout, advance man, choreographer, and consultant as well as "any costs for horses or cowboys provided by Darrell Winfield."

His contract had a confidentiality clause threatening his immediate termination if he talked about terms, so he wouldn't, and neither Philip Morris nor Leo Burnett will say a word. In cowboy terms, he did well, but in terms of the advertising industry, his pay was a mote. People in development and production made more, as did models for other products. In the late 1980s, he averaged $165,000 a year. According to a Marlboro compensation review, a model for Virginia Slims cigarettes, working the same number of days and selling the same number of ads, would have averaged four times that amount.

His work with Marlboro may have allowed him the freedom to become an independent rancher instead of a hired hand, something that might have happened anyway, or maybe not. Either way, Darrell made the point how he was no different than he ever was. He still went to work every day. He still wore the same clothes. His friends from past years were still his friends. The only difference was he didn't smoke, drink, or dip, and he ate mostly bison instead of beef. In every other way he lived much as he did when he was a hired cowboy.

—⚬⚬⚬—

When Holly and I arrived at the ranch in the summer of 2005, Darrell and Lennie lived in the same double-wide house trailer mounted on cinder blocks as when we'd stayed with them in 1975. During that earlier visit Darrell had just moved his parents from Oregon into the ranch's white wood-framed house. While we waited for him to come in from his evening chores of feeding the horses, his thirteen-year-old son, Brian, came out of the house with his right arm in a cast. He'd broken it while practicing team roping for a rodeo. "I was trying to head a steer," he said, "and my arm got caught." He was going to withdraw from the roping competition. "My dad told me to learn to rope with my left," he said. He had three weeks to do so. How did he do? "Good," he said. We later learned he and his team-roping partner had won the event.

Thirty years later, as we again waited for Darrell to come in from feeding the horses with his daughter Linda, we sat in a large den with wall shelves full of books, an addition to the log-sided mobile house, along with a porch. "Darrell's dad built that room and porch for me," Lennie said. She'd had two knee replacements since we'd seen her, but she was still working in the garden, chasing after grandkids, baking, and cooking. I remembered her homemade butter and homemade bread. Buffalo stew was on the night's menu.

In the den, Darrell's books ranged from Mari Sandoz's *Old Jules* and *Cheyenne Autumn* to Frances Fuller Victor's *River of the West*, about mountain man Joe Meek. There were books on General George Crook, or "Grey Wolf," as the Apaches reportedly called him, and Pancho Villa; books on *Cowboy Work, Cow*

Country, Horse Trading, The Cowboy, The Western Peace Officer, Powder River Country, The Journals of Lewis and Clark, Andy Adams' Campfire Tales, Ben Green's *Wild Cow Trails*, and Jo Mora's *Trail Dust and Saddle Leather*. Many on Native Americans included *A History of Utah's American Indians, The Crow Indians, On the Rez, Shoshone Mike*, and *Crow Dog: Four Generations of a Sioux Medicine Man*.

Unlike mountain men of the Old West, Darrell didn't hunt, and unlike gunslinging cowboys of legend, he didn't shoot. On the den wall, an 1894 Winchester Legendary Lawman Commemorative .30-30 Carbine was mounted on a custom plaque, a gift from his son and daughters on his sixtieth birthday. Another gun displayed in a custom frame was a Double-Barrel 12-Gauge Stagecoach Shotgun with dual triggers and hammers that Brian gave him on his sixty-second birthday. Brian, who owned a gun shop for ten years, gave his dad several vintage guns, often as birthday gifts, like an 1873 Silver-Engraved Single Action Army Colt .44-40 revolver, fitted into a basket-weave holster that Darrell's grandson Zane made and engraved with the WD brand.

Darrell enjoyed the guns as collectibles, just as he liked Indian beadwork, spurs, bits, and saddles of the Old West. "As long as I own these guns," he said, "they won't be shot."

Back in Pinedale, he used to join Sonny and other guys on hunting trips into the high country for elk, deer, and moose, but he wouldn't shoot. He liked being around wild animals but didn't want to kill them. "I don't think he ever shot an animal in his life," Lennie said.

After Darrell arrived in the den and kicked off his boots, he explained how it was Lennie's fault that they'd been stuck in the same house for thirty years. "I told her we could move down there to the other side of the ranch, but she didn't want to go.

Lennie has been a very successful woman. She has succeeded in making my life completely miserable."

A great-granddaughter and her mother appeared and kissed Lennie and Darrell. Other kids came and went. It was hard to keep track. An irony of Darrell's image as the iconic American cowboy is his lifelong distance from the legendary Western hero as the isolated, unattached, individualistic loner. Lots of family have always been around him. At last count, Darrell and Lennie had six children, twelve grandchildren, twenty-six great-grandchildren, and eight great-great-grandchildren. During one of my visits, their son and four of their five daughters lived on the ranch in trailers and a camper, as did some spouses and part-ners, grandchildren and great-grandchildren, while several oth-ers weren't far away, making the Winfield ranch at times appear less a ranch than a veritable commune. One daughter worked in the hospital pharmacy, another in the office of Devon Energy, another at State Farm Insurance, another in physical therapy at the senior center. Several of the grandsons had headed to nearby oil fields.

One grandson, who lived in Paradise Valley, was a farrier and also a Marlboro on-camera wrangler. He'd just returned from a shoot in Moab. He'd met his wife, who's from Minnesota, when she was working on a Marlboro trip as a caterer.

In 2005, Darrell remained on the Marlboro payroll as a con-sultant, going out on shoots, though he typically downplayed his involvement. "I don't do nothing," he said. In the previous ten years Colorado cowboy Billy Walck had become the most pho-tographed feature cowboy, along with Chuck Morris and Jerry Dominick, though Darrell still appeared in ads and commercials. You can see him at sixty-eight on YouTube in an international commercial called "Rope Dance." Marlboro last filmed him when he was seventy-nine, forty years after his first ad.

At noon in 2005, Holly and I ate sandwiches with Darrell and Lennie outside under the cottonwoods amid the clang of chutes and the thuds of hooves as grandkids and other young cowboys practiced roping in the corrals near the house. It was July 3rd, Lennie and Darrell's fifty-seventh wedding anniversary. She was seventy-three. Later that month he would turn seventy-six. I asked whether he'd wished his wife happy anniversary. He assured me it wasn't necessary, repeating to Lennie what he'd said to her that morning, "Darling, I told you before I love you. And that should last you until I say differently."

Family and friends planned an afternoon barbecue across the ranch at the home of the oldest Winfield daughter, Janet. Her fifty-seven-year-old cowboy husband, who'd trained horses with Darrell, had Alzheimer's. "He doesn't know where he is," Darrell told us matter-of-factly, adding how one day he'd noticed his son-in-law not remembering how to saddle his horse. Darrell pointed in the direction of his two-year-old great-granddaughter. "She has more attention span than he does." Darrell's grandson, Mike, who was the Marlboro wrangler, wouldn't be at the barbecue. He was laid up in the house with two broken wrists. His mother told us he'd come off his horse during the last Marlboro shoot. Darrell appeared unconcerned. "He really has West Nile," he said.

Darrell's parents had died. Other family darkness from drugs, alcohol, divorce, jail, and even prison time lingered behind the day's celebratory mood.

I sat with Darrell in a wide outdoor lawn swing under the cottonwoods. Above us, on the iron bar supporting the swing, he'd fastened a plastic replica of a human skull. He'd been diagnosed the previous fall with lung cancer. The doctors presented him with a grim prognosis. "They supposedly found a little tumor on my lung," he said. "They told me I'd be dead in two months. One of them was a little nicer. He gave me eight months. After a PET scan they looked so sad I told them, 'I guess you think I better go home and get my stuff in order?'"

No, they said, but he needed an operation right away followed by chemo and radiation. "I don't need to do any of those things," Darrell responded. "Tell me," he asked a doctor, "what are the odds after an operation that I'd have to carry around one of those little oxygen tanks." Fifty-fifty, he was told. "Well, I'm not going to do it." The doctor looked mournful. "Give me the name," Darrell said, "of someone my age"—he was seventy-five—"my age," he repeated, "who was alive a year after all your chemo and radiation." They couldn't give him a name but emphasized his dire predicament.

"Can't you people be positive?" Darrell asked sternly. "Why do you want to instill in someone he's going to die?"

A doctor spoke about how Lennie and the three Winfield daughters, also in the room, were concerned. "Everyone here seems concerned," he told Darrell, "except you." He again tried to make Darrell understand he could possibly be dead in two months, if he didn't do something.

"I will do something," Darrell said. "I will treat myself."

His daughter Nancy told me, "You should've been in the car with us after we saw the doctors and Daddy refused all treatment. We rode home in complete silence."

Darrell treated himself by eating what he calls "the black medicine," or Compound X. He knew the man who'd developed it, Howard McCreary, and for years he'd used the salve to remove tumors from horses, cows, and other ranch animals. Many of the Winfield family, it seemed, had also used it for warts, moles, and skin lesions, but Darrell took it internally. He gets it from a friend of Howard's who uses the original formula. "You can go to the health food store and get some but it's not the same."

"The Indians also doctored me with sweats and herbs," he said. "Now the Indians, they're positive: You got a problem? We're going to treat you, they say, and you're going to get all right."

Another irony of Darrell's opposition to the legendary cowboy, who battled Indians in fiction and film, is his closeness to Native American life. I recall a moment at the Quarter Circle 5 when we were on horseback during a mountain roundup and we'd surprised a herd of pronghorns. Darrell said wistfully, "Imagine what this country was like when only the Indians were here—the amount of wild game there must've been." As if catching himself for becoming too serious in revealing what he really thought and felt, he added, "What a great life they had. The women did all the work, and the men sat around bragging how brave they were."

Lennie is an enrolled member of the Choctaw Tribe of Oklahoma, listed with the Talihina Agency as having "11/64 Indian blood" from her father's side. She doesn't have documentation of her mother's Cherokee heritage. Darrell's ranch is surrounded by the Wind River Indian Reservation, where he'd made several friends and was adopted into an Arapaho family. For years he took part in sweats on the reservation, often as the only non-Indian. "Something kept calling me back," he told me. He also built his own sweat lodge next to his ranch house, and Indians joined him there.

After his diagnosis with lung cancer, the Arapaho conducted a series of healing sweats for him. Never reliant solely on whim or intuition as either a cardplayer or a horse trader, Darrell likewise saw his response to doctors as rational, given the possible effect of medical treatment on someone his age. He told his doctors that he knew three or four of his old friends who underwent chemo and radiation. "They didn't last a year afterward," Darrell said, "and they went through hell. Why don't the medical profession see the light on that?"

No fool, he went back twice for scans during the six months between the time of his diagnosis and the wedding anniversary barbecue. "Whatever you're doing," a doctor told him, "keep it up." The tumor had shrunk from 2 to 1.7 centimeters.

Six months later Nancy's husband died from a massive heart attack at her breakfast table. He was fifty-seven. Four years later, in 2009, Janet's husband with dementia died in a nursing home. That same year I heard that Darrell, who was then seventy-nine, was having problems. I called, worried that his cancer had returned, but his problem, I was told, was with his back. Celia Stenfors-Dacre, M.D., a neighboring horsewoman, who was giving Darrell acupuncture treatments, told me in an email, "He hurt it years ago coming off a horse so it flares up now and then." He was looking into having an operation.

"I thought the Marlboro Man was dead," someone said when I mentioned that Holly and I were again heading to the ranch to see him, causing me to think, *Someone is bound to be right one of these days.*

—⁓—

Holly and I arrived at the ranch the afternoon before Darrell's eightieth birthday. Lennie said, "Darrell comes in around five or five-thirty after his chores. In the morning he's at the barn until eleven."

In his barn office, on the morning of his birthday, I asked Darrell what happened to the lung tumor, diagnosed five years earlier. "Gone," he replied. He had tests when he went in for his back operation. "All's I got is a little scar tissue." He talked about the black medicine. His youngest daughter, Darlene, had just used it to get rid of her son's warts after a dermatologist had failed. "You used it, too, Floyd," Darrell said to the then ninety-year-old cowboy he'd brought from California to live in Riverton, "for that mole on your head. You don't have any hair, but otherwise you're all right." He talked about the Arapaho sweats and herbs. "You can say there was a connection or a coincidence," he said, "but something worked."

His six-year-old great-granddaughter, Aspen, came into the barn office with some feathers she'd pulled from a peacock's tail. "Don't do that," Darrell told her. "That hurts. What if I pulled your hair?" He added to us so she would hear, "We've become uncivilized."

Regarded in the family as the most affectionate of grandfathers, Darrell regularly had tea in the afternoon with Aspen. After tea, they danced.

Darrell asked her, "Did you say good morning to Floyd?"

"Good morning, Floyd," she said, also greeting the rest of us in the same way. "Grandpa, can I ride bareback today?"

"Yes," he said, "but not until we eat."

His daughter Debi was cooking his birthday lunch that day. With blue eyes, blonde hair, and girlish high energy, she arrived at the barn, looking, like other Winfields, ten years younger than her age. She was fifty-one. "I just heard on the radio," she announced, "that they're looking for men between sixty-nine and ninety to pose nude for a calendar."

"I'll do it," Darrell said. "I don't even want to get paid. I just want to pose in the nude."

Debi had cooked lamb for lunch, not the mutton Darrell wanted. Lennie had mistakenly given Debi a package of lamb chops from the freezer. "I might have to find you a new mother," Darrell told his daughter.

Debi took a taste of the lamb after cooking but didn't eat lunch with us. She rarely ate any meat except bison. "We took a buffalo in to butcher last week," she told me. "I will eat some of that. I definitely know it's as organic as I can get." She also doesn't smoke. "I just say, if it's legal, it's your choice, but I don't think it's good for you." Normally she juices three to five times a day. In February, five months earlier when she was fifty, she was diagnosed at the University of Colorado Hospital with a rare stage-three melanoma originating in her big toe. After her toe was amputated and the hospital offered her a clinical trial, Debi refused further treatment.

Her sister Nancy told me, "She's her father's daughter."

I was alarmed. There's a big difference, it seemed to me, between a seventy-five-year-old man making such a decision and someone twenty-five years younger. I knew the University of Colorado Hospital in Denver was expert in dealing with melanoma. My sister-in-law was treated there after being diagnosed with stage-four melanoma and given nine months to live. She remained free of cancer eighteen years later. One of my closest friends, diagnosed with the same melanoma as Debi's in her toe, had received successful amputation and treatment at the hospital. I put Debi in touch with her.

Debi, though, like her father, wasn't acting on a wing and a prayer. The hospital offered her five different chemo treatments, she told me, but none with a high percentage of helping. "At that point, I decided not to do any of their treatments. I didn't want to destroy my immune system."

She went down to Arizona to work with a doctor for six weeks to build up her immune system with herbs and natural remedies. (Doctors she worked with at the hospital pharmacy checked out the Arizona physician and told her he was good.) She returned to take part in four sweats with an Arapaho healer on the reservation. "The Medicine Man's father and mother adopted my dad into their family years ago," she told me, "and I thank God for that. My dad being so involved with the Native ways is one reason I chose the natural healing, not to mention he cured his cancer that way."

Each healing sweat had a different emphasis with different tasks for her. Her toe was painted with animal fat, her foot wrapped in a blanket she then kept in her bed, her body brushed with an eagle feather, her hands held sage she carried with her at all times. She learned various prayers. Most important, she said, was how the shaman taught her to strengthen her mind to heal her body. "It is truly amazing the power you feel in the sweat lodge," she said.

The incredible emotional waves she experienced during the sweats, how she learned to slow down, to appreciate life in a different way, to accept her path on the Red Road—to walk it slow and strong through ups and downs—"I really would have never known without this cancer. I never thought I would ever think of it being a blessing in my life." The Arapaho healer had told her during the first sweat that she would be blessed in a special way. "I now know that special blessing," Debi said.

In August of 2009, she told me in an email, "We had my last healing sweat with the Medicine Man last night. It was powerful and awesome."

The next day, she wrote, "I am celebrating! My test results came back GREAT! No cancer activity showing up!" All her subsequent scans have been normal.

When I next saw Darrell three years later, he'd experienced some setbacks. Two more operations on his spine had gone well enough for him to ride horses again. Everything returned to normal at the ranch. He was at the barn every day until June 2011, when he was eighty-one and had a stroke, slurring his speech and paralyzing his right arm and leg. He was in a rehab hospital. "All of us girls are taking turns staying with him," Nancy wrote me in an email. "He is never without one of us. He can't even roll over by himself."

Five days after the stroke Debi wrote to say that Darrell was moving his toes and leg, and his speech was getting better. "His spirits are high and of course he is still pulling jokes on us."

After three more weeks of therapy in the hospital, he insisted on going home, where he would continue therapy. Although his speech was back to normal and he could move his leg, his right arm remained immobile. The hospital wanted him to stay a couple of more weeks. Darrell said he had work to do at home.

Eight months later, in March of 2012, he had a heart attack. In the hospital he was in such pain he told the doctors, "Do something or kill me." They inserted two stents. Back home, he was getting down to the barn for an hour or so in the mornings, but he'd had an episode a couple of days before I arrived that September. Lennie said he'd been awake all night with bad chest pains but hadn't said anything until the next morning at the breakfast table. She put a nitroglycerine pill under his tongue, but when she turned around and asked, "Do you want some eggs?" he was unconscious. "His blood pressure had bottomed out," she told me. She called 911.

Now he was home in his living room chair, eighty-three years old, feeling better. "Everything's going okay," he told me, "considering." His mustache was gray, but his hair remained astonishingly brown. "I see one gray hair," Debi said.

Darrell acknowledged everyone coming into the room for lunch, "Debi and Dave take care of me, and Grandma, Linda and Dailen. It's nice being an invalid." Then he asked me, "How's Holly? Do you still have a wife?"

Debi aimed her camera at Darrell, Lennie, and me to take a photo for her Facebook page. "One, two, three," she told us, "everyone say, 'Chicken shit.'" We laughed, and the camera flashed.

Darrell sounded mournful. "That's not very nice. I hate to hear you girls talking that way."

Debi later told me, "My dad said he didn't like to hear his daughters cussing. If only he heard me when I was drinking!" I wondered: *Doesn't even his own family always know when he's joking?*

The teasing would go on to the end. Four months before he died, Debi asked Darrell what he wanted for lunch. He answered, "Pig ears," a request I didn't understand until we were all eating Lennie's homemade bread and Debi's Portuguese soupish (she couldn't find pig ears). I'd churned ice cream for Debi's Palisade peach pie and for Lennie's apple pie, made with fall apples she'd picked from the tree in her front yard.

We added vinegar to our bowls of soupish. "My mom's sister and brother married Portuguese," Debi said. "I remember going to Hanford and they'd have this big pot of *sopa* at Portuguese celebrations. Aunt Barbara cooked it in a pot as big as this table."

"We lived in Ripperdan then," Linda said.

"Remember that magic show you did for us there?" Debi asked me.

"He did one at the Eastside Ranch, too," Linda said. "In Ripperdan the Russians around us wore dresses like the Amish."

"Russian Mennonites," Debi said. "We lived right on the river in Ripperdan. We had a boat with a hole in it, and we'd take it across the river for horses"

Darrell asked me, "You're mostly Basque, aren't you?"

"More than half," I said. "My mother was a hundred percent Basque and my father part. I still have relatives in the Basque Country."

"There used to be a lot of Basques in Buffalo, Wyoming," he said. "I don't know if there still is. I imagine there's quite a few, but I see where a lot of the older ones died. I had a Basque guy working here but I had to get rid of him 'cause him and Linda sat around mooning."

Lennie added, "I went to a birthday party one time and he started singing in his language and smiling at Linda. And we finally asked what's he singing, and he was singing to Linda some love song."

"He could cook pig ears good," Darrell said.

"They were horrible," Linda said, "but he made really good sheepherder's bread."

"I would make him crazy," Darrell said, "when I asked: 'Are you Spanish Basque or French Basque?' and he said, 'Neither one. I am one-hundred-percent Basque.'"

"He was born on one side or the other," I said, "but Basque is Basque."

"His name had twenty-six letters in it," Debi said. Sebastián Legarretechevaría.

"Well," Darrell said, "Sebastián was lost in a snowstorm—he was herding sheep out here—he was lost for six days—"

Linda interrupted, "I think it was seven, wasn't it?"

"Seven," Debi said.

"Six days," Darrell repeated. "They couldn't fly to look for him because of the weather. On the fifth day they gave up looking for him, and the camptender said, 'Look one more day. He's a Basco. He'll be alive. If he's a Mexican, an Indian, or a white man, he wouldn't make it.' And they looked one more day and they found him underneath a log—a tree that fell down—with his two dogs—and all he lost was some fingers and toes. I think what kept him alive is he was thinking of Linda."

—⁂—

On a Saturday morning, two years earlier, Darrell was telling me how he'd only lost one time after betting on Lennie in a footrace back in California. We talked about his early days in the San Joaquin Valley. When he was sixteen he'd met the actors Tex Ritter and Wild Bill Elliott. They knew the old rancher Darrell worked for before he ran off with the carnival. Elliott played the cowboy Red Ryder in the movies, and I'd often thought how Darrell could've been the cowboy model for the comic-strip character of Red Ryder, their squared-jawed features were so similar. I asked how he felt about meeting Tex Ritter and Wild Bill Elliott. Had they been cowboy models for him? He veered away from my leading questions, saying, "Yeah, it was like a kid today meeting a movie star. They were two nice guys. Really nice."

We talked about his decision to leave California and move to the Pinedale ranch in Wyoming, where the Marlboro people found him. He grew reflective. "It's funny how you go through life—the different walks of life guys take—and how things turn out." He brought up the time after his boss at the Eastside Ranch killed himself and he'd wanted to go to Australia. "I had a job offer there. Grandma didn't want to go. She flat refused. I should've left her and went to Australia and got my aborigine woman and lived happily ever after. I ended up coming to Wyoming. She didn't want to come to Wyoming either. She didn't want to leave California. She hated it here the first year. Hated it. Grandma, tell how back in California you liked to go to that nudist colony."

"That's not true," Lennie told me.

"It is the truth," Darrell said.

Lennie still had two sisters in the San Joaquin Valley, one in Manteca and one in Hanford. After Darrell was diagnosed with a lung tumor, they drove back to the San Joaquin Valley, especially to visit Hanford, where they'd grown up. Debi and Dave went along. "I had to go," Darrell said. "They have the best milkshakes in Hanford. With a double-decker ice cream cone you get four scoops." Superior Dairy started serving ice cream in 1929, the year Darrell was born. "I don't have to go back again," he said. "Everything else was gone. I got to Pinedale just in time."

Lennie left us to drive to the rodeo at the casino to see a granddaughter and their great-granddaughter Aspen in the barrel races. Darrell and I talked about the history of the Okie migration as part of the Scots-Irish movement westward. "From what I read," he said, "all this country around here was settled mostly by Scots-Irish." He talked about how they were always on the move, unlike others, as in Pennsylvania, where "a lot of the Germans settled. They did quite well, but they didn't move in the same way. My grandma—my mother's mother was Scots-Irish. She was red-headed." His other grandmother was "big and domineering. Her word was law. You stepped lightly around her."

At 2 p.m., an Arapaho healer and some of his family—his wife, son, daughter, and two grandchildren—arrived from the reservation to hold a cedar ceremony for Darrell. The Arapaho said, "You're looking good, Darrell."

"I'm still kicking," Darrell said. "I feel good. My arm don't work. My leg don't work. Half the time my brain don't work."

The Arapaho healer, George Moss, talked with Darrell for a while about his cattle on the reservation and his own illness the previous winter. He was a tall, wiry, soft-spoken man, sixty-six years old with black hair and gentle eyes, wearing a green-checked cowboy shirt, cowboy belt, and cowboy boots. "Well, Darrell, I'm losing my hearing. My eyesight ain't worth a damn. I stay in the saddle all day long, I can't get off my horse."

"You been cowboying a lot?" Darrell asked.

"Yeah, tomorrow I'm going to move my cows down close to the house. No feed out there."

"It's dry everywhere," Darrell said.

As the men talked about previous sweats and how hot the

lodges could get, George's son Preston wearing thick glasses, put a stone brazier on the floor and lit charcoal. "The doctors," Darrell said, "they don't want to believe in the old ways."

Lennie returned from the rodeo to say that Aspen was "sitting number one so far. She made a real pretty run."

Debi, Linda, Dailen, and Janet arrived. The living room began to fill with other Winfields. Aspen came in with her aunt. "Hi, Grandpa," she said. She kissed and hugged Darrell. I asked how she did.

"I did good," she replied. She took second in the open barrel races.

When it came time for the ceremony, George said, "Darrell, I'm going to cedar you." He carefully pulled off his boots. Wearing white cotton socks, he knelt on the floor, while Preston sprinkled cedar on hot coals. George spit on his hands, rubbed his palms together, and with his eyes closed, seemingly transformed from an aging Indian cowboy into an old shaman, he began a slow, deep-voiced prayer in Arapaho. With measured words and deliberate movements he untied hide-wrapped pouches of herbs and brushed Darrell with an eagle-wing fan.

Smoke filled the room. I felt elevated, heady, and wondered what might be in that smoke but realized it was the dignity invested in the ceremony by the old Arapaho healer himself that was so moving. He applied the eagle wing and pressed a heated pouch of medicinal herbs to Darrell's forehead, chest, and paralyzed arm, causing me and others in the room, as I learned afterward, to feel the swelling in our chests. Because the healing ceremony is communal, we all took our turns kneeling in front of the brazier, waving our hands through the smoke as if it somehow clung to our palms as we rubbed our faces, our chests, our arms. George's grandson chanted in a wavering, high-pitched voice.

Darrell hunched forward in his big chair, with a blanket wrapped around his shoulders, silent, thoughtful, absorbed, looking in profile much like an old Arapaho himself, an elder sachem.

I recalled the rhyming couplets Darrell's brother Bud wrote about his thirty years of living in the religious Brooklyn community of Jehovah's Witnesses. People had commented on how totally different the brothers were, one a rural cowboy—the Marlboro Man—the other an urban evangelist. I came to realize how much alike they really were in what they shared: a facility with language, a commitment to communal life, and a spiritual dimension. Neither judged success by worldly standards. Both were, in that sense, religious.

After the ceremony, George Moss told Darrell, "What I did for you will make it a little more easier for you. The sweat is the best place to do what needs to be done, but that medicine root that I used on you comes from our sacred pipe. It's our most powerful medicine. It grows high up in the mountains. Preston and I go out every year to pick this root. It's hard to find. That's going to help you a lot."

"Good," Darrell said.

"Keep standing strong in terms of where you're at."

"Grandma takes good care of me," Darrell said.

"Anytime you need me to come down, let me know. I'm always thinking of you, my friend. You're always in my prayers, you and your family."

"Thank you very much." Darrell said. "Something helped before. One doctor gave me two months to live. The other one gave me eight months. I'm still here. You probably saved my life."

The two men talked about their good friends on the reservation who'd recently died, with Darrell naming them as if in a dirge from *Deor's Lament*. "Big Rock, he's gone. Juan Roman, he's gone. You know, it's sad in one way: Big Rock, myself, Juan, and Leo Harrington—four or five of us—were going to have a get-together and a feed." All the men were the same age, eighty-three. But then, Darrell said, "I had the stroke. Big Rock got sick. Juan got sick. It shows, don't put off things with friends."

Only five days had passed since Juan Roman's death at his home in the town of Arapahoe. Richard "Big Rock" Shakespeare died on the reservation a month earlier. In another six months, Leo Harrington would also be dead. Darrell would live almost another two and a half years before his heart gave out.

—⁂—

The morning after the cedar ceremony, at the barn, things were back to normal. Linda picked up the phone on the desk to call the house. "Daddy might be wanting to come down," she said. "Usually he wants to come down around this time."

When I asked how the ranch was run with Darrell laid up, she said, "He's still the boss, but we're taking care of it, Dailen and I. He still makes the final decisions; otherwise, we just take care of things the way he always did before. Nancy helps us."

"It's wonderful," Dailen said about Linda, "because she knows exactly how he likes things done, how he likes things fed, how he likes things watered, what he likes as far as when people come. If there's anything that we have a question about that he hasn't already stipulated 'Okay, this is what I want'—if there's a question that comes up—we ask him. Whatever he wants, that's the way it is."

A Marlboro photo on the wall showed Darrell on horseback. Dailen talked about a nearby "shoot over by the lake," when Darrell ran five hundred horses with their manes all going one way and their tails all long. He mentioned another photo showing Darrell on horseback chasing cattle downhill while swinging a rope. "He's coming off this real steep hill and he's got a great big loop swinging over these cattle. It reminds you of that movie—" Dailen paused to think of the title.

"*Snowy River*," Linda said, "but don't tell him that because he doesn't like it. He says it's too far-fetched. 'That's not real,' he says." She went on. "Daddy never watched TV until he had this stroke." He was always reading history and realistic books about the West. "Now he'll watch some of the old-time Westerns from the Gene Autry era. He doesn't like spaghetti Westerns. There's some he likes, some he doesn't, but he always loved Indian movies."

I mentioned watching a Western with him forty-two years earlier at the Quarter Circle 5 Ranch in Pinedale, at a time when we'd both left the valley we'd grown up in. As night fell on the ranch, after the cow was milked and the dogs, calves, pigs, horses, and pet antelope fed, Linda, who was then fifteen, pulled off her father's boots. We all ate dinner and settled back to watch Richard Widmark in *Death of a Gunfighter*.

"Darrell told me he'd got to Pinedale just in time," I said, "because in some ways the San Joaquin Valley was leaving him, except for the milkshake stand."

"Pinedale," Dailen said. "Darrell says that was the best time he ever had."

In 1991, in the final installment of his eight-part *Denver Post* series, titled "In Search of the Marlboro Man," Jim Carrier says his search ended in Pinedale. He'd traveled all over the West looking for the Marlboro Man with no help offered by the Philip Morris Company. Finally, he arrived at a ranch, where he found a man in a barn, wearing a farrier's apron, bent over, shoeing a horse. The man looked up. It was Darrell Winfield. "I knew I'd found the Marlboro Man," Carrier said.

Certainly a legend-engendering scene, but it fits the man.

"Let's go have a sandwich," Darrell told Carrier.

Carrier closed his article by saying that after he'd spent some time with Darrell in his sweat lodge and at a goat roast he realized the cowboy he'd found had nothing to do with his looks, his hat, or his set in the saddle. It was how he embodied the soul of the West. "Philip Morris had no reason to hide this man," Carrier wrote, "a man of depth and compassion, a grandfather, a family man, a history buff, a gentle, joking presence."

On an executive's office wall in the Leo Burnett Agency in Chicago hangs a quotation from Darrell: "A cowboy is a guy who fetches life."

In Pinedale, after I'd watched the Western on TV with Darrell and his family, we were, as the song goes, back in the saddle again, combing 3,000 mountain acres the next morning in search of 400 head of cattle. In the mountains a sporadic wind rattled the few leaves attached to white aspens and swept snow from the higher pines. Darrell and I separated when we entered a marshy meadow, where we surprised a herd of pronghorns. Alone, I nervously drove some cattle from a water hole up a grassy hill, maneuvering my horse, "Hot Lips," into wide cautious sweeps, quite certain I eventually would rejoin the cowboys and have to confess every one of the damned beasts in my care had escaped back into the hills. But all went well. From a crest Darrell soon rejoined me. Sonny Clement and other cowboys came into sight, the herd swelled—balking, bellowing, and breaking back more frequently now—until we drove them into a fenced field to water and feed. After sorting, most of them would later be taken down the country road to the home ranch on a two- or three-day drive.

When the fence gate was closed, it was time for fun. We broke into a gallop toward the horse trailer, reminding me of races back to the home barn after a roundup when I was a kid. Darrell rode turned in the saddle, laughing and yelling back at me, "Pass

Clampetts, don't let him win. Pass him!" I kicked Hot Lips in the flanks.

Debi told me how she remembers Darrell saying to her as a child, "Every day is a great day. Some are even better."

Acknowledgments

Tall thanks to Jim Unti, my friend since the first grade, for his help and knowledge during the making of this book and for connecting me with people, as did my other lifelong valley friends Frank April, Kay Frauenholtz, and Ray April. My friend Joe Claassen's experience and advice about the valley have been immense as has been the help and support of our high school classmates Bill Sterling, Fred Franzia, John Filice, Joe Spaulding, John Cahill, John Scandizzo, Tom Abts, Laurie Abrahamsen, and Tony Morici.

Thanks to those who read this book in manuscript, Mark Bergon, Ann Vernon, Barbara Frick, Zeese Papanikolas, and Jack Vernon—with special thanks to Roser Caminals and Bill Heath, who read every draft and variation as they came off my computer.

My heartfelt thanks to those who gave me support or information along the way: Debi Winfield Walters, Lennie Winfield, Marie Grace, Aleksandra Mendive, Michele Karpov, Kon Karpov, Madeline Bergon, Sonny Clement, Warner Berthoff, Fred Massetti, Dave Walters, Brian Winfield, Sal Arriola, Mitch Lasgoity, Rosemary Lasgoity, Michele Lasgoity, John Lasgoity, Chris Fenner, Michael Berryhill, Bill Coate, Tina Unti, Albert Wilburn, Heather Hartman, Gene Dellavalle, Chantal Sagouspe, Nancy Cook, Paul Russell, David Means, Cecilia Massetti, Joe Alvarez, Josephine Filippini, Holland Wines, Elisha Fisch, Janet Winfield Mendes, Diane Massetti, Irene Waltz, Linda Winfield Saunders, Dailen Jones, Nancy Winfield Eppler, Ken Krom,

Bill Thompson, Gerald Haslam, Jerry Weinberger, Denny Grant, Dan Montero, Nancy Turner Gray, Celia Stenfors-Dacre, Polly Owens, Jim Barsotti, Clay Daulton, Amy Elquist Nelson, Monika Madinabeitia, David Rio, Alfred Bush, Iñaki Arrieta, Xabier Irujo, Joseba Zulaika, Edurne Arostegui, Sylvan Goldberg, Eddyann Filippini, Dan Filippini, Jayne Tichnor, UCSF Tobacco Documents Library, Randy Buffington, Dusty Daulton, Kathy Ring, Denis Prosperi, Ken Schmidt, Joey Franzia, Steven Baker, Scott Walters, Ramona Frances, Katie Baker, Renata Franzia Price, Gordon Schwabacher, Susie Schwabacher Modic, Susan Bernardin, Darlene Raymond, Susie Hauge, Noel McElhany, and Tony Diebold.

At the University of Nevada Press I'm grateful to Sara Hendriksen, JoAnne Banducci, Iris Saltus, and Alrica Goldstein for shepherding this book into print and to readers. In my return to Nevada I want to thank my first editor at the press, Tom Radko, for publishing four of my early books, and to my even earlier editors and in cases continuing supporters Karen Mitchell, John Thornton, Nicholas Bakalar, and Michael Millman.

Special thanks to my friend Journie Kirdain for the cover painting and for working with me to bring to fruition a design showing Darrell Winfield overlooking California's Coast Range and a Franzia vineyard during a grape harvest in the San Joaquin Valley. Once again, my deepest thanks goes to Holly St. John Bergon, for the gift of her presence and judgment from the beginning to the end.

About the Author

FRANK BERGON was born in Ely, Nevada, and grew up on a ranch in Madera County in California's San Joaquin Valley. He is the author of the novels *Jesse's Ghost, Wild Game, The Temptations of St. Ed & Brother S,* and *Shoshone Mike,* a historical novel about the Nevada Indian massacre of 1911. He is also the author of *Stephen Crane's Artistry,* the editor of the Penguin Classics edition of *The Journals of Lewis and Clark, The Western Writings of Stephen Crane, The Wilderness Reader, A Sharp Lookout: Selected Nature Essays of John Burroughs,* and the co-editor with Zeese Papanikolas of *Looking Far West: The Search for the American West in History, Myth, and Literature.* With his wife, Holly St. John Bergon, he has published translations of the Spanish poets Antonio Gamoneda, José Ovejero, Xavier Queipo, and Violeta C. Rangel. He has taught at the University of Washington and for many years at Vassar College.